AMERICANS ALL!

Number Seventy-three:
Williams-Ford Texas A&M University Military History Series

AMERICANS ALL!

Foreign-born Soldiers in World War I

NANCY GENTILE FORD

TEXAS A&M UNIVERSITY PRESS
COLLEGE STATION

The paper used in this book
meets the minimum requirements
of the American National Standard for Permanence
of Paper for Printed Library Materials, Z39.48-1984.
Binding materials have been chosen for durability.

Library of Congress Cataloging-in-Publication Data

Ford, Nancy Gentile, 1954–
    Americans all! : foreign-born soldiers in World War I / Nancy
Gentile Ford.—1st. ed.
        p.   cm.—(Texas A&M University military history series ; 73)
    Includes bibliographical references and index.
    ISBN 1-58544-118-X (alk. paper)
        1. United States. Army—Minorities—History—20th century.
    2. World War, 1914–1918—United States.   3. Immigrants—
    United States—History—20th century.   4. United States.
    Army—History—World War, 1914–1918.   5. Sociology,
    Military—United States.   I. Title.   II. Series.
    UB417.F67   2001
    306.2'7'097309041—dc21   00-011797
    ISBN 13: 978-1-60344-132-2 (pbk.)
    ISBN 10: 1-60344-132-8 (pbk.)

First published as Number Seventy-three:
Texas A&M University Military History Series

To Jackie

& Sam Gentile,

Mom and Dad

Contents

Illustrations

Acknowledgments

I became interested in both ethnic studies and military history while in graduate school at Temple University. At first, researching immigrant soldiers of the American Army during the First World War proved difficult, and this book, an exciting journey through a variety of archives, almost came to an abrupt end with my first investigation. I was about to admit defeat at locating any information about these men, when an archivist at the National Archives suggested that I examine the Military Intelligence Division records since "unusual things have been found in the MID files." Unfortunately, the organization of MID correspondence, filed alphabetically by the name of the correspondent, proved yet another obstacle. Since I did not know the names associated with foreign-born soldiers, I began with "A" and continued through days of tedious searching looking for clues concerning the treatment and training of immigrant troops. Fierce determination kept me focused on my mission and gave me the energy to fight off hundreds of genealogists eyeing my microfilm reader. Finally on the third day, success. Under the name D. Chauncy Brewer (thank God his name wasn't Zimmerman) was a list of MID files on alien soldiers. The game was afoot.

I have many people to thank for their efficient and professional assistance during my research: Mitchell Yocelson of the National Archives and Records Administration, Washington, D.C.; Louise Arnold-Friend and David Keough of the United States Army Military History Institute, Carlisle Barracks, Carlisle, Pennsylvania; Josephine Crossley, Nancy Weyant, and Alice Getty of the Andruss Library, Bloomsburg University, Bloomsburg, Pennsylvania; and the staffs of the American Jewish Historical Society, Waltham, Massachusetts; the Balch Institute for Ethnic Studies, Philadelphia; the Historical Society of Pennsylvania, Philadelphia; Seeley G. Mudd Library, Princeton, New Jersey; the Free Library of Philadelphia; the YMCA Archives at the University of Minnesota; and the YWCA Archives in New York City.

Since this book grew out of my dissertation, I must thank the United States Army Center of Military History in Washington, D.C., and Temple University for their dissertation fellowships. A very special thank you goes to my dissertation committee: Kenneth L. Kusmer and Russell F. Weigley of

Temple University and Randall Miller of St. Joseph's University—you all helped mold me from a raw recruit into a fighting soldier. A personal thank you goes to my graduate-school friends who read all or part of my work: Kim Juntunen, David Reichard, Deborah Prosser, Mike DiPietro, and Doug Karsner. Jennifer Keene—a fellow World War I researcher—and I kept stumbling across each other in various archives, and we have since become good friends. I am grateful for the many inspiring conversations we had on the Great War.

Since receiving my doctorate, I have spent a considerable amount of time continuing my research, and I have found a significant amount of new material that helped reshape the direction of my work. Thanks to Bloomsburg University of Pennsylvania for reassign time and research and disciplinary grants that allowed me to turn a dissertation into a book. Thanks to the following Bloomsburg friends for their assistance in reading all or part of the manuscript: Kim Humphrey, Eileen Kovach, and Mary Ellen Zeisloft. Special thanks go to my former department chair, Jim Sperry, whose constant support and kind words helped me endure the long hours of teaching, research, and writing. Noel Parsons, Diana Vance, Gabriel Salas, and Mia Sanders from Texas A&M University Press and freelance editor Kevin Brock have been a delight to work with, and I thank them all for their dedication and professionalism. Kevin and the two anonymous readers offered invaluable suggestions that helped me fine-tune the manuscript.

I have been blessed with many good friends along the way, particularly Cindy Lotz O'Connell—who encouraged me to follow my dreams when we were freshmen in college—and Kara and Ron Shultz—who have never stopped encouraging me since that first academic year. A very special gratitude goes to my wonderful husband, David Ford, who I met in the early stages of my research. David, thank you for reading over my work, sharing many an all-nighter, and especially for retiring your commission with the United States Navy to join me in Bloomsburg, Pennsylvania. Thanks also to my stepdaughter, Miranda, who has grown from a mischievous kindergartner into a beautiful teenager—all while I was working on this book! I must also thank my family for their love and encouragement: my parents, Sam and Jackie Gentile, and the rest of the Gentile clan, Frank, Lorrie, Kristi, Julie, Jim, Denise, Jessica, Dan, Nicole, Corrina, Jake, and Mickey. Thanks also to my in-laws, Pat and Bob Ford, my sister-in-law, Robin, and to Sherilyn Glass.

My grandfather, Francesco Gentile, came to America from Italy in 1920 seeking the American Dream. What he found was hard work—digging sewers and laying railroad track—with little opportunity to get ahead. My father followed him to the railroad working as a station agent, and both he and my mother put aside their personal dreams to dedicate their lives to their children. I would not be writing these words today if not for the love and support of my parents, who taught me that anything is possible, if you believe, even achieving the American Dream. Mom and Dad, my biggest accomplishment in life would be to successfully follow your example of love and commitment to your family. I dedicate this book to you.

AMERICANS ALL!

You could not imagine a more extraordinary gathering than this american [sic] army, there is a bit of everything, Greeks, Italians, Turks, Indians, Spanish, also a sizable number of boches. Truthfully, almost half of the officers have German origins. This doesn't seem to bother them. . . . Among the Americans are sons of emigrated Frenchmen and sons of emigrated boche. I asked one son of a Frenchman if these Germans were coming willingly to fight their brothers and cousins, he squarely answered me: "yes!"

—A French soldier referring to American troops in France, 1917

Introduction

During the First World War, the U.S. government drafted into military service nearly half a million immigrants of forty-six different nationalities, creating an army with over 18 percent of its soldiers born in foreign countries. In addition, thousands of second-generation "immigrants" also served. This new influx of Old World soldiers challenged the cultural, linguistic, and religious traditions of the American Army and forced the military to reexamine its training procedures. The military invited Progressive reformers and leaders of various ethnic groups to assist them in formulating new military policies. As a result, these policies demonstrated a remarkable sensitivity and respect for Old World cultures while laying the foundations for the Americanization of these immigrant soldiers. Cooperation between military officers, Progressive reformers, and ethnic-group leaders allowed the military to avoid a conformist path of "100 percent Americanism" and helped foster an atmosphere in which immigrants could express both pride in their ethnicity and patriotism to their newly adopted country.[1]

Prior to World War I, the United States military experienced an unprec-

edented modernization. Much of this was motivated by the expansion of
the American empire in the late nineteenth century and the chaos associated with the Spanish-American War. Military reformers studied European
models and examined the history of the military in the United States.
Changes included the formation of the U.S. Army General Staff, new training methods, tighter reserve regulations, improved military education, and
the use of modern technology. By the early twentieth century, leaders like
Secretary of War Elihu Root and Maj. Gen. Leonard Wood helped shape a
"new army."

Historians have long debated whether civilian reforms also helped transform the United States military and whether general trends in civilian society matched those in the armed forces. The new military training methods
of World War I addressed many of the same social concerns prevalent in
civilian society, and Progressive reformers played a key role in training,
educating, and socializing the army. In training camps, prominent civilian
Progressive agencies did battle with the same negative influences they
sought to destroy in civilian society. The military's new emphasis on the
"management of men" was similar in many ways to the trends of the corporate scientific mangers who attempted to control the growing labor force.
In addition, the military methods of Americanizing immigrant soldiers
closely matched techniques used by social justice leaders in the nation's
settlement houses. Looking at these similarities in the civilian and military
societies does not exclude Europe's important influence on the new American military, nor does it exclude the efforts of military reformers who carefully studied past conflicts in their quest for reforms. However, this examination does allow us to see the symbiotic relationship between the civilian
and military communities.

The linkages between Progressivism, ethnic organizations, the military,
and the experiences of immigrant soldiers were interwoven and complicated.
To understand the connections, we must first explore the Progressive Era.
Progressivism was not a unified movement but was instead characterized
by a number of crusades designed to combat the enormous problems created by the rapid industrialization and modernization of the late nineteenth
and early twentieth centuries. These transformations caused a demise of
the earlier community-centered value system and left society searching for
order and identity. Reformers struggled to deal with economic chaos associated with an unregulated economy, the physical deficiency of unplanned
cities, the far-reaching consequences of new technology, massive immigration from southern and eastern Europe, and the waves of disruptive strikes

and urban riots. Proposed solutions varied but included replacing "machine" politicians with knowledgeable professionals, improving the urban environment through city beautification, offering positive social and recreational activities to replace negative influences, and restricting or Americanizing the foreign born. Other solutions included regulating corporations, developing corporate welfare, and setting standards for businesses, educational institutions, and the government.[2]

Two major trends dominated the Progressive Era: the social welfare and scientific management movements. Social welfare reformers saw themselves as moral guardians and attempted to end problems by reordering society in their middle-class image and by morally uplifting the lower classes. Their leaders engaged in crusades against prostitution, alcohol, gambling, and social disease and worked to educate the working classes in what they deemed was "proper" moral behavior. These Progressives hoped to reshape the dirty, unsanitary, and crowded cities with playgrounds, sports fields, gymnasiums, and public libraries. Their goal was to provide positive alternatives to negative urban influences by recreating the urban environment and building a new "urban citizenry" who would be "moral, industrious, and socially responsible."[3]

With millions of immigrants dominating the nation's urban areas, social welfare leaders unsurprisingly often targeted immigrant communities for their reforms. However, unlike reigning nativists who sought total conformity, social welfare reformers developed new Americanization methods. The Americanization movement of the late nineteenth and early twentieth centuries was hardly a new phenomenon. The "fear" of the foreign born can be traced back to the beginning of U.S. history. Writings of eighteenth-century political leaders spoke of their apprehension over non-Anglo immigration and discussed the concern that the foreign born would never understand democratic principles. Over the decades, the intensity of Americanization and the push for strict conformity became magnified, especially during times of economic, political, or military turmoil. Similar to Progressivism, the Americanization movement never stemmed from a unified source or focus. Throughout its history, advocates of Americanization took very different approaches in their attempts to restrict or acculturate immigrants. During the Progressive Era, plans ran the gamut from harsh Americanization methods to gradual acculturation. Those who supported immediate and complete Americanization sought to destroy a cultural belief system that endured over the immigrants' lifetimes, including traditions and values passed down through a multitude of generations. Those who promoted gradual acculturation acknowledged the importance of retaining aspects of ethnic traditions while adopting valuable elements of the American culture. While some reformers supported immigrant restrictions, others saw no need to close America's "golden doors."[4]

During the Progressive Era, many social welfare reformers moved into settlement houses in the nation's worst ghettos and worked with immigrants. Here, settlement-house workers advocated gradual acculturation and "sought to temper . . . assimilation by providing a receptive environment for Old World heritages." Jane Addams, founder of the "settlement house" movement, recognized the delicate balance between cultural recognition and Americanization and sought "to preserve and keep whatever of value [the immigrants'] past life contained and to bring them in contact with a better type of American." In their gradual assimilation efforts, settlement houses featured pageants and festivals that emphasized ethnic cultural heritages, gave lectures on the contributions of different nationalities, and exhibited artistic talents of the area immigrants. "American" cultural evenings provided immigrants the opportunity to listen to the music of classical composers, peruse reproductions of renowned artists, visit area museums, and participate in plays written by the ancient Greeks. Settlement-house reformers Americanized immigrants through classes in English, civics, American history, and citizenship. They also taught the women about "proper" housekeeping, table manners, sewing, and cooking skills designed to show them how to run "neat middle-class American homes." Ultimately, "the settlement's greatest contribution lay not in its teaching history or English, but in its insisting that immigrants preserve the customs and traditions of the old country, assuring immigrants that it was not necessary to reject the past to become an American."[5]

During the late nineteenth and early twentieth centuries, new, self-confident, and professional business and government leaders launched the scientific-management movement, which promoted efficiency by applying innovative management techniques to restructure the rapidly changing urban-industrial society. Scientific-management experts preached the virtues of efficiency and standardization, utilized professional experts, set regulations, streamlined systems, and conducted endless timesaving studies to uncover causes of problems and develop solutions. These ideas, however, went far beyond maximizing mechanical efficiency, since scientific managers, like other Progressive reformers, sought to impose social order on the urban environment, and their efforts often focused on the "management of men."

Developing scientific-management theories also lead to the redesign of business practices, the addition of new technology, and the adoption of time-saving work habits. Reformers such as Louis D. Brandeis, Herbert Croly, and Walter Lippmann discussed the virtues of scientific-management concepts in speeches, books, and well-known journals. These reformers applied efficiency theories to such diverse social and political issues as municipal efficiency, labor-management relations, class issues, and democracy. What began as a way of reorganizing the factory developed into an attempt by Progressive efficiency experts to restructure all aspects of their society. Soon, these men began to take on a moralistic tone. Personal efficiency became synonymous with discipline, hard work, and thrift: concepts found traditionally in the Protestant work ethic and continually repeated in Progressive rhetoric. Once they took on moral overtones, theories of scientific management expanded far beyond their industrial application and found their way into homes, churches, schools, the government, and the military.[6]

As historian Peter Karsten noted, the military in the late nineteenth and early twentieth centuries "underwent a virtual revolution . . . a revolution involving new missions, managerial and technological streamlining, professionalization and sheer growth." Many historians have clearly linked this military modernization to European military traditions (especially the German), and there is no denying these important influences. Modernization and professionalization of the military, however, did not take place in a vacuum but resulted from a joint civil-military effort that coincided with the Progressive Era. Historian John Gates notes the connection between the civilian and military societies and concluded that military officers were "intellectually and philosophically very much a part of the American mainstream" and that military professionals were often among the "most progressive of the nation's leaders."[7]

Secretary of War Elihu Root transformed the military at the turn of the century by studying European military traditions, past American military experiences, and the writings of military reformers. Root expanded the size of the army, supported new technological development, initiated educational reforms, and improved the reserve system. However, his greatest reform came with the establishment of the U.S. Army General Staff, based on the model of Germany's military organization. Although he considered himself a Progressive "only in a very limited degree," Root recognized the need for military modernization brought about by dramatic social and industrial changes as well as America's new colonial responsibilities. Root rethought military leadership qualities and management styles and helped transform them from "heroic leadership" to "managerial" leadership, a style similar to new civilian leadership trends. This transformation helped close the gap between the military and society and promoted the rapid growth in civil-military cooperation. Maj. Gen. Leonard Wood also embraced the idea of America as a world power, calling for the army to be prepared for its new global status. Wood's appointment as the chief of the army's General Staff in 1910 reflected, in part, similar aspects of professionalism and corporate management. Wood worked closely with civilian supporters of the "Pre-paredness Movement" in his effort to train civilians for the eventuality of war. Wood also regarded scientific-management principles as an "effective instrument of national policy" and supported many "progressive efficiency reforms" designed to professionalize and modernize the armed forces.[8]

Prewar military literature captured new scientific-management theo-ries. World War I journals also discussed positive aspects of the new effi-ciency methods and promoted the "administration" and "management of soldiers" along with ideas to increase soldier morale. The *Manual of Inten-sive Training* (1916) for infantry soldiers, noncommissioned officers, and the infantry squad called for the "application of the 'scientific management' of the industries to the process of soldier development and training." The au-thor, Lt. Elvid Hunt (later colonel), applauded civilian time and motion studies that resulted in improved efficiency and worked against the "duplication of efforts, misdirection of energy, waste of time . . . and misassignment of indi-vidual tasks." Hunt called for standardization in army training, physique, and morale efforts. By 1917 the United States military had introduced scientific management, or Taylorism (after Frederik W. Taylor, the civilian efficiency expert who started the scientific-management movement), into its navy yards and army arsenals. Scientific-management expert Frank Bunker Gilbreth enlisted in the army and applied his timesaving and fa-tigue studies to the efficient training of soldiers in machine-gun assembly methods. The United States military utilized the writings of Maj. William E. Dunn who employed new management theories to training in field artil-lery. Dunn studied the principles of scientific management that had "revo-lutionized modern industry" and applied the concepts of "industrial efficiency" to military efficiency.[9]

Brig. Gen. Edward Lyman Munson advocated the "management of men," and he warned military officers of otherwise "grave" morale problems in his 1917 article, "The Soul of the Army." During World War I, Munson worked with the Morale Branch, War Plans Division, where he embraced scientific-management philosophy and called for both the "systematized education and training in the psychology of the soldier and of war" and the "systematized psychological stimulation of troops in the promotion of fighting efficiency." In his postwar book, *The Management of Men*, Munson devoted a section to "Morale Methods and Scientific Management."[10]

During the war, the War Plans Division of the General Staff distributed a copy of Maj. Gen. David C. Shank's *The Management of the American Soldier* to all officers responsible for morale, since the book contained "valuable suggestions . . . of assistance to those who have charge of the education, recreation and character building of the Army."[11] According to Shank's book, officers should know the names of all men in their companies, treat the soldiers in the same manner they would like to be treated, discipline without nagging, and avoid destroying self-respect by instilling pride. Shank regarded efficiency as the key to the success of any officer and concluded that true efficiency came from managing men as a way of preserving harmony.

In early 1917 the War Department acted on this important connection between combat performance, morale, and the management of men. To this end they worked closely with both the Commission on Training Camp Activities (CTCA) and the Military Intelligence Division's (MID) Military Morale Section (MSS). Social welfare leaders worked with the CTCA in socializing and "morally uplifting" soldiers. The MSS instilled the men with a fighting spirit while bolstering troop morale.

At the start of conflict, the War Department hired a number of well-known Progressive reformers, among them Raymond Fosdick (former settlement worker and New York's commissioner of accounts), Joseph Lee (president of the Playground Association of America), and Joseph Mott (secretary of the Young Men's Christian Association [YMCA]). Secretary of War Newton D. Baker had previously been a municipal Progressive reformer during his days as mayor of Cleveland. Leading social welfare organizations assisted the military in the socialization of both native-born and foreign-born troops. This included the YMCA, the Young Women's Christian Association (YWCA), the Salvation Army, the Playground Association of America, the American Social Hygiene Association, and the American Library Association. The War Department also enlisted the help of the Knights of Columbus and the Jewish Welfare Board to provide for the needs of its Catholic and Jewish soldiers. Similar to their work in the civilian societies, the goal of these social welfare organizations was to keep soldiers away from negative influences such as prostitution, alcohol, and gambling and direct them to positive alternatives like sports, music, and reading. As venereal disease quickly spread through the ranks and crippled several divisions in the Allied armies, socializing

American soldiers became even more imperative. Adopting a social welfare philosophy resulted in revolutionary changes within the military structure, including innovative training methods that emphasized social, educational, recreational, and character-building activities, all designed to socialize and "morally uplift" the soldiers to create an effective military.[12]

Increasing the morale of soldiers also became an important part of their military training. The war years marked the extraordinary reorganization and expansion in the scope and size of the Military Intelligence Division. The MID had been terminated in 1908, and its staff dispersed to various positions in the War College Division. It was reactivated in May, 1917, as the Military Intelligence Section (MIS) under the War College Division of the Army's General Staff with only two officers and two clerks. By war's end, the section had 282 officers and 1,159 civilian employees. Maj. Gen. Ralph Van Deman served as the chief of the MIS until June, 1918. During that time, Van Deman concentrated much of the organization's efforts on counterintelligence and internal security issues in America's communities. The MIS also designed manuals and periodicals for agents that outlined procedures for fighting pro-German influences with counterespionage activities in both the army and the civilian population of the United States. In addition, they focused on censorship, propaganda, codes and ciphers, labor disputes, and sabotage. Increasingly, however, the Military Intelligence Section also began to shift its focus to morale issues since "military intelligence personnel operating in the field on counterespionage missions kept running across information showing that many American soldiers were seriously discontented and lacked any true understanding of the war aims of the Nation."[13]

By May, 1918, bolstering of morale became a regular part of military training. In June the War Department expanded its focus on morale issues with the creation of the Military Morale Section (MMS), which soon reported to the newly reorganized Military Intelligence Division. The MID, directed by Brig. Gen. Marlborough Churchill, became a "separate and co-equal unit of the War Department General Staff." The reorganization of the MID reflected the new understanding of the crucial role morale played in creating an effective fighting force. This was evident in the creation of the Military Morale Section, "charged with the 'psychological stimulation of troops to promote fighting efficiency.'"[14] Capt. Grafton Brookhouse Perkins served as chief of the new MMS, and the organization closely studied morale issues and implemented innovative policies designed to increase morale and instill an esprit de corps within the troops.

All these factors—Progressive socialization and Americanization, the "management of men," and the new emphasis on morale—came together with the training of foreign-born soldiers during the First World War. The War Department approached the training of immigrant soldiers with a rational pragmatic approach in the "managing of men," and they also adopted social welfare techniques in socializing, Americanizing, and bolstering the morale of these foreign-born men. World War I foreign-born soldiers were part of the largest group of immigrants to arrive in the United States in its history. Between 1880 and 1920, over 23 million people, primarily from southern and eastern Europe, came to the United States. They were alienated from their homelands by severe economic, political, and religious conditions and attracted to America with the promise of economic security and the hope for religious and political freedoms.

Historians traditionally portray the immigrant experience in the First World War as one of forced assimilation, ruthless xenophobia, and harsh Americanism. Historians David M. Kennedy's *Over Here* and John Higham's *Strangers in the Land* depict the superpatriotic atmosphere of suspicion and mass hysteria directed toward the civilian ethnic groups during World War I and illustrate how nativists attempted to strip immigrants of their ethnic culture. Immigrants often became victims of a society bent on, in Kennedy's words, "stamp[ing] out all traces of Old World identity among the foreign-born."[15] National and local nativist leaders, the American mainstream press, and members of the entertainment community joined the government's war propaganda machine, the Committee on Public Information. Together they demanded total conformity to white Anglo-Saxon Protestant values and lifestyles and called for demonstrations of absolute and unqualified patriotism.

Recently, however, historians have begun to investigate the reaction of ethnic groups to Americanization. Many now challenge both the traditional idea that immigrants assimilated easily into a dominant American culture and the revisionist concept that ethnic groups successfully fought off assimilation through fierce cultural resistance. Instead, scholars now contend that ethnic groups engaged in an active process of reshaping and reinventing their own identity in response to changes both internal and external. In this way, historian Kathleen Neils Conzen (among others) contend that immigrants participated in "defining their group's identities and solidarities." Immigrant leaders often straddled the line between their ethnic community and the outside world. Leaders of ethnic organizations protected their communities from the harsh encroachment of the dominant culture and helped preserve important Old World traditions and values. Concurrently, ethnic leaders also worked to help their community members accept important elements of the dominant culture. Historian Victor Greene notes that these leaders were motivated both by their own "self interest," power, and a "public objective" to help their people adjust to America, and they "answered the question of how simultaneously to be a foreign-born member of an immigrant community *and* an American." In his investigation of American immigrant leaders from 1800 to 1910, Greene called ethnic leaders "traditional progressives" who "synthesized past and future" and demonstrated that "a dual identity was possible." He wrote, "It became customary to describe this condition at German American festivals by exclaiming that in order to be loyal to his bride [the United States], an immigrant did not have to forsake his mother—*'Germania meine Mutter, Columbia meine Braut.'"*[16]

In considering World War I, it would be wrong to assume that immigrant groups were simply accommodationists falling in step with local nativists or the U.S. government's propaganda machine. Many ethnic leaders had their own goals and agendas, and ethnic patriotism became a complex issue. John Bodnar recently examined the intricacies of public memory, commemorations, and patriotism in the twentieth century. Although his discussion on immigrants focuses primarily on the decades after the Great War, his findings help one understand the complexities of ethnic patriotism during that conflict. Bodnar found that all patriotic commemorations contain "powerful symbolic expressions—metaphors, signs, and rituals—that give meaning to competing interpretations of past and present reality."[17]

Likewise, Robert Zecker's study of the Czech and Slovak communities in World War I confirmed that we cannot simply look at patriotism as a "top-down campaign" since ethnic groups often "used public ceremonies to achieve their own goals, not just the agenda of governmental or economic elites."[18] Although there is no doubt that ethnic group participation in World War I served as a way for immigrants to express loyalty to their adopted country, demonstrations of patriotism were often connected to ethnic political aspirations and international goals. For many of the new immigrants born under the oppressive reign of the Central Powers, expressions of American loyalty also translated into a converted effort to gain the freedom of the immigrants' homeland. The rhetoric coming from ethnic enclaves often combined the language of American patriotism with hope for a European nation-state. For many immigrants, service in the United States was one way to work toward these goals.

Many of the foreign-born soldiers could not read, write, or speak English, and the military faced the immense task of organizing, training, and educating these immigrant troops. As with native-born soldiers, the military was also concerned with morale issues. Most of the foreign-born recruits came from southern and eastern Europe, and many belonged to the Jewish and Catholic religions. These men created unique cultural and religious challenges for a military previously dominated by Anglo-Saxon Protestants.[19] The situation became even more complicated when many of the immigrants, labeled "enemy aliens" because they originally came from territories controlled by the Central Powers, wanted to fight with the American Army to free their homeland from the oppressive Austro-Hungarian and German Empires.

The United States military did not simply attempt to transform the foreign-born soldiers into "Anglo-Saxon Protestants." Instead, the War Department turned to Progressive reformers and ethnic leaders to help them in training, educating, Americanizing, socializing, and bolstering the morale of these men. Many Progressive reformers had substantial experience in working with the new immigrants in various civilian social welfare agencies. Ethnic leaders came from the professional classes: editors, clergymen, doctors, lawyers, businessmen, and heads of social and fraternal organizations. They were also very instrumental in formulating and implementing military policy toward immigrants.

In January, 1918, the secretary of war, Newton D. Baker, took an important step in his department's policies toward immigrant soldiers with the establishment of the Foreign-speaking Soldier Subsection (FSS) under the Military Intelligence Section. The prime responsibility of the FSS was to bring "improvement in the treatment of alien personnel within the army."[20] For the first five months, D. Chauncy Brewer, a prominent Boston lawyer and president of the North American Civic League for Immigrants (NACL), headed the agency, reporting to Van Deman. However, the two men soon tangled over policies, and Brewer resigned. His departure coincided with the reorganization of the Military Intelligence Division, and the FSS transferred administratively to the Military Morale Section. The War Department put Lt. Herbert A. Horgan in charge of the FSS, but both Perkins and Horgan signed most of the correspondence. A significant amount of the FSS correspondence also came directly from the new director, Marlborough Churchill. The new FSS continued to work closely with ethnic leaders and Progressive reformers, and it eventually reorganized immigrants into ethnic-specific companies commanded by immigrant and second-generation officers.

What made the training of immigrant soldiers complex was the military's desire to both increase the morale of the foreign-born soldiers and instill American patriotism and loyalty. The military was, therefore, faced with two serious challenges that at first seemed to be practically contradictory: instilling Americanization and building morale. Ultimately, the War Department did not simply force a choice between America and one's native culture. Instead, they used Americanization methods similar to those of social welfare reformers who respected Old World ways while laying the foundations of Americanization. This required a complex alliance between military officers, Progressive reformers, and prominent ethnic leaders. New civil-military relationships forged a union between the United States military and hundreds of prominent leaders of immigrant groups who played a key role in helping define military policies concerning foreign-born soldiers.

Ethnic community leaders gave patriotic speeches, taught English, translated social hygiene literature and war propaganda material, and worked to counter enemy influences. Much of this effort had the underpinnings of American patriotism. However, these leaders participated on their own terms; they also pressured the military to recognize and meet important cultural and religious needs of the foreign-born troops and demanded fair and just treatment of the men. Immigrant leaders argued that celebrating ethnicity and meeting the cultural and religious needs of the foreign-born troops could only increase troop morale. They successfully convinced the military to grant special leave for religious holidays, secure immigrant clergymen, celebrate cultural holidays, hire foreign-speaking secretaries in hostess huts, and forbid officers to use ethnic slurs. Leaders alerted the War Department to specific problems faced by foreign-born soldiers and protested unjust treatment by officers or civilians that affected the morale of these troops. Prominent members of the ethnic communities also acted as intelligence agents in immigrant communities and in army training camps with large immigrant populations to assist the military in countering enemy influences. Did their army experience Americanize immigrants? The answer is more complex than forced conformity, for in many ways ethnic leaders "negotiated" the Americanization process by helping promote patriotism and loyalty while retaining key cultural traditions.

The question remains why did the United States military treat immigrants in a rather enlightened fashion, yet at the same time preserve the "second-class" status of black soldiers? The answer may be found in a study by Jennifer Keene. She demonstrates that both white and black soldiers brought with them "distinctive racial agendas." Keene notes that "army authorities often lost control of white and black troops in racially charged situations, and therefore feared that, if unchecked, racial conflict might paralyze the nation's war campaign." Although the racial situation in the military was extremely complex, Keene found that the army "unhesitatingly accepted the limitations which civilian communities placed on the role black soldiers could assume in the military." Although nativism was put aside, even a serious military manpower shortage could not shake the powerful hand of racism.[21]

This book explores the training and treatment of immigrant soldiers in the American Army during World War I. Chapter 1 examines the complexities of immigrant patriotism, especially in the midst of the harsh atmosphere of Americanization prevalent during the First World War. Chapter 2 focuses on the intricacies of drafting in a multiethnic society. Chapter 3 looks at how the military reorganization brought immigrant troops into an effective system of ethnic-specific units under immigrant leadership. Chapter 4 reveals the War Department's attempt to socialize and "morally uplift" both native-born and foreign-born troops and to lay the foundations of Americanization for immigrant soldiers. Chapter 5 explores the important role that ethnic-group leaders played in establishing military policy and how the War Department attempted to meet the cultural needs of the foreign-born soldiers.

A Victory Liberty Loan poster acknowledged the contributions of immigrant soldiers who served in the United States Army. Entitled "Americans All!" it included an "honor roll" of ethnic names: Du Bois, Smith, O'Brien, Cejka, Haucke, Pappandrikopolous, Andrassi, Villoto, Levy, Turovich, Kowalski, Chriczanevic, Knutson, Gonzales. Yet the World War I experience did not simply transform immigrants into white Anglo-Saxon Protestants. Instead, it redefined what it meant to be "Americans All." In the end, United States military policies did not create a melting pot, but they instead provided an atmosphere of dual identity that made both American and ethnic pride acceptable. As the editor of one ethnic newspaper put it, "We may consider ourselves happy for being in a position where we can harbor love for both America and our old country, without doing injustice to ourselves."[22]

Only the war could have established the fact that living in the same country does not mold the various nationalities into one nation. They are a gathering of peoples in the family of one nation. . . . America is now learning its most important lesson: That it is not at all necessary for liberty, security, and prosperity of America to fuse all the nationalities here to a point where they will lose their identity entirely. On the contrary, it is much better that they should treasure dearly the inheritance which they brought with them from the old world—their language, their songs, and the beautiful traditions of their past.

—"The Fire Beneath the Melting Pot," *Daily Jewish Courier,* June 5, 1918

CHAPTER 1

"In the Family of One Nation"

The Complexities of Ethnic Patriotism during the Great War

America in 1917 was a nation in the throws of wartime mobilization. This went far beyond mustering in men for the military forces. The initial unpopular nature of the war, the threat of draft resistance, and the diversity of the United States transformed World War I into a "war for the American Mind."[1] In its attempt to sell the war, the United States government implemented a national propaganda campaign that utilized new mass-media communications. The dark side of this effort was the encouragement of a society that manifested itself in mistrust and suspicion. The nation's immigrants were particularly targeted. Many scholars have examined the oppressive nature of the American home front during World War I, noting the superpatriotic atmosphere that led to mass hysteria. Their works tell of immigrants falling victims to harsh Americanization efforts designed to strip them of their native culture and loyalties. Some argue that ethnic displays of loyalty were forced upon immigrants with stinging assimilation policies by reigning nativists. However, for far too long historians have lumped together very different ethnic experiences. Although there is no denying the oppression of immigrants or the power of Americanization during the war, ethnic groups should not be viewed simply as isolated and powerless victims cowering to a barrage of nativist bullets. The story of ethnic patriotism during the Great War is complex. In many ways, ethnic loyalty was influenced as much by their own leaders as by government-sponsored demands for conformity.

Even before the United States declared war, many ethnic groups organized in an attempt to influence America's foreign policy or to draw attention to the plight of their war-torn homelands. While some pushed for the strict neutrality of the United States, others sought American involvement in the European conflict. The German and Irish communities in particular joined forces to try and keep the United States out of the war and attempted to use ethnic political power to force the nation into abiding by international laws of neutrality. For immigrants from southern and eastern Europe (Czechs, Slovaks, Jews, Poles, and others), the American entrance into the war offered the hope of independence for their homelands. Ethnic demonstrations of patriotism were complex and often utilized the "language of Americanism." But many times these expressions entwined symbols and rhetoric of American patriotism with ethnic cultural pride and homeland-liberation agendas. Therefore, "ordinary people" redesigned the patriotic culture of America as they, in John Bodnar's words, "acknowledge[d] the idea of loyalty in commemorative events and agreed to defend the symbol of the nation but often use[d] commemoration to redefine that symbol."[2]

American German and Irish community leaders worked diligently to keep the United States out of the First World War and pressured the government to maintain strict neutrality. Americans of German descent represented one of the oldest and largest ethnic groups in the United States and one of the best organized and politically powerful. German immigration began in the seventeenth century and steadily continued well into the 1900s. Although considered "Americanized" by the turn of the century, many of the nation's German Americans lived in ethnic enclaves and preserved cultural traditions along with their native language. It would be inaccurate to portray the entire German American community as unified in their politics, religion, and culture or even in their response to the First World War. Nor can

it be assumed that the opinion of national German American organizations absolutely reflected the belief of all their constituents. But the power
and influence of ethnic leadership cannot be ignored, and their actions reveal a great deal of solidarity in their response to U.S. diplomatic policies
prior to the American entrance into the First World War.[3]

The National German-American Alliance, incorporated in 1907 as an
educational society, included in its goals the preservation of the German
language, literature, and culture in the United States, and the organization
actively encouraged German immigrants to become naturalized U.S. citizens. As early as 1914, the National German-American Alliance numbered
over two million members in forty states. Eventually, it would become the
most influential of all the German American organizations and the largest
of all similar alliances in the United States. News from the "old country"
remained important, and in the early years of the European conflict, subscriptions to German American newspapers and journals increased dramatically.[4]

As the war continued, a number of ethnic groups became increasing
concerned with the possibility of America entering the fighting on the side
of the Allies. In response, the National German-American Alliance and ethnic journalists, through speeches, rallies, demonstrations, resolutions, and
newspaper editorials, became energetic lobbyists and powerful proponents
of strict American neutrality. Many of the nation's cities with large German American populations protested against British violations of international law. German societies responded with fury to Great Britain's refusal
to honor German Americans' passports, expressed great condemnation
when British sailors removed German American citizens from ships, and
vigorously questioned why the United States did not respond with outrage
to the British "raiding" of American merchantmen. The National Alliance
also sent international-law experts to Washington to object to the shipping
of United States munitions and equipment to the Allies and to note the in-
equity of loans that clearly favored Great Britain. The National German-
American Alliance continued to pressure for strict American neutrality and
sent a number of resolutions to both the U.S. House and Senate (including
150,000 telegrams). German-Irish coalitions for peace and neutrality demonstrated in major cities throughout the United States.[5]

Editorials in the German American press argued that British violations
of international laws had pushed Germany into adopting aggressive re-
sponses such as submarine warfare. After concluding that the British government dominated American war news through an active propaganda

campaign, the German American press responded in an attempt to balance the war coverage by providing news from Germany and reprinting official statements from German leaders. Some of the more radical papers predicted a Central Powers victory over British forces.[6]

The pinnacle of German American political pressure came with their powerful campaign against the reelection of President Wilson. Ethnic leaders established the National Organization of German Newspaper Publishers and called for a mass meeting in Chicago to organize an ethnic voting block against Wilson. The editors put their support behind Associate Justice Charles Evans Hughes, the former governor of New York and the Republican presidential candidate. However, in the end, the German American community did not vote in a solid block. Some clung to their traditional Democratic loyalties, some threw their support toward the charismatic Theodore Roosevelt, while others voted for a more radical candidate. Hughes lost by a narrow margin.[7]

Once the United States broke off diplomatic relations with Germany in early 1917, most German American organizations and newspapers tabled their protests but made a last emotional plea for neutrality. Within a few months, the United States and Germany tumbled into war. With jingoism on the rise and ethnic Americans facing harassment and even violence, the majority of German American organizations made the decision to keep a low profile for the remainder of the war; membership in the National Alliance declined rapidly. The National German-American Alliance withdrew from politics after the U.S. Congress began an investigation of the organization. By April, 1918, members of the alliance voted to dissolve their organization and subsequently transferred their remaining treasury to the Red Cross.[8]

While many German American newspapers continued to report on the freedom campaign in Ireland, most limited their war protest to the reprinting of quotations from respectable mainstream English-language papers opposed to the end of neutrality. The *Philadelphia Gazette-Democrat* began publishing all its news and editorials in English, ending a forty-year tradition of the exclusive use of the German language. This action, according to the papers, was a voluntary act to "best serve the interests of the United States." The newspaper did retain the German language in some sections, with the self-proclaimed "result" of spreading American "government aims and activities" to the subscribers who could not read English. The *Gazette-Democrat* also donated free advertising space for the Liberty Loan campaign and produced a patriotic booklet, *Liberty is Alive!!*, which expounded the good deeds of the paper.[9]

e efforts to demonstrate "absolute loyalty," circulation in
can newspapers dropped and advertisers began to distance
ntually, subscriptions would decline by almost 50 percent
nbers.[10] Some German American newspapers chose not to
:ourse of action. The *Milwaukee Seebote* continued to blame
Britain for causing the war, and the *Cincinnati Freie Presse* pushed the enve-
lope by publishing articles on the German war effort alongside articles on
American efforts. Some stopped their presses for the duration of the war. Others such as the *Philadelphia Tageblatt* were shut down by the federal government, caught up in the emotional turmoil of the day, for alleged violations of
the Espionage Acts of 1917, which authorized the postmaster general, Albert
Sidney Burleson, to refuse material "advocating treason, insurrection, or
forcible resistance to any law of the United States." Burleson defined these
acts loosely in order to shut down ethnic newspapers and crush radical
dissent. Only a minority of German American organizations continued to
openly oppose America's policies after the country entered the fighting.
Once war was declared, many German Americans served in the U.S. Army
(see chapter 2).[11]

Similar to the German American community, Irish Americans worked
industriously to keep the United States out of the war and protested violations of neutrality that obviously favored the British government. Many
Irish American leaders resented British imperial policies and worked to free
their homeland from oppressive colonial rule. Millions of immigrants came
to the United States from Ireland beginning in the early nineteenth century to flee poverty and starvation. They were met with harsh nativism
and claims that Catholicism threatened American institutions and undermined democracy. But by the late nineteenth century, many Irish Americans had made substantial inroads into the country's political and economic
structure, although most remained barred from total acceptance into the
Protestant society by anti-Catholic prejudices. For Irish Americans, the onset
of the First World War brought a resurgence of the question of Irish nationalism and a reluctance to accept Britain as an American ally. It also
created an opportunity to demonstrate their loyalty to the United States
and break the last barriers of nativism. But the war divided the Irish Americans and fragmented the opinions of radicals, moderates, and Roman Catholic Church leaders.[12]

Prior to the First World War, moderate mainstream Irish Americans, led
by Catholic religious leaders, had moved away from the radical notions of
Irish nationalism. In an effort to gain "respectability," these leaders advo-

cated temperance, called for boycotting plays and shows that caricaturized Irish Catholics, applauded the social moiré of the time, and tied Catholic religious virtues to American patriotism and citizenship. They also tended to support Home Rule of Ireland over the more radical position of complete independence. As the American claim of World War I neutrality increasingly gave way to British support, the Irish American community struggled to respond.[13]

While many Irish Americans were unified in their resentment of British power and their call for the strict neutrality of the United States government, the community split apart over other issues of importance. As early as January, 1907, the Ancient Order of Hibernians and the National German-American Alliance met in Philadelphia "to oppose a widening current of Anglo-Saxon internationalism" and adamantly protest "an alliance of any kind, secret or otherwise, with any foreign power on the part of the government of the United States."[14] The meeting resulted in the union of a number of Irish-German leagues, formed to ensure United States neutrality, to pressure for American endorsement of Ireland's freedom, and to fight British propaganda infiltrating the American press. Joseph McLaughlin, president of the Hibernians, backed the Irish-German pact. Other Irish nationalists rallied around similar issues with varying intensity, including the radical secret society, the Clan-na-Gael. Likewise, the more radical Irish American newspapers such as the *Irish World, Gaelic-America, Irish Nation*, and the *Freeman's Journal* published pro-German articles and editorials in an effort to balance pro-British influences.[15]

Pressure applied by Irish nationalists eventually led to a crucial and heated interchange between President Wilson and Jeremiah O'Leary, the founder of the American Truth Society. The society, a national organization with a mission to counteract British propaganda and combat the Anglo-Saxon influences felt to be deeply rooted in the country, sent a telegram to President Wilson registering disapproval of America's "pro-British policies." O'Leary called Wilson's domination over Congress a "dictatorship," accused the president of leniency toward the British Empire, and strongly opposed Wilson's approval of war loans and ammunition supplies for Great Britain. Finally, O'Leary warned Wilson that these positions would become burning issues in the coming election. Wilson's response was short and to the point. "Your telegram received. I would feel deeply mortified to have you or anybody like you vote for me. Since you have access to many disloyal Americans and I have not, I will ask you to convey this message to them, signed Woodrow Wilson." O'Leary was so outraged by Wilson's response that he issued a twenty-three-page public statement of defense and sent several telegrams to the president. In his statement, O'Leary provided "evidence" of his loyalty to the United States, including his service in the 69th New York Irish Regiment during the Civil War.[16]

Other Irish American nationalists such as the National Trustee for the Friends of Irish Freedom, the Clan-na-Gael, and the Irish Progressive League pressured the president and Congress to recognize Ireland's freedom and demanded that Great Britain do likewise. The groups sent a number of delegates to Washington, D.C., for the "Great Irish Meeting." That gathering, held on April 13, 1918, was also intended to remind the administration that the "Irish are heart and soul with President Wilson for the principle of self-determination."[17]

Although far less radical, the Catholic press and mainstream Irish newspapers also pushed for the strict neutrality of the United States and objected to British violation of international law and its domination of the war coverage in the American press. The Catholic publications supported Ireland's home rule and attempted to provide a balanced coverage of the war by including "news favorable to the Central Powers." But Catholic leaders James Cardinal Gibbons and Archbishop John Ireland objected to the radicals' attack on the U.S. government, fearful that it would exasperate anti-Catholic nativism and slow up the acceptance of Irish Americans. Throughout their campaign, mainstream Irish Catholics such as the Irish dominated Knights of Labor consistently promoted loyalty to the United States organized around the principles of American patriotism. Once the nation entered the war, much of the Irish American community, although obviously uneasy about America's alliance with Great Britain, unified in the "chorus of unbridled patriotism."[18]

The U.S. Declaration of War on April 6, 1917, dashed the hopes of the German American and Irish American communities. While these groups failed to successfully affect American foreign policy, their efforts were important, nonetheless. Ethnic editors, lawyers, and political leaders used their skills in an attempt to force the United States to stay the course of neutrality. These two groups organized and sometimes joined forces to try to achieve goals tied directly with their ethnicity and homeland politics.

In the early years of the war, American political leaders and the general public agreed to stay out of the European conflict. Pres. Woodrow Wilson even ran for reelection in 1916 with a campaign that promised to keep the nation out of war. But as the conflict progressed, many political, economic, and military factors made the issue of intervention more complex, and the

United States soon found itself at war. Faced with deeply divided public opinion concerning America's involvement in Europe, Wilson created an official propaganda agency, the Committee on Public Information (CPI). The CPI hired an impressive group of writers, photographers, historians, and entertainers to "sell" the war to the public. In addition, the United States attorney general, Thomas W. Gregory, worked with local nativist groups and empowered them with the mission of uncovering "disloyal" Americans. One of the largest of these citizen-detective groups, the American Protective League (APL), had over 250,000 members. Other such organizations included the American Defense Society, the Boy Spies of America, and the National Security League. Members of these groups watched over neighbors, colleagues, and strangers; broke into homes; opened private mail; slandered innocent people; and physically assaulted and arrested alleged "disloyal" Americans. The leagues also focused on foreign-born groups. "[W]rapped in the mantle of patriotism, extremist groups such as the American Protection League and the Sedition Slammers threaten to whip out political dissent and nonconforming behavior. Acting as self-appointed vigilantes and espousing 100% Americans, these groups persecuted so-called hyphenated Americans."[19]

In a high-pitched, emotionally charged campaign, the Committee on Public Information exploited and ignited strong feelings of nativism, xenophobia, jingoism, and superpatriotism, and war hysteria soon gripped the nation. National, state, and local nativist organizations pressured immigrants for total conformity. *The Meaning of America,* one of the booklets produced by the CPI, provided instructions and speaking suggestions to the Division of Four-Minute Men, a group of over 75,000 volunteers who provided short patriotic speeches to move-theater audiences and social clubs throughout the United States, and included specific information on how to talk to foreign-born groups. It directed speakers to persuade immigrants to speak "the English language . . . salute the flag . . . cultivate patriotism in [their] children . . . [and learn the] words of [The] Star Spangled Banner." The agency contended that some of the nation's immigrants "expected too much from the land of liberty," and therefore, it was CPI's goal to remind America's ethnic groups of their duty to the United States.[20] In addition, CPI produced thirty different propaganda bulletins and distributed over 75 million copies in various languages. They also reprinted President Wilson's "A Tribute to the Foreign Born," which revealed his increasing anxiety over America's ethnic diversity and the divided opinion of the immigrant communities over the war. Wilson claimed to be in "a hurry for an opportunity to have a line-up and let the men who are thinking first of other countries stand on one side, and all those that are for America first, last, and all the time on the other side."[21] Immigrants from enemy states (people known as "enemy aliens") were expected to register their names with the government.

Postmaster General Burleson instigated a personal crusade against alleged war dissenters and justified his actions with the espionage laws. Burleson frequently overstepped his delegated authority by cutting off the second-class mailing privileges for many ethnic presses without due cause, an action that subsequently bankrupted the papers that could not afford to use first-class mail. He also indirectly censored ethnic publishers by forcing them to submit English translations of all articles (prior to publication) that referred to the war. These actions fostered a fear among foreign-language presses of a shutdown for what might be construed as "disloyal" materials. Moreover, the delay in publication crippled many papers that could not bear the added expense.[22]

In order to help raise money to pay for the war, the government initiated the Liberty Loan campaign. This drive capitalized on the superpatriotic fever of the day and quickly tied the purchase of war bonds with a demonstration of loyalty. Liberty Loan posters that draped the cities also promoted conformity. One poster read: "Are you 100% American? Prove It! Buy U.S. Government Bonds." Liberty Bond advertisements, written in various languages, made extensive use of patriotic and emotional symbols such as the Statue of Liberty, the American Flag, and Ellis Island. One popular theme was to remind immigrants of their arrival in America and the reasons why they came. Heading one poster that pictured immigrants on the deck of a ship steaming past the Statue of Liberty was the message: "Remember Your First Thrill of American Liberty—YOUR DUTY—Buy United States Government Bonds."[23]

Specific ethnic groups became key targets for harassment, particularly German American communities. Hamburgers, sauerkraut, and German measles became liberty sandwiches, liberty cabbage, and liberty measles. School boards instructed students to cut out all references of Germany from their textbooks and canceled German language classes. Officials in many of the cities forbade the playing of Bach and Beethoven in public orchestras, and German art was removed from some city museums. For many German Americans, war hysteria resulted in violence and even death. Throughout the United States, nativists called upon foreign-born citizens to prove their allegiance to America.

The late nineteenth century marked the largest flow of immigrants into America. Most of the nation's "newcomers" arrived from southern and eastern Europe, where they fled from political, economic, or religious turmoil in their homelands. Like many other immigrant groups throughout American history, they tended to live in ethnic enclaves where they could speak their own language, eat ethnic foods, read news of their homelands in ethnic newspapers, and find support in ethnic fraternal and social organizations. Immigrants continued to retain important parts of their native ways, but they also adopted key elements of the dominant American culture.

During World War I, ethnic communities actively demonstrated their loyalty to the United States with resolutions, parades, and fundraisers that were wrapped in American symbolism and steeped in patriotic language. However, it is too simplistic to view these acts of loyalty as purely a response to a harsh nativism that forced immigrants to conform in their expressions of loyalty. This is especially true when one considers that these patriotic demonstrations were often fused with messages of ethnic cultural pride and were frequently connected to issues of homeland independence. Therefore, immigrants not only clearly expressed loyalty to the United States but also "liberally employed the rhetoric and imagery of American patriotism . . . and used the iconography of `100% Americanism' to obtain their own ethnic community goals."[24]

In May, 1918, a committee representing many of America's foreign-born groups sent a petition to President Wilson "announcing plans for a great demonstration on the Fourth (of July) of loyalty to the United States and the cause for which it is fighting and asking the entire country to join with them." Wilson responded with "heartfelt appreciation" and encouraged nationwide "Independence Day" celebrations designed to show unity, loyalty, and patriotism, and many cities responded by hosting "Americanization Day" events. The *New York Herald* reported that all over the nation, foreign-born Americans planned Fourth of July celebrations with parades, mass meetings, pageants, and speeches. The New York multiethnic celebration resulted in a coalition of twenty-two nationalities and a petition addressed to Wilson with a declaration of their loyalty: "Let us on July 4, 1918, celebrate the birth of a new—a greater spirit of democracy—by whose influence we hope and believe, what the signers of the Declaration of Independence dreamed of for themselves and their fellow countrymen shall be fulfilled for all mankind."[25]

Another Fourth of July broadside, printed in Philadelphia and designed to copy the Declaration of Independence, expressed the loyalty of twenty-four different ethnic groups. In the declaration, the groups "pledged their lives, fortunes, and sacred honor to support the United States." Delegates from the different immigrant groups signed the document, including representatives from the Armenian, Assyrian, Belgian, Chinese, Danish, Norwegian, Swedish, Dutch, French, Greek, German, Hungarian, Italian, Jewish, Latvian (Lettish), Lithuanian, Bohemian-Moravian, Slavish, Carpatho-Russian, Polish, Russian, Serbian, Romanian, and Ukrainian communities. The Bohemian National Alliance and the Slovak League distributed a written declaration representing forty-eight ethnic groups entitled "The Solemn Declaration of the Czechoslovak People to the Republic of the United States of America and Its Great President Woodrow Wilson." The declaration expressed their great respect for the American people and their leaders, emphasized the urgent need to make the world "safe for Democracy," and declared a "solemn pledge" of loyalty to America. Earlier patriotic events included a June, 1918, New York City parade that lasted twelve hours and included representatives from the Italian, Hungarian, and Czechoslovak national councils as well as "Jugo-Slav" organizations. The festivities included the "League of Foreign-Born Citizens," consisting of 1,000 men and women from twenty-one different nations who declared their intentions to become U.S. citizens in a united attack against "Kaiserism."[26]

Many demonstrations of immigrant loyalty entwined ethnic pride and homeland agendas with the language of democracy and national symbols such as the American flag, Uncle Sam, and Independence Hall. About sixty Slovene immigrants in Rock Springs, Wyoming, participated in a Fourth of July parade to express their loyalty to their new country, carrying both the American flag and the flag of their homeland. The marchers, some dressed in native costumes, also displayed a large sign that read, "Your Allies the Jugo-Slavs."[27] Many immigrant groups also participated in Indianapolis's Fourth of July parade. "Following units of city police, military bands, Boy Scouts, and the Daughters of the American Revolution carrying American flags, immigrants marched in native costumes and rode on floats as they presented themselves to the dominant society." The design of an Italian American float showcased children waving American flags with a "caricature of the 'Queen of Italy.'" Romanian immigrants in the same parade featured both "Uncle Sam" and the flag of their homeland. Over 350 Slovenians demonstrated their loyalty by marching in the Indianapolis parade. A group of Slovene American women dressed in ethnic costumes held a sign that answered Wilson's request: "We Are For America First, Last and All the Time."[28]

Sometimes, the words of ethnic leaders mirrored the "language of Americanism" used by leading nativists.[29] The Czech National Alliance suggested that parents "tear the obnoxious pages" of the "Kaiser Story" from their children's schoolbooks. The Czech National Alliance and the Polish National Alliance collected the "ripped" pages to send to the various school boards in protest. The Bohemian newspaper *Denni Hlasatel*, which called for immigrants to become naturalized citizens and celebrated the loyalty of "Czechs, Slovaks, Jugo-slavs, Poles, and other Slavonic nations," blamed American Germans and the German American press for the "antagonism shown toward the immigrants and . . . the attempts made to Americanize them instantly." Many ethnic leaders also joined in the Liberty Loan Crusade in the Foreign Language Division. Community leaders organized Liberty Loan parades, and editors recounted emotional war stories to elicit contributions. An editorial promoting the Third Liberty Loan noted, "Czech-Americans have never forgotten their motherland, and yet they have always shown that they are good citizens of this country who can be relied on in the critical days of war as well as in times of peace."[30]

While German and Irish immigrants expressed concern over the United States joining the Great War, other ethnic groups encouraged American involvement in the conflict. For those from southern and eastern Europe, the defeat of the Central Powers became directly tied to their dream of independence for their homelands. Many of these ethnic groups used American patriotic symbols and language in their efforts to show loyalty to their new country and to regain nation-state recognition of their native lands. Others hoped to create new nations out of the rubble of the war.

Even before the United States entered the conflict, the Czech and Slovak communities in America supported a war against the Austro-Hungarian Empire—an empire that had long strangled their ethnic groups. Over 1.5 million immigrants lived in the Czech and Slovak enclaves of America. As early as 1914, Czechs in New York created the American Committee for the Liberation of the Czech People. That same year, Czech ethnic leaders joined with the American National Council, the Czech Press Bureau, and other Czech organizations in a unified effort to free their homeland. Czech Sokols and the National Mutual Aid Organization soon joined in the cause. The Slovak League, organized in 1915, worked with the Slovak-American press, Slovak Sokols, and Slovak Catholic and evangelical groups to gain support for an independent Czechoslovakia. By October, 1915, many of these Czech and Slovak organizations united into the Czechoslovak (Bohemian) National Alliance. The alliance was headquartered in Chicago but had branches in other major cities including New York; Cleveland; Cedar Rapids, Iowa; Boston; and Omaha, Nebraska, and it grew rapidly to include over 80,000 members in nearly 350 branches throughout the United States. The alliance worked to rally public support for the cause of Czechoslovakian independence through lectures, pamphlets, leaflets, and newspaper articles that educated people to the plight of European Czechs and Slovaks.[31]

The Slav Press Bureau, established by the Bohemian National Alliance and the Slovak League of America, kept the Allied war cause in front of the immigrant public years before the Committee on Public Information began its propaganda campaign. In January, 1917, the Czech Catholic community joined in the call for independence when they unified into the National League of Czech Catholics. Ethnic newspapers and literature worked to keep the public informed. The Slav Press Bureau sent out anti-German and anti-Austrian articles to the American press two or three times each week. The *Bohemian Review* recalled, "on the very day when Austrian cannons were first fired against Serbia, Bohemians in Chicago organized a relief fund which in a few months collected nearly $20,000." Similar fundraisers took place in New York City, Cleveland, Omaha, Chicago, and Cedar Rapids that together collected over $320,000. Ethnic organizations sold arts and crafts at Bohemian bazaars and "Allied Bazaars" and solicited donations throughout the United States to raise money for the independence of their homelands. Czech and Slovak artists designed buttons, stamps, badges, postcards, posters, and maps, which were sold to raise funds for the fight for independence. Estimates put donations from American ethnic communities "into the millions."[32]

Once the United States declared war, ethnic leaders saw their peoples' participation in the fighting as a way of demonstrating loyalty to their adopted country and bringing "liberation and independence" to their homeland. An April, 1917, article in Chicago's *Denni Hlasatel* summed it up best: "We live in America as free citizens[, and] we enjoy here freedom of speech and of the press. . . . It was the people from the lower class and the middle class who have benefited considerably by the conditions in the new country. . . . The immigrant should constantly keep all this in mind, especially now that his new homeland is at war. . . . If America with the Allies annihilates Germany, it will have done away with our deadliest enemy, and advanced us nearer to the fulfillment of our sacred dream, the rescue of our motherland and the nation of our ancestors from the paws that have been on them in bondage for centuries."[33]

Ethnic leaders carefully incorporated American symbols and rhetoric with their homeland agendas. The *Bohemian Review* noted that the Czechs and Slovaks were "acting consistently with the Declaration of Independence, which maintains that governments are instituted among men to secure the right to life, liberty and happiness, deriving their just power from the consent of the governed." The *Review* concluded, "the Czechoslovaks were worthy heirs to the American Revolution."[34] The Czech National Alliance in Chicago compared President Wilson with Abraham Lincoln when it discussed the struggle for freedom of the Czech and Slovak peoples: "Just as Abraham Lincoln's voice called for a government of the people, your voice is imparting strength to millions of subjugated men and women who are, however, determined to protect their ancient, inalienable rights. . . . As Americans of Czech descent, we doubly feel the power in your decision. . . . We rejoice over America's entrance into the war, for we know that . . . it means help to the Czechoslovak people in their unequal struggle against the tyrants."[35]

Immediately after the United States entered the conflict, ethnic leaders called for members of their community to enlist in the armed forces and later supported the national draft. Czech and Slovak women gathered together to knit sweaters and other warm clothing for soldiers fighting in Europe. These ethnic sewing "bees" later joined the American Red Cross efforts as auxiliary groups. As early as April 8, 1917, the Bohemian National Alliance addressed members through some fifty ethnic newspapers: "We want to impress upon all members of the Bohemian National Alliance the duties which war lays upon all citizens of the country. Above all, it is your duty to fight for the land you made your own, to which most of you swore allegiance, the land which is dedicated to the eternal principles of justice and rule by the people."[36]

Czech and Slovak leaders mixed the symbols and rhetoric of American patriotism with cultural pride in their efforts to recruit immigrant soldiers for the American Army. This was done both to express loyalty and to achieve ethnic community goals. The Czech and Slovak leaders promoted voluntary service in the U.S. Army and Navy through social and fraternal organizations. Sokols hosted gatherings and mass meetings at which "all the societies, associations, and clubs [were] urged to work diligently, taking the names of all men willing to enlist." Recruitment rallies featured pictures of life in the army, military equipment, and patriotic Czech, Slovak, and American songs. Ethnic leaders from various organizations (the Bohemian National Alliance, the Czech and Slovak Sokols, the Czech Protestants, and the Czech National Alliance, the Union of Czech Ladies, and the Sisterhood

of Aid Societies) worked with recruiting officers from the American military to provide immigrant soldiers with inspirational speeches. The Czech
National Alliance, the National Alliance of Czech Catholics, and the Slovak League also held meetings with a "twofold" purpose: first, "to demonstrate our irreconcilable opposition to the Government of Austria; and
second, to proclaim our loyalty to America, which has declared war on
decayed Austria." As the Bureau of the Czech National Alliance of Catholics put it: "In this critical time, when we feel compelled to draw the sword
for the defense of human rights and the liberation of the oppressed peoples
by autocratic governments, our duty stands out clearly to us. . . . Our place
is under the Star Spangled Banner, the symbol of equality and liberty. . . .
Let us show that we have grasped the meaning of duty and intend to has-
ten to the colors to increase the number of those willing to lay down their
lives for the country."[37]

From April to June, 1917, ethnic newspaper articles listed the names of
immigrants who volunteered in the United States military. Some recorded
the gradual emptying of the Sokol gymnastic societies as members answered
the call of their nation. Other articles boasted that the "so-called 'hyphenated Americans,' that is Czechs, Poles, Slovaks, Croats and others of Slavonic
blood. . . . [offered] his services, and perhaps his life, to his new homeland."
The editor of the *Denni Hlasatel* claimed that information from the recruiting office and the War Department indicated that "more than two-thirds of
the volunteers hailed from the strata of the immigrant populace."[38]

Once the national draft was implemented in June, the Bohemian press
reminded Czechs and Slovaks to register with the U.S. Selective Service Board
and continued to tie the war effort to independence of the homeland. "Thousands of Czech families will soon have to part with their sons. We feel the
painful throb in a mother's heart, . . . but her son is going to fight for a
cause dear to Czechs and Americans alike." Parades featured Czechs and
Slovaks in "Uncle Sam's Army" such as the Chicago march that ended at
the Sokol Havlicek-Tyrs Hall to the sound of "The Star Spangled Banner."[39]

By November, 1917, the United States expanded the conflict with Germany by declaring war on that nation's partner, the Austro-Hungarian
Empire. This action also "technically" excluded noncitizen Czechs and Slovaks from serving in the army since they had been born in the empire. Not
surprisingly, this brought resentment from the ethnic groups who had long
called for the defeat of the Central Powers and had worked diligently for its
demise. Various Czech and Slovak groups rallied to demonstrate continued
support for the war, and leaders worked to have the "technical enemy alien"

status removed from noncitizen members of their community. While the situation was being straightened out, Czech and Slovak organizations in America began to raise money and recruit for the Czechoslovak Legion to serve with the French Army.[40]

The founder of the Czechoslovak Legion, Thomas G. Masaryk, was a former member of the Vienna Parliament and a professor of philosophy at Prague's Charles University; he would later become the first president of Czechoslovakia. With the outbreak of World War I, Masaryk decided the time was right to fight for the independence of the Czech and Slovak peoples and to break the bondage of Austro-Hungarian control. On May 30, 1917, the Czech Coalition sent a resolution to the Austrian Parliament asking for "home rule" and emphasizing "the principles of self-determination for a democratic Czech State united with the Slovaks."[41]

Edvard Benes, a former student of Masaryk at Charles University and lecturer in a Prague college, and Dr. Milan Rastislav Stefanik, a Slovakian scientist and son of a Lutheran pastor, assisted with Czech enlistments. Stefanik became the vice president of the Czechoslovak National Council, the official recruiting organization for the Czechoslovak Legion. In the fall of 1917, Stefanik spent a few weeks in the United States to raise funds and lay a "firm foundation" for recruitment of nondeclarant immigrants for the Czechoslovak Legion. Even though France did not officially approve of the legion until December, 1917, Count de Montal, a French Army aviation colonel and military attaché in Washington D.C., accompanied Stefanik. The United States did not officially sanction recruiting for the Czechoslovak Legion until the spring of 1918, but according to newspaper accounts, the government had given its consent for raising funds and early recruitment the previous October.[42]

On October 14, 1917, Chicago's Sokol Havlicek-Tyrs auditorium was crowded with the largest group ever assembled in the hall. The stage was set with the flags of the Allied countries, photographs of thirty-two members of Havlicek-Tyrs already fighting in Europe (probably with the Canadian Brigade), and a memorial to another member, Anton Nedelka, who was killed fighting in France. Dr. Ludwig J. Fisher, president of the Czech National Alliance, introduced Dr. Stefanik and Colonel de Montal, both of whom wore French uniforms. According to a newspaper account of the meeting, Stefanik's "chest glittered with four medals which he had won by his daring exploits in the French Army." Stefanik announced his goals: rally support for Czechoslovak independence, raise funding for the Czech and Slovak cause, and enlist Slavs from the United States. The speaker pleaded

with Czech and Slovak women not to "place obstacles" in front of volunteers. The responsibility for this liberation, he said, "rests upon the soldiers
of the Slavs in America." Fisher followed with his own address, in which he
predicted that Czechoslovak forces "should become an efficient cog in the
gigantic wheel of the international struggle and work for the Allies. . . . It is
up to every Czechoslovak who is not burdened with care for his family to
prove that his patriotism is honest and sincere." Fisher ended his dramatic
speech by announcing his willingness to "give his life for the old motherland" and his service to the Czechoslovak Army. Colonel de Montal noted
the common ideals of the French, Czechs, and Slovaks. After the program
ended, the speakers headed to a Pilsen Brewery Park pavilion to address a
large "Czechoslovak" Catholic crowd. A representative of the Czech National Alliance stayed behind to organize the volunteers, one hundred men
who stepped forward. To ensure that soldiers could return to the United
States after the war, community leaders pushed for immigration laws that
would allow foreign-born soldiers to be repatriated.[43]

Czech and Slovak Americans who helped in the recruiting efforts carefully selected images that express both loyalty to their adopted country and
pride for their ethnicity. For example, at a farewell to legion volunteers in
November, 1917, performers dressed in ethnic costumes and sang the Czech
National Alliance battle song, "Vyzva" ("The Call") while standing before a
replica of the Statue of Liberty. A singer performed the Czech national anthem, and "an apotheosis of Slovak volunteers serving in the various Allied armies, and also of Slovak girls rendering homage before a Statue of
Liberty, closed the memorable evening to the strains of the 'March of the
Czechoslovak Army.'"[44]

The situation became even more complex with the declaration of war
between the United States and the Austro-Hungarian Empire, especially
when the U.S. Selective Service Board started to record all noncitizen immigrants born in the empire as "enemy aliens." Czech and Slovak leaders urged
the government to remove this status so their men could continue to serve
in the United States military. As Congress and military leaders discussed the
situation, recruitment for the Czechoslovak forced in France continued.[45]

In the spring of 1918, Masaryk traveled to the United States in the hope
of securing recognition for his country's independence, raising funds for
the legion, and securing volunteers from the Czech and Slovak enclaves.
Stefanik accompanied him. They recruited in New York, Boston, Baltimore,
Cleveland, Pittsburgh, and Washington, D.C., but Masaryk and Stefanik
particularly targeted Chicago because the city had the largest Czech popu-

lation outside of Prague. Czech leaders, "well-known" businessmen, professors, editors, physicians, and leaders from American Czech and Slovak organizations helped in the recruiting efforts. According to Masaryk, Chicago greeted him with open arms, and thousands of people lined the streets in national costumes, waving flags with the Czech and Slovak "colours."[46]

In June, 1918, a huge crowd shouted *"Na Zdar!"* (to success!) as they welcomed the leader to Pilsen Park in Chicago. The Czech Catholic Alliance and the Slovak League called the Czechoslovak Army "the crowning of our national patriotic efforts."[47] Most of the recruiting drives clearly combined American patriotism with ethnic pride. In a moving speech, Lieutenant Horvat, a Slovakian clergyman serving in the Legion, told the audience, "There are no differences in the Czechoslovak Army. Czech and Slovaks stand as equals, and shoulder to shoulder, with one aim—to humble the age-old common enemy. . . . .You in America know what liberty means. We want to build the independent Czechoslovak State upon the same principles."[48]

The Chicago Military Committee for the Czechoslovak Army recruited in the Midwest. The committee asked its "ladies" and the area businessmen to provide a send-off reception for fifty volunteers from Nebraska, Wisconsin, and Illinois and asked the Czechoslovakian public to "appear in large numbers to give our boys our last greeting." At a send-off for forty Czech volunteers in August, 1918, performers sang "The Star Spangled Banner" along with "old country" Czech songs. The Workmen's Chorus sang "Kdo Jste Bozi Bojovnici" ("Soldiers of the Lord") followed by the American anthem. Guest speakers included First Lieutenant Holy of the Czechoslovak Army and Dr. Knapp, editor of the *Chicago Journal.* In an emotional speech in September, 1918, Masaryk told new Czech and Slovak recruits: "We are now fighting on all battle-fronts. Our blood is being shed with the blood of American soldiers as well as with the blood of the other allied soldiers. Out of this mixture of bloodshed . . . there will be, we hope, a brotherhood of allied nations."[49]

Recruiters also circulated colorful enlistment posters and postcards in Czech and Slovak. The postcards depicted soldiers in action with catchy slogans: "Fall in rank! Brothers join your bothers here! All ye who bear the name of Slovak!"; "Fatherland, oh Fatherland! To conquer or die!"; "Seize arms and join our ranks, all ye of Czechoslovak birth!"; "The country calls! Prepare to act." Recruiting also took place in ethnic newspapers that called the Czechoslovak Army of France "crusaders of modern times" and encouraged noncitizen immigrants to do "their duty to serve the old homeland."[50]

The Czechoslovak National Council called on physicians and nurses to volunteer with Czechoslovak forces in Siberia. The council required applicants to have knowledge of the Czech and Slovak languages. The Czechoslav Aid Committee also raised funds for the legion and raised enough money to purchase an ambulance for shipment to Vladivostok through the American Red Cross. Fund raising for the Czechoslovak national cause continued throughout the war and netted hundreds of thousands of dollars.[51]

When the United States officially recognized the independent Czechoslovak state in September, 1918, ethnic communities rejoiced in their success, and Czechs and Slovaks were taken off the enemy alien list and once again allowed to serve in the U.S. Army. To celebrate, Czech and Slovak communities in Chicago held a "gigantic parade" to express "joy over President Wilson's declaration . . . and testify to their gratitude and loyalty to the United States Government." Community organizers requested that servicemen from their areas be furloughed from Camp Grant and the Great Lakes Naval Training Station to honor the occasion. Ethnic leader and Congressman Adolph J. Sabath telegraphed the commanders of the two camps, and the soldiers and sailors soon joined the celebratory parade. Some 17,000 soldiers at Camp Dodge, Iowa, ended their independence parade with a special formation symbolizing the Statue of Liberty as the regimental bands played patriotic music.[52]

Recruiting for the Czechoslovak Legion lost its momentum after Congress recognized Czechoslovakia's independence and declared the new country an ally. Masaryk understood the desire of most Czech and Slovak Americans to enlist in the army of their adopted country, although he did not give up trying to recruit immigrants into the French Army. In the end, the Czechoslovak Legion in France consisted of over 15,000 soldiers including about 3,000 volunteers from America's ethnic enclaves.[53]

With the end of the Polish-Lithuanian Commonwealth in the late eighteenth century, Poland experienced a long period of occupation. By 1772 Prussia, Russia, and Austria began to divide the country. Poles revolted many times during the century, but although boundaries and politics changed, they remained under foreign imperial control. As political oppression mounted in the late nineteenth century, almost one million emigrants left for the United States. Once in America, many remained intensely interested in the freedom of their homeland. Polish patriotic societies even trained young recruits for the eventual day when they would return and Poland would be independent.[54]

To ensure that the fight for freedom would continue, these patriotic societies conducted military training programs so they would be ready to defend their homeland when the opportunity arose. A number of patriotic fraternal organizations including the Polish Falcon Alliance, The Polish National Alliance, the Polish Youth Alliance, and the Polish Military Alliance worked toward the restoration of Poland's independence.[55]

The First World War brought a renewed interest in the old country. Similar to American Czechs and Slovaks, Polish Americans also hoped that the Great War would lead to the independence of their homeland. Their leaders organized a number of fundraisers designed to assist this cause. Polish patriot and famed pianist Ignancy Jan Paderewski and his wife headed many of the fund-raising activities. At most of these events, Poles sold flags of their native country and "Polish Refugee Dolls" to raise money for the Polish Committee for Emergency Aid. As the situation in Poland worsened, the Polish American community sharply stepped up its efforts through such groups as the Polish Central Relief Committee (PCRC) and the Polish National Council. President Wilson assisted these efforts when he dedicated January 1, 1916, to the Poland war-relief effort. The American Red Cross also worked hard to bring food into the devastated country. Once America's entrance into the war became certain, Polish Americans expressed their loyalty through resolutions, parades, Liberty Loan campaigns, and fundraisers. Over 138,000 of them served in the American Army.[56]

Many immigrants not subject to the American draft chose to support the development of the Polish Legion. The Polish Falcons met in a special meeting in Pittsburgh in April, 1917, where 187 delegates discussed recruiting an army to fight with the French to free Poland. Despite the connection with the French government, the Polish American community concluded that "the Polish army [was] to be considered as an appendage to the regular United States army; its flag should be the Stars and Stripes, only the regimental banners ought to display national Polish colors in order to make the nationality of the fighters more obvious to their kin on the opposite side."[57]

In June, 1917, Polish leaders in Pittsburgh began a preliminary search for officers for the legion. Qualified candidates had to be between the ages of eighteen and thirty-five, be physically fit, have a basic knowledge of mathematics, be of good character, and speak and write both Polish and English. Each officer also had to supply his own uniform, rifle, and bayonet. The response was so great that by July 5 the Pittsburgh Falcons announced that no further candidates would be accepted. Excitement over the legion grew in other Polish communities throughout the United States. Polish leaders Dr. Teofil A. Starzynski, Ignace Jan Paderewski, C. W. Sypniewski,

Dr. Adam Wolcyrz, J. Sierocinski, W. Sulewski, F. Boguszewski, and many other prominent Polish doctors, lawyers, and leaders formulated plans for training their fellow immigrants.[58]

The only thing that remained was to convince the United States government to officially recognize the legion, and Polish American leaders put pressure on Pres. Woodrow Wilson to approve of their army. They were joined in June, 1917, by the French government, which presented a decree calling for the creation of the Polish Army of France. The British government also helped when they agreed to open up its Canadian training camps to the Polish American recruits. The U.S. State Department and War Department discussed the possibility of creating a separate Polish legion attached to the American Army and considered officially recognizing the nation-state of Poland. But due to the political complications of Poland's independence, the United States took no immediate action. Growing impatient, some Polish Americans joined the Canadian Army. After initial training, the soldiers were sent to the "Polish Division" of the French Army.[59]

By September, 1917, the U.S. government announced that recruitment of the "Polish Army in America" could begin: "The War Department has been advised that no individual of Polish nationality resident in the United States who is in any way subject to the draft will be accepted as a recruit by this military commission. Having in mind the attitude of this Government toward a united and independent Poland, the War Department is glad to announce that it is entirely in accord with the proposed plans of this military commission."[60]

Recruitment almost ended when the U.S. Fuel Administrator, Harry G. Garfield, expressed concern over the possibility of losing too many Polish American miners in the coal fields. Garfield supporters argued that Poland, controlled by German forces, was technically an enemy of the United States and sought to stop development of the Polish Legion. Secretary of War Baker quickly put an end to these obstructions and recruitment in the legion continued. "Thus the stage was set for the long anticipated organization of [an] American contingent of the Polish Army in France."[61]

Polish enclaves organized "citizen committees" to promote recruitment and raise money for the American Polish units. The Polish Roman Catholic Church, Ladies Auxiliaries, and other Polish organizations also solicited support for the cause. Polish leaders set up recruiting offices in Milwaukee, Chicago, Detroit, Cleveland, Buffalo, Pittsburgh, Wilkes-Barre (Pennsylvania), New York City, and Boston. Mass rallies drew attention to the legion, complete with Polish folk songs and music from Polish military bands. Movie theaters in ethnic neighborhoods showed films of the legion training in their Niagara camp, and recruiting officers spoke at various community functions. Approximately 20,000 Polish American volunteers served with the Polish Army in France. When they enlisted, new Polish American legionnaires signed a statement of dual loyalty: "I, the undersigned, declaring my readiness to fight for a united, free and independent Poland and for the honor of the Star-spangled Banner of the United States."[62]

Many Jewish Americans connected the American war effort with the freedom of European Jews and the establishment of a Jewish homeland in Palestine and also actively served in the American Army. Eventually, over 250,000 Jews served in the United States military. In early April, 1917, Rabbi Buchler of New York led a movement to enlist Austro-Hungarian Jews in the U.S. Army and Navy. He planned a mass movement as an "initial step in a whirlwind recruiting campaign among men of foreign birth."[63] Prominent Jewish leaders organized the American League of Jewish Patriots in April, 1917. The League's committee members included Samuel Untermyer (president) and Joel Slomin (secretary) along with a number of Jewish editors: Judge Aaron J. Levy (from *The Warheit*), Leo Moissies (from *The Day*), Peter Viernick (from *The Jewish Morning Journal*), Leo Kamaki (from *The Jewish Daily News*), William Edlin (from *The Day*), Louis Miller (representing Jewish weeklies published in Yiddish), and Herman Bernstein (representing Jewish weeklies published in English). The committee announced that its purpose was to encourage enlistment of Jewish men into the army of the United States. The committee organized offices throughout New York City from which Jewish men and women would aid in registering Jews into the American military. Jewish American leaders even tied their war effort to "Americanization" issues and concluded that only the "un-Americanized Jew" would fear the war, since they would inadvertently connect the American draft with the Russian draft: "When the Jew becomes Americanized, however, he then becomes entirely different. Then he understands that the Constitution of the United States gives all citizens of the country equal rights, and that this country affords every inhabitant equal opportunity. Then he who originally was a 'slacker' is among the first to volunteer, and on the field of battle he is the renowned hero."[64]

But concern over the homeland issue continued. Many editorials treasured the Old World traditions but expressed their love and patriotism for America and "prayed" for a "victory of the American ideal of liberty and democracy over the evil powers of autocracy." American Jewish newspapers express dual loyalty—that is, pride in fighting for both America and the

Jewish cause. The subtitle of one Chicago newspaper, the *Sunday Jewish Courier,* read: "Help America to Victory! Help the Jewish People to Victory!" The article went on: "If America wins, every Jew throughout the world wins—he will have won a new status in life, the respect and esteem which he deserves as the son of an ancient people with great classical traditions. . . . The moment has also arrived for us Jews in America to prove that we love America, that we are thankful to America, and that we love our own people, and wish to make them free and happy."[65]

Jewish American Zionist leaders also worked diligently to raise funds to help their European brothers. Philadelphia-area Jews raised money at various patriotic events such as the Opera House fundraiser, which received pledges for over $200,000 to aid Jewish war victims. At a conference in March, 1918, New York Jewish leaders raised $50,000 toward the community's goal of $1,000,000 for the "restoration of Palestine" to the Jewish people.[66]

Similar to the Czechs, Slovaks, and Poles, Jews also organized a foreign legion. The development of the Jewish Legion resulted from the persistence of a young Russian Jewish journalist, Vladimir Jabotinsky. Prior to the war, Jabotinsky served as chief editor in Constantinople for four different Zionist newspapers. In 1914 he became a correspondent with the *Russian Monitor.* His on-going assignment was to report on the "mood and sentiments" of the war rather than the actual fighting, and he traveled to England, France, Norway, Sweden, Egypt, Algiers, and Morocco. In his memoirs Jabotinsky reported that his trip to Britain was to determine the truth behind "the biting quip," then popular in Russia, that "the British Lion [was] prepared to fight to the last drop of Russian blood." But it was in France where Jabotinksy turned from a "mere observer" into a war activist after he read that Turkey had joined the Center Powers: "Turkey's move transformed me in one short morning into a fanatical believer in war until victory; Turkey's move made this 'my war.'"[67]

The young Zionists realized that the only hope of restoring Palestine was in the defeat of the Ottoman Empire. The answer seemed simple: the formation of a Jewish military force to help the Allies destroy the Turks and ultimately free Palestine, which would become a Jewish homeland. The idea of a legion became even more crucial when the Turks began to clamp down on Jewish settlers. However, British politics, military strategy, and Jewish Zionism complicated this simple answer, and it would take four years of struggle before the Jewish Legion came into existence. After a long and difficult journey through a political maze, Jabotinsky finally got the attention of

British war secretary Lord Derby. When he met with Derby, Jabotinsky's friend Joseph Trumpeldor, captain of the Jewish Mule Corps attached to the British Army, accompanied him. When asked by Derby if the two men could promise enough Jewish soldiers to form a regiment, Trumpeldor replied: "If it is to be just a regiment of Jews—perhaps. If it will be a regiment for the Palestine front—certainly. If, together with its formation, there will appear a government pronouncement in favor of Zionism—overwhelmingly." Lord Derby "smiled charmingly and said, 'I am but a War Secretary.'"[68]

Shortly after the meeting, the War Department announced the formation of the Jewish Legion to fight in Palestine. Soon thereafter in November, 1917, the British minister for foreign affairs, A. J. Balfour, announced what became known as the Balfour Declaration, a promise by Britain to open up Palestine as a Jewish homeland.

Major recruitment efforts soon followed. Hebrew signs welcomed young men in the London enlistment office. The British signed up Jews in both Palestine and the United States. Recruiters reported a "spontaneous movement among the young Jewish Colonists [living in Palestine] . . . who felt it to be their duty to share in the task of liberating their home from the hated Turk." Recruiters noted that efforts were helped by the Balfour Declaration. In fact, several hundred Jewish soldiers serving in the British military requested transfer into the legion.[69]

Recruiters headed to the United States, where they hoped to convince American Jews to join the legion. The American government made it clear that only Jews ineligible for the U.S. Army could serve with the British Army in Palestine. National Jewish leaders in America demanded four conditions for Britain's legion recruitment: "That the units had to be sent to the eastern front for active service in Palestine; that they be integrated in the British army as Jewish units under Jewish commanders; that they employ Jewish national emblems and symbols for their identification, such as the Jewish flag; [and] that the language of command be Hebrew."[70]

Jabotinsky traveled to America to help with these efforts. Recruiting offices sprang up in New York, Chicago, Cleveland, and other American cities. Maj. C. Brooman White directed the operation with the help of the British-Canadian Recruiting Mission and two British officers, Capt. T. C. Dolthin and Col. J. S. Dennis. They were assisted by the Zionist Organization of the United States, which greeted the Jewish Legion "enthusiastically."[71]

By February, American recruitment for the Jewish Legion of Palestine was well underway. Over 200 young Jews, wearing the Star of David, were honored at a New York restaurant on February 25, 1918. A few days later,

another group of 150 newly recruited New York Jews listened to a welcome speech by Prof. William Bradley Otis, who equated service in the Jewish Legion to a "religious movement greater than the Crusades." Some recruiting efforts were quite dramatic. In March the British tank "Britannia,"
commanded by a Captain Haigh, drove through the streets of New York
"seeking recruits." Roman Freulich heard about the legion from a young
British solider standing in Union Square making an "impassioned appeal
for volunteers to fight the Turks and free Palestine, the ancient Jewish homeland." Freulich was drawn to the young speaker since he was wearing the
Star of David on his uniform. Legionnaire William Braiterman recalled
another recruiting method. A group of volunteers in Baltimore, Maryland,
would stand on the sidewalk of a busy intersection and sing Hebrew songs.
After catching the attention of passers-by, the soldiers would hand out recruiting literature in both Yiddish and English. They would also stand on a
"soap box" and speak to the audience about creating a Jewish homeland.
The speakers would "appeal to the listeners to join the Jewish Legion and
fight in a Jewish Army, under a Jewish Flag, with Jewish officers, and with
Hebrew commands. An article in the June 5, 1918, *Daily Jewish Courier* noted
that the men fighting "under the British flag in Palestine . . . still cling with
their souls to Jewish hopes and Jewish traditions." The newspaper observed,
"In helping America to win—and win fast—we are not only doing our duty
as citizens, not only expressing our appreciation to the country which accepted us when we were running away from the enemy, and which has
given us freedom and a thousand opportunities to develop our strength,
but we are also helping ourselves as Jews; we help the Jewish people to ob-
tain their old homeland and become a nation equal to other nations."[72]

Jewish Americans who joined the legion came from different socioeco-
nomic backgrounds of both native-born and foreign-born Jewish communities. Some spoke Hebrew or Yiddish, others English. Their occupations
were various and included "shop workers, artisans, storekeepers, professionals, students, white-collar workers, teachers, and writers." Many recruits were "ardent Zionists," while others were seeking adventure or es-
caping problems. The Zionist Labor Party also helped recruit from within
their ranks. The British government later learned that a number of soldiers
had lied about their age in order to serve, and others were too old to be
drafted into the U.S. Army. Zionist organizations "wined and dined" the legionnaires and gave them gifts of warm clothing and various foodstuff.
Zionist leaders hosted a number of "send-off dinners" for Jewish American
recruits at their Zionist Lunch Club at the New York Hotel Imperial.[73]

Carrying the Jewish flag, the first group of 150 recruits paraded down Fifth Avenue to the sounds of a military band. Thousands of supporters turned out to celebrate the event. American Zionists leaders Dr. Shmarya Levin and Louis Lipsky spoke to the young men, and Levin closed his remarks with, "go and take the country and never give it back." Reuben Brainin, the well-known Jewish writer, accompanied his two sons, Joseph and Moses, on the train ride to their training camp. Brainin told his sons he wished he were young enough to serve with them and spoke to the group of recruits. "Boys, listen to me: it is better that you die in the Land of Israel, than that you should return into Exile."[74]

Within a few weeks, another squad, this time with 350 Jews from New York, Philadelphia, and Cleveland, marched through the Bronx after being sworn in to the British Army. Several thousand people cheered them as they paraded by wearing David's "shield" (the Star of David). Jewish legionnaires from Chicago, Baltimore, Syracuse, Newark, and small towns in Connecticut and New Jersey soon joined other Jewish Americans to fight for Palestine. "At the railroad stations, there were speeches, pats on the back from the elders, and kisses from the ladies, many of whom cried."[75]

To thank the Americans for their help, Lord Reading, the British ambassador, sent a telegram to Major White welcoming the "new contingent of the Jewish battalion" and said he felt "sure they [would] contribute worthily on the field of battle to the cause of democracy and liberty throughout the world." To ensure that Jewish soldiers enlisting in foreign legions could return to America, Congressman Adolph J. Sabath worked on a repatriation bill, which passed in June, 1918. The British and Jewish recruiting team told American Jews they could either come back to the United States or stay in the Holy Land to "make new homes for themselves in the ancient land of their fathers."[76]

Eventually, the Jewish Legion would boast 10,000 Jewish soldiers, of whom about 5,000 came from the United States. Legionnaire William Braiterman explained: "Some felt that we were not expressing our full allegiance and our appreciation to America for their kindness to us . . . that we should enlist in the American Army. Some were afraid that we would risk our American citizenship, but America was big enough and strong enough not to miss a mere 5,000 American Jewish volunteers, many of whom were not yet citizens or too young for the draft."[77]

The American Jewish women's organization, Hadassah, sent over thirty doctors, some nurses, and medicine to help build the "Jewish State." American Jewish women also organized the Red Magen David to give aid to the

Jewish Legion in Palestine. From their headquarters in New York City, volunteers raised money through Yiddish theaters and publications. The women also established sewing and knitting bees during which they made warm clothing for the soldiers. Red Magen David volunteers "cared for the families of the Jewish Legion volunteers and otherwise provided services to the Jewish soldiers, akin to Red Cross, Y.M.C.A., or Salvation Army."[78]

The end of the First World War did not result in a Jewish homeland in Palestine as so many had hoped—it would take another world war and continued bloodshed afterward. However, in the conclusion of his memoirs, Vladimir Jabotinsky ends with a stirring message for all the Jewish legionnaires who served in Palestine: "Far away, in your home, you will one day read glorious news, of a free Jewish life in a free Jewish country—of factories and universities, of farms and theaters, perhaps of M.P.'s and Ministers. Then you will lose yourself in thought, and the paper will slip from your fingers; and there will come to your mind a picture of the Jordan Valley, of the desert by Raffa, of the hill of Ephraim by Abuein. Then you shall stand up, walk to the mirror, and look yourself proudly in the face. Jump to 'attention,' and salute yourself—for 'tis you who have made it."[79]

In July, 1917, the American ambassador in Rome forwarded a request from the "Armenia Indipandents" committee. This group of Armenians, seeking the independence of their homeland, asked the United States to organize a legion of Armenians from that nation, Greece, Egypt, and the Aegean Islands to fight with Allied forces. Four months later in a related matter, the British Embassy in Rome expressed concern about the troops in northern Persia and the Caucasus front, concluding that the Armenians were the only ethnic group with a commitment to help the Allies. The British diplomats requested that the United States work with Russia to send Armenian recruits into the Russia Army to fight in the region. The British also suggested that American officers and American money would help in this mission. However, these did not convince the U.S. War Department to create an Armenian Legion, and the secretary of war, Newton D. Baker, expressed his regret that the United States would be unable to send munitions or army officers.[80]

In December Britain tried again, this time with a letter from Lord Bryce suggesting that the United States government send American officers to help "organize and drill the Armenians so that they might be able to defend the Christian populations against an advance by the Turks or an uprising of the Tartars in the eastern region of Trans-Caucasia."[81] Lord Bryce understood that Armenian immigrants in America wanted to fight against the Turks, and he noted that many Armenians had already begun to enlist in the American Army. The War College Division recommended that the chief of staff deny the request since the United States was not officially at war with Turkey. The division also noted that Armenian officers were needed in the United States Army, and that the Armenian American population was too small to support a large enough force to accomplish this military action. For the second time, the War Department concluded that an Armenian legion was "impracticable."

In October, 1917, Judge Joseph Buffington of the United States District Court in Pittsburgh joined forces with the Russian counsel to inquire about the establishment of a "Russian Legion" made up of Russian immigrants in America. They suggested that this unit be attached to the French Army. Secretary of War Baker noted that a creation of such a force had to have congressional approval and would take away some ten thousand Russian laborers needed in the Pittsburgh area. Baker also reminded Judge Buffington that the United States was in the process of training Russian American soldiers to fight in the U.S. Army. As with the proposed Armenian Legion, this all-Russian force never gained United States support.[82]

Other ethnic groups also fought diligently for the freedom of their homelands. Many with roots in Central Europe published pamphlets, conducted meetings, and held public fundraisers for the benefit of their war-torn homelands or to elicit support for their independence. American Serb, Croat, and Slovene communities pressured the U.S. government to help establish a democratic state in the Balkans. The Philadelphia Committee for Armenian Relief gathered contributions throughout the city, and the Slavs met at Independence Hall in a symbolic gesture to declare the independence of southeastern Europe. The American Committee for Armenian and Syrian Relief conducted a national fundraiser in an effort to help three million destitute countrymen. America's Allies Co-operative Committee (an alliance of English, French, Italian, Belgian, Serbian, and Polish war relief committees) raised funds to help the "suffering Allies."[83]

The Lithuanian newspaper *Lietuva* applauded the "thousands of Lithuanian-American Youth" who served in the United States Army despite the neutral status of Lithuania. The paper reported on their "enthusiastic participation" in the Liberty Loan campaigns and Red Cross drives, noting: "in America, Lithuanians are loyal to all the American ideals and acknowledge them as their own. Overseas, they cannot be neutral because the Germans hold Lithuania by the force of arms." As with other ethnic groups in America, Lithuanians sought recognition of the independence of their homeland. In May, 1918, Wilson informed a "delegation of the Lithuanian-American Council that he was in full sympathy with Lithuania's efforts for independence." Norway's declaration of neutrality during the Great War left many Norwegian American communities "eager" to express their loyalty to America. These commemorations were "as much a demonstration of an ethnic group's loyalty to the United States as it was a continued celebration of ancestors and ethnic pride."[84]

During the Great War, ethnic patriotism in America was complex. Despite an organized and harshly poignant conformity campaign, ethnic groups did not simply give up their ethnicity and assimilate to the "official culture" of the dominant society, nor did they blindly demonstrate their loyalty under nativist threat. Instead, immigrants utilized patriotic rhetoric and imagery employed by both reigning nativists and the government propaganda machine to prove their own loyalty and make their ethnicity acceptable. However, they also used the language of patriotism to achieve their own international goals and express ethnic pride.

Prior to the United States entry into the war, German and Irish immigrants attempted to pressure the government to keep America out of the conflict and actively promoted a course of strict neutrality. Other immigrants advocated American participation in the war. World War I provided American Czech, Slovak, Polish, and Jewish immigrants an opportunity to fight for the independence of their homeland from the bondage of the German, Austro-Hungarian, and Turkish Empires. They did so through their service in the United States military, through ethnic community war-relief fundraisers, and through ethnic legions assigned to Allied armies. Ultimately, immigrants did not simply learn to "speak the English language, . . . salute the flag," and learn the words of "The Star Spangled Banner" as nativists suggested, but instead they learned to redefine the patriotic culture of the United States as they honored their adopted country and fought for their homelands.[85]

From out of the melting pot of America's admixture of races is being poured a new American, a soldier man who, wearing the khaki and covered with the dust of the parade ground, is stepping forth into the ranks, file upon file of him, to make the world safe for democracy. . . . He is the "non-English speaking soldier," who along with his American-born brothers, had been selected through the draft to drive the overseas barbarians back into their lair.

—Capt. Edward R. Padgett, October, 1918

CHAPTER 2

Drafting Foreign-born Doughboys into the American Army

The U.S. Army has traditionally consisted of both native-born and foreign-born troops. The best way to understand the influence and experience of immigrant soldiers in the First World War is to begin by tracing the evolution of the American Army as it grew from a small, decentralized military force into the massive, national conscription force of 1917. This examination can provide important insights into the evolution of American society and the history of immigrants in the United States military. Two strong military concepts grew directly from the American colonial experience: the need for local defense in the form of citizen militias and the recognized dangers inherent in a permanent, powerful standing army. Circumstances created the need for colonies to form militia units as local communities joined in a common defense due to conflict with Indians and competition with European colonial powers. However, defending one's home was a far cry from the establishment of a permanent class of professional soldiers or the idea of mandatory military service. The colonists knew from their previous European experiences that the formation of a permanent army financed by taxation was expensive. Also, many colonists had left their European homelands to escape various forms of oppression, among them, repeated obligatory military service and tyranny associated with military autocracies. Therefore, the question of universal military service and the creation of a national army of professional soldiers stood as possible threats to individual freedom and became highly debated issues throughout the early history of the United States.[1]

The American Declaration of Independence represented a break not only from the British government but also from its military structure. Concerns over a large national army of professional soldiers explain the make-up of the Continental Army, which relied heavily on temporary multistate forces of long-term regular soldiers (two to three year enlistments) and short-term state volunteer militiamen put into national service. The use of primarily state-raised soldiers allowed leaders to bypass a national draft and a powerful central government but resulted in a temporary, weak "coordinating authority" to oversee the multistate force. This organization reflected the dominating ideologies concerning the fear of a strong standing army, the importance of maintaining local and regional autonomy, and the reluctance to implement a national conscription. A military draft did occur in many states, but the system was far from the virtuous organization of citizen-soldiers envisioned by its republican founders. Instead, the system of state drafts allowed for the hiring of substitutes, which primarily resulted in the exemption of the middle and upper classes and created a national army of predominantly poor "farmers, laborers, indentured servants, vagrants, and immigrants."[2]

The assistance of foreign officers in the American Revolution is well documented and included Marie Joseph Paul Yves Roch Gilbert du Motier, Marques de Lafayette, Tadeuz Andrzej Bonawentura Kosciuszko, and Friedrich Wilhelm Augustus Freiherr von Steuben. But foreign-born participation in the revolution was far more involved. Recent scholarship challenges the legendary myth of the "yeoman" Anglican farmer who left his community and family farm to fight for the freedom of America. Instead, "African Americans, ethnic minorities, and 'free white men on the move' [untied to community or family farm,] eventually formed the bulk of the

Continental army." Immigrant soldiers came primarily from two ethnic groups, "Irish" (Celtic or Scotch-Irish) and German immigrants. The promise of a steady wage appealed to foreign-born recruits. However, for many immigrants the revolution also reflected an ideological connection with the mutual fight for freedom they understood from experience in their native lands. According to muster records, between 10 and 20 percent of New England recruits had Irish surnames. Not surprisingly, the number of "Irish" recruits from the Middle States, who made up about 45 percent of regiments from the region, was much higher due to the large Irish, primarily Scotch-Irish, population there. Germans constituted the second-highest ethnic group in British North America. German-born recruits could be found in both belligerent armies. Those serving in the Continental Army came primarily from among German immigrants living in America, although the rebel forces also recruited Hessian deserters, and together made up approximately 12 percent of Washington's total forces. Not surprisingly, due to high levels of immigration many American Germans came from Pennsylvania, where they constituted some 25 percent of that state's total recruits. One revolutionary soldier, Joseph Plumb Martin, described the Continental Army in this way: "There was the Irish and Scotch brogue, murdered English, flat insipid Dutch [German] and some lingoes which would puzzle a philosopher to tell whether they belonged to this world or some undiscovered country."[3]

At various times in the history of the United States military, Congress restricted immigrant service. The first began shortly after the War of Independence when various government restrictions technically forbade the enlistment of aliens (noncitizen immigrants) in the United States armed forces. In reality, these restrictions were inconsequential, since the pre–Civil War peacetime regular army consisted of a small number of soldiers (under 10,000), and immigrants could technically be eligible for enlistment by obtaining state citizenship. More important, these restrictions were repeatedly suspended during national crises when manpower shortages were acute.[4]

The first exception to the restrictions occurred during the War of 1812, when Congress rejected Pres. James Monroe's push for national conscription. Federalists, who openly opposed the war, called conscription an "unconstitutional and a tyrannical instrument of Napoleonic despotism." Instead of a national draft, Congress attempted to increase the size of the regular army by doubling bounties (money paid to entice men to enlist) and considering extending enlistment to include both noncitizen immigrants and free African Americans. Although a compromise allowed aliens to enter the ranks, a congressional act of 1808 prevented noncitizen immigrants from becoming officers.[5]

In the years following the War of 1812, immigrants continued to enlist in both the peacetime and wartime armies. Economics motivated many of the newly arrived Irish and German immigrants to find steady employment in the military despite its low wages. Additional crises such as the Mexican War also drew immigrants into the ranks. In fact, Irish and German immigrants composed some 47 percent of the army's recruits during the 1840s as Congress continued to ignore enlistment restrictions. In addition to enlisting in the regular army, immigrants began to form their own local militias, which created anxiety among nativists, who regarded their historic militia units as "purely American" social and political institutions not open to the foreign born. By the 1850s, under pressure from native-born groups, "foreign militia" units were disarmed in Massachusetts and Irish Catholic units dissolved in Connecticut.[6]

The question of aliens serving in the military became more complex with the implementation of a national drafting system. The first national conscription occurred during the Civil War and represented the continuation of the long-standing debate over drafting in a democratic society. Ironically, the Confederacy, fighting for state rights, implemented the first "national" draft. Its Northern counterpart, initiated through the Enrollment Act, came only after substantial debate and ultimately contributed a small addition of soldiers (6 percent) to Union forces. The Militia Act of 1862 was the first attempt at conscription in the North. However, a series of protests from governors combined with violent draft riots permanently postponed implementation of the act.[7]

As the devastating war continued to take its toll on human lives, and as the terms of Northern volunteer soldiers expired, a crucial manpower shortage developed. By March, 1863, a new conscription effort, the Enrollment Act, made all able-bodied male citizens between twenty-one and forty-five years old eligible for the draft. In addition to drafting native-born and naturalized citizens, immigrants who formally declared their intention of becoming citizens (defined as "declarant aliens") became eligible for conscription. By 1864 an amendment to the draft laws expanded eligibility to include any immigrant who had either voted in past elections or held public office despite their status as "nondeclarants." Some states allowed declarant immigrants to vote; however, mix-ups did occur and in some cases nondeclarants voted in local elections, which made these nondeclarants subject to conscription. Allowing drafted men to hire substitutes or make a commutation payment of $300 (purchased exemptions) substantially weakened the original intent of the Enrollment Act. Those who could afford it overwhelmingly took advantage of the payment exemption. Of the 249,259 draftees called up, 86,724 paid their way out of service while another 116,188 hired substitutes. Therefore, the Northern draft directly affected only 46,347 of the 2,666,999 men who served the Union Army.[8]

Despite the small number of actual draftees, Civil War conscription was "widely denounced as tyrannical, oppressive, and un-American."[9] Certainly, the draft exemptions represented class privilege, as only those who could afford the cost could escape military service. The exemptions also undoubtedly reflected the prevailing negative attitudes toward the implementation of obligatory national military service in a democratic society. The drafting of noncitizen aliens, however, reveals a significant contradiction to Americans' attitudes toward immigrants. Clearly, old-stock Americans, while objecting to immigrants in their traditional and prestigious militia units during peacetime, thought nothing of allowing aliens to serve and possibly die for their adopted country in times of crisis—a theme that would be repeated in wars to come.

In addition to conscription laws that made declarant aliens eligible for the draft and allowed immigrants into wartime militia units, Congress also encouraged aliens to enlist in the regular army. Of course, nondeclarant immigrants always could hire themselves out as substitutes for anyone desiring to avoid military service. Immigrants found their way into the Civil War military by other means as well. For instance, private organizations as well as local, state, and federal governments offered bounties to entice the foreign born into joining the service. This inadvertently created a class of "unscrupulous bounty-brokers" who cheated naive recruits and pocketed much of the soldiers' allotted bounties. Europeans anxious to emigrate to the United States often fell victim to this group of thieves by selling their service in the military in exchange for passage to the New World.[10]

Other motivating factors included harsh laws regarding draft resistance, which often singled out aliens. The 1864 amendment announced that declarant aliens or any immigrants who had voted in the past and who refused to be drafted could be stripped of their political rights and possibly be deported. However, this provision did not pertain to native-born or naturalized American citizens. During the war, Congress did lift restrictions against noncitizen officers and allowed immigrants to secure commissions in both the regular and ethnic regiments in the Union Army. Ultimately, foreign-born soldiers composed 25 percent of the Northern Army. By the end of the war, African Americans made up 10 percent of the Union Army. Since draftees represented only 6 percent of the army, the bulk of the immigrant soldiers were volunteers in ethnic and, more commonly, ethnically mixed units.[11]

Immediately after the Civil War, the United States once again substantially reduced the size of its armed forces and concentrated its small army primarily in the western frontier. However, dramatic changes during the latter years of the nineteenth and the early years of the twentieth centuries quickly altered the size, strength, and role of the United States military. Profound changes caused by the penetrating forces of imperialism, industrialization, immigration, and urbanization drastically changed the role of the federal government and subsequently the relationship between the military and society. Along with these dramatic changes came a reevaluation of American military forces. This was particularly necessary due to the nation's new role in international, economic, political, and cultural affairs.

Beginning in the late nineteenth century, the United States joined other imperial powers by expanding its influence and power into Latin America, several Pacific islands, and parts of Southeast Asia. As the country became increasing involved in international events, including the Venezuela dispute, the Boxer Rebellion, the Russo-Japanese War, the Spanish-American War, and the Philippine War, it became clear that a modernization of the military was imperative. As the United States became a leading industrial power, enormous technological changes also pushed the military toward reforms in modern organizational skills, communication methods, and the development of new weaponry.

Other transformations contributed to a change in attitude toward the military and at the same time altered its relationship with civilian society. The rise of nationalism in the late nineteenth century promoted the growing acceptance of the changing nature and modernization of American armed forces. Nationalism had been slow to develop due to the country's exceptional nature. However, in the decades after the Civil War, a growing national consciousness formed as a result of the unifying nature of the war (North vs. South), global expansionism, and domestic modernization. This evolving sense of nationalism was reflected in the relatively slow legalization of "national" citizenship, which finally crystallized after the Civil War with the adoption of the Fourteenth Amendment. Events at the turn of the century such as the Spanish-American War and the Philippine War magnified the sense of nationalism reflected in the rallying call for Americans to "civilize" the world. In April, 1898, Congress authorized the expansion of the regular army to 64,719 soldiers with an additional 10,000 in volunteer units. Researchers have neglected the history of immigrant soldiers in the Spanish-American and Philippine Wars. However, heavily multiethnic areas such as New York recruited volunteers and National Guard regiments to serve in these conflicts. Therefore, it is very likely that immigrants participated in these two wars.[12]

The experiences of both native and foreign-born soldiers in the American Army during World War I represented a dramatic difference from previous military duty. To begin with, the First World War had a profound impact on American society. It expanded the size and power of the United States government, restructured the work force of industrial America, and brought the inadequacies of a national laissez-faire policy to the forefront of politics. The Selective Service Act of 1917 affected an unprecedented number of men and quickly turned some four million civilians into soldiers. While the Civil War draft had been met with some dramatic resistance, the First World War drafting system was facilitated by a new public discipline associated with the modern industrial society. Industrialization created a growing sense of group consciousness and helped change the relationship between the "people" and the "state" and between the military and civilian society. The development of a time-orientated, disciplined, and hierarchical work force contributed to the increasing acceptance of national conscription. The reevaluation of the draft system and the rise of a strong central state that intensified a growing sense of nationalism allowed for the relatively smooth execution of conscription. It did not occur, however, without some complications related to the multiethnic nature of the country. Finally, draftees who entered the U.S. Army in World War I entered a substantially more complex military organization than in any previous period in American history. Significant political, social, economic, and cultural changes had propelled the country from a rural-based household economy toward a centralized urban-industrial nation-state.[13]

With its declaration of war in April, 1917, the United States began to mobilize an effective fighting force. Since the nation traditionally maintained a small standing army, drafting citizen-soldiers was imperative. The number of conscripted men in the American Army during the First World War was unprecedented in the history of the United States. Eventually, the Selective Service registered a total of 23,908,576 men through 4,648 local draft boards. Of the approximately 3,500,000 men in military service during the First World War, 2,758,542 were drafted into the armed forces, the remainder voluntarily enlisted. Unlike the Civil War's Union Army, of which about 6 percent were conscripts, draftees made up 67 percent of armed forces in World War I.[14] The General Staff carefully studied the Civil War draft system in order to avoid that era's catastrophic draft riots and decided to end the option of substitutions, purchase exemptions, and bounty payments. As a result, First World War conscription transpired with relative ease. Still, there was some confusion and conflict, especially concerning the drafting of immigrants into the U.S. Army.

Initially, after a review of international law, the Selective Service Act of May, 1917, divided immigrants into four groups: diplomatic, declarant, nondeclarant, and enemy aliens. The Selected Service exempted alien diplomats from the draft since they did not technically reside in the United States. As in the Civil War, declarant aliens included immigrants who had filed their first papers of intention to become citizens and were waiting to fulfill their five-year residency before completing the naturalization process. The Selective Service Act made declarant immigrants from friendly nations eligible for the draft since it was felt that they received the benefits of their adopted country and should, therefore, share the nation's burdens.[15]

The status of nondeclarant aliens, as in the Civil War, applied to immigrants who did not file their papers of intention for citizenship. Selective Service considered this group transitory, and technically this group could not be drafted due to their temporary resident status. It was understood that this transitory consideration would also protect American visitors and businessmen living in other countries from becoming drafted into foreign armies. The final category, enemy aliens, included both declarant and nondeclarant immigrants from enemy nations. According to a provost marshal general's report, enemy aliens could not be compelled to serve since they would be put in a position of fighting against their own countrymen.[16] Although the four classifications seemed clear, the Selective Service immediately faced several challenges. The problems included complaints over an unequal draft quota system, diplomatic concerns over the drafting of neutral and allied immigrants, and the desire of many enemy aliens to serve in the United States Army.

The first dilemma arose over public dissatisfaction with the quota system, which mandated that local boards draft a percentage of the total population in each district. Since the total population in many board districts included a substantial number of nondeclarant immigrants and enemy aliens who were technically ineligible for conscription, many feared that citizens and declarant aliens of these areas would be disproportionately drafted. This was particularly true in the Northeast and Midwest, where the bulk of the immigrant population resided. For instance, nondeclarant alien status made up 70 percent of the registrants in one Chicago district and 25 percent of a Brooklyn district. These large groups, although added into the total population of each area, were legally exempted from the draft. The situation in Brooklyn, according to Sen. Henry Cabot Lodge, resulted in the drafting of "every eligible American" in that New York district.[17]

Expressions of discontent over this system reached the press, local conscription boards, Congress, and the Selective Service Office. Major newspapers and journals including *The Literary Digest, The Morning Telegraph, St. Louis Globe Democrat, Macon Telegraph, Chicago Daily Tribune,* and New York's *Tribune, Sun,* and *Globe* echoed the growing resentment over the "alien slacker" issue and stood behind congressional proposals to make every immigrant of military age eligible for the draft despite their legal status. Most editorials were similar to the *Chicago Tribune*'s comments: "America has welcomed these strangers and given most of them a measure of prosperity they did not possess and could not hope for in their native lands. . . . If they are to enjoy the advantages of life in America they should be compelled to meet its responsibilities." The *New York Sun* noted: "The apparent injustices of stripping the land of American youths to furnish a fighting force in Europe while leaving millions of aliens at home to enjoy the rewards of peaceful industry has undoubtedly got on the people's nerves."[18]

Provost Marshal General Enoch H. Crowder, who headed the Selective Service Office, echoed this sentiment when he declared: "It is not too much to say that the spectacle of American boys, the finest in the community, going forth to fight for the liberty of the world while sturdy aliens—many of them born in the very countries which have been invaded by the enemy—stay at home and make money has been the one notable cause of dissatisfaction with the scheme of military service embodied in the selective service act."[19]

Many of the local boards strongly expressed the widespread popular belief that aliens should be forced to serve in the army. Congressional resolutions and hearings also echoed these opinions. Under pressure from the public, Congress made several attempts to pass legislation making all aliens, regardless of their status, liable for the draft. Sen. George E. Chamberlain, an Oregon Democrat, led the charge as the chair of the Senate Military Affairs Committee. The senator had already earned a reputation as an ultranationalist with his relentless drive to implement universal military training and with an attempt to pass a bill that would have placed dissenters who endangered the success of United States forces before a military tribunal.

According to Chamberlain's bill, a person found guilty would bypass all aspects of the civilian legal system and be executed by a firing squad.[20]

By August, 1917, Chamberlain began a new crusade with the introduction of a bill to make all immigrants, except enemy aliens, eligible for the draft. Immigrants unwilling to serve in the military would be deported. Congressmen seemed torn between the protest over "alien slackers" and the realization that the drafting of nondeclarants would cause international problems. This dilemma was raised during congressional debates:

> Hon. John Jacob Rogers (Mass.): I do not think that the United States exists in order to give privileges to aliens. . . . If he [an alien] does not think it is worth while to serve the United States why should we go out of our way to favor him? Why should we give him citizenship and why keep him in the United States?

> Hon. William Gordon (Ohio): Because we need his labor, I suppose. . . . The fact that a man is an alien is an absolutely legal bar to military service.[21]

The bill actually passed through the House, but the Senate stopped it only after Secretary of State Robert E. Lansing testified before the Committee on Military Affairs regarding the serious diplomatic and economic implications of the bill. The secretary emphasized the international ramifications of drafting aliens into the U.S. military and noted the diplomatic problems that would result. In addition, Lansing reported that deportation of foreign-born residents "would disorganize commerce and, to a large extent, industry" and force a significant number of foreign students and businessmen who did not want to secure permanent residency in the United States to leave the country. In addition, he emphasized that the deportation of migrant laborers from Mexico, "who had no intention of becoming citizens," would have a "disastrous effect" on the economy of southwestern states that relied heavily on this labor source. The conscription or deportation of aliens would very likely subject Americans living abroad to the same treatment (draft or deportation). Lansing further testified that to his knowledge none of the belligerent nations were currently drafting the foreign born into their military forces.[22]

The secretary of state continually emphasized the delicate diplomatic nature surrounding the issue of drafting aliens and adamantly contended that problems should be handled through diplomatic channels by international treaties and not by congressional legislation. In fact, Lansing reported that the State Department was engaging in negotiations with Allied nations to give both declarants and nondeclarants a choice of serving in the army of their resident country or returning to their native land for military duty. In the matter of drafting neutral aliens, Lansing reported that this practice had never been implemented in previous American conflicts, and it would no doubt cause great difficulties. The secretary suggested that the United States should "avoid every cause of irritation that is possible at the present time" since such action could send neutral nations into the enemy camp. Finally, Lansing testified that enemy aliens should not be forced into the service of the U.S. government, either in a military or war-industry capacity, and pointed out that Germany was receiving world criticism for compelling the Belgium people to work in the German industrial service.[23]

After the completion of the hearings, Congress agreed to temporarily table the issue of drafting aliens pending negotiations with Allied countries concerning the drafting of nondeclarant immigrants into the United States Army. The issue of unfair draft quotas was resolved by congressional legislation introduced in January, 1918, and passed in May, 1918. The act outlined a classification system that placed native-born and naturalized citizens and declarant aliens who were physically and mentally fit into Class I and all nondeclarant aliens and enemy aliens into the Class V exemption category. Nondeclarants eligible for draft through treaty agreements would also be included in Class I. The service, thereafter, computed the quota systems based only on Class I and, therefore, eliminated the problem of disproportionate drafting.[24]

However, the problems did not stop with the new classification system. In order to expedite the drafting process, the Selective Service put the burden of proof for nondeclarant status on the immigrant himself. How the alien was to prove that he had never filed his "first papers" was not made clear. Therefore, although local boards were required to give every alien a "full and fair hearing" concerning any draft exemptions and were instructed to inquire into the status of any registrant whom they believed eligible for draft exemption, numerous mix-ups did occur. In an effort to eliminate the confusion, local board officials in heavily populated immigrant areas hired "men of foreign race stock" and social welfare workers who, according to the provost marshal general, understood the exemption rules and "took pains to inform the ignorant and to protect the helpless."[25]

Despite the efforts of the Selective Service, the erroneous registration of nondeclarants into the Class I status occurred, resulting in the drafting of some resident aliens. Of the 123,277 immigrants selected in the first draft, some 76,545 had not declared their intention of becoming United States citizens. The service blamed administrative errors, overzealous local boards caught up in the "slacker spirit," and the ignorance of the aliens themselves for the oversights (many did not speak English or did not understand their legal rights).[26]

Many countries protested the drafting of aliens into the United States military. In fact, 5,852 diplomatic protests inundated the State Department concerning the induction of nondeclarants. Government officials from thirty-four foreign countries requested the immediate discharge of their countrymen from the U.S. Army. Beginning in December, 1917, the federal government attempted to quietly handle each of the diplomatic protest cases. However, because of the army's widespread circulation of a letter based on a presidential order of April 11, 1918, authorizing the discharge of nondeclarant aliens directly associated with these diplomatic requests and the extensive publicity by major newspapers of the nondeclarant conscription problem, the situation turned into a major fiasco.[27]

Eventually, the government's original intention to apply the order only to diplomatic request cases was extended to all nondeclarants. Thereafter, the number of requests for discharge by nondeclarant aliens rose from one or two cases per week in December, 1917–January, 1918, to over one hundred per week during February and March, 1918. By October, 1918, a total of 6,000 cases had reached the Selective Service Office. By the end of the war, the army had discharged 1,842 men "on the grounds of alienage or upon diplomatic request." An additional 14,019 declarant and nondeclarant British subjects received exemption status in accordance with an agreement with Britain and Canada dated June 3, 1918. Despite these diplomatic pressures, thousands of nondeclarants willingly waived their right to exemption and accepted conscription into the U.S. Army; 191,491 nondeclarant aliens by September 12, 1918.[28]

Diplomatic problems also arose over the status of declarant immigrants from neutral countries. The State Department received numerous protests from nonaligned nations that considered the drafting of their countrymen a violation of international law and existing treaty obligations, which forbade the drafting of aliens from neutral countries regardless of an immigrant's intention to become a U.S. citizen. Although Pres. Woodrow Wilson could not override the Selective Service Act and exempt neutral declarants from the national draft, he could enforce exemption status within the military. Thus, acting as commander in chief, the president ordered that "both declarants and nondeclarants of treaty countries . . . be promptly discharged upon request of the accredited diplomatic representative of the countries of which they [were] citizens."[29]

The conflict between treaties with neutral countries and the Selective Service laws ended on July 9, 1918, when Congress agreed to exempt declarant neutrals from military service if they withdrew their intention of becoming United States citizens. Any declarant who requested conscription exemption or discharge from the army would automatically "cancel his [citizenship] declaration, and . . . be forever debarred from becoming a citizen of the United States." Some 2,035 immigrant subjects of neutral countries withdrew their intention to become citizens of the United States. Although this congressional stipulation was originally intended for neutral aliens who had not yet been drafted into military service, the army, by order of the War Department, extended this practice to declarant immigrants already inducted. Thus, neutral declarant alien soldiers who asked to be discharged under the presidential order of April 11, 1918, would also be required to give up their right to future United States citizenship. Despite this way out, thousands decided to remain in the U.S. Army.[30]

Treaty negotiations with Allied nations over the immigrant question also proved to be difficult. Between June and November, 1918, the State Department obtained reciprocal treaties of conscription with Great Britain, France, Italy, and Greece. The agreements allowed alien residents the opportunity to enlist first in the service of their homeland before being automatically eligible for the draft in their country of residence. Other treaties with Argentina, Costa Rica, Honduras, Japan, Paraguay, Serbia, Spain, Switzerland, and Persia outlined liabilities for compulsory military service as well. Over 48,000 aliens who came to the United States from the United Kingdom joined the British Army. Other immigrants joined foreign armies in an effort to free, protect, or establish their homeland.[31]

The question of enemy alien service in the American military also became complex. The provost marshal general declared this group "not subject to draft" in the hope that this would leave "the Selective Service regulations free to impose an absolute prohibition upon the local boards to accept for military service any enemy alien, declarant or nondeclarant, in spite of his waiver of nonliability."[32]

At first, the enemy alien exemption status included only immigrants born in Germany, since an official declaration of war did not exist with the Austro-Hungarian Empire until November 11, 1917. In the draft of June 5, 1917, 41,000 German registrants were supposedly exempt from the draft due to their enemy alien status. However, when soldiers arrived in training camps in December, they included 1,000 nondeclarant German draftees and an "appreciable" number of declarants. In addition, a significant number of German immigrants had joined the American Army prior to the war. Although Provost Marshal General Crowder reported that all German aliens were discharged from the service, this never occurred. Instead, the adjutant general of the army contacted all commanding generals to explain that despite the "Selective Service Regulations of Section 79, Rule XII, Note 4," enemy aliens currently in the military could continue to serve if the commanding officers considered them loyal. Officers interviewed all enemy aliens and noted their loyalty in reports to the camp commanders. Soldiers who wanted to leave because they feared they would end up fighting against their family in their homeland received discharges. The War Department also allowed unnaturalized German soldiers to stay in United States combat divisions located in France if they were determined to be "of undoubted loyalty" by their division commander. The adjutant general also insisted that officers explain to their German American soldiers that "on account of his nationality, he runs the risk of being shot as a traitor upon falling into the enemy's hands." These soldiers also had the option of being discharged or transferred into a noncombat supply division. The War Department instructed that any German-born soldiers deemed dangerous should be turned over to the Department of Justice for possible internment.[33]

German and Austrian immigrant soldiers in the military created a unique dilemma when the question of whether or not these soldiers could list family members from their homelands as beneficiaries. The adjutant general of the army, E. H. Crowder, concluded, "these men are members of our military force and are entitled to all the benefits of the War Risk Insurance Act." However, he warned that although the soldiers have an "absolute right" to name German and Austrian residents as beneficiaries, immediate payment upon the policy's maturity was "another question." Crowder pointed out that the government had no "legal objection" to such remittances, but noted, "whether it is expedient or polite to do so is to be determined as a political and not as a legal question."[34]

Immigrants born in the Austro-Hungarian Empire continued to be drafted into the United States Army until they too were classified as enemy aliens in November, 1917. Between June and November, 1917, many ethnic leaders and newspaper editors continued to call on the immigrant community to serve in the American military and often tied the Allied cause to the hopes for a free homeland. Local Selective Service boards in heavily populated ethnic areas included and sometimes were dominated by local ethnic leaders from the professional classes (doctors, lawyers, and newspaper editors). Those who originally came from the "oppressed races" under Austro-Hungarian rule viewed that empire as the enemy and wanted to serve in the American Army. An article in the Czech American paper *Denni Hlasatel* reflected this position. It told of the thousands of Czech families who would soon send their sons off to fight for the United States and reminded immigrant mothers of the terrible crisis in Europe. "Just let her think of Czech mothers in the old homeland who must sacrifice their sons and see them slaughtered for the benefit of Austria, which is bent upon murdering and destroying our people."[35]

In addition to the thousands of declarant immigrants from the Austro-Hungarian Empire drafted into the United States Army, some 9,000 nondeclarant aliens waived their exempt status so they could fight too. The Selective Service registered an additional 239,000 immigrants who were eligible for further draft calls.[36]

With the U.S. declaration of war on the Austro-Hungarian Empire in November, 1917, the drafting of noncitizen immigrants from its subject lands was suppose to stop since, in spite of their willingness to serve, these people were technically from enemy territories. Yet, a September, 1918, article in the *Infantry Journal* about the drafting of enemy aliens noted the confusion as the U.S. government classified Greeks and Armenians born under Turkish rule, Romanians born in Austria, Germans and Austrians born in Poland, "Czecho-Slovaks" (Bohemians and Slovaks), and "Jugo-Slavs" (Slovens, Croatian, and Serbians) as "technical" enemy aliens. The article concluded that these groups were very bitter about having been classified as enemy aliens and predicted that a "great number" of them would make good soldiers.[37]

In reality, this "absolute prohibition" on drafting enemy aliens did not work as planned because a large number of noncitizen enemy aliens continued to be drafted in the American Army. Confusion over whether "technical" enemy aliens could waive their right of exemption from the draft continued in the months after the declaration of war with the Austro-Hungarian Empire, as ethnic leaders encouraged service in the American military: "All our fellow countrymen who are not citizens, and who on these grounds ask for exemption from military service, are, thereby, proclaiming themselves to be 'alien enemies.' They ought to think the matter over very thoroughly before deciding to take the step. By asking exemption they announce themselves as belonging to the 'undesirable element,' as people who consider the United States to be a country just good enough for making money. They show that they would not make any sacrifices for the preservation of existing conditions or for their betterment. These people testify that they are nothing more than greedy egoists and parasites. . . . This is the time for a showdown. May the proof be a splendid success which will do us honor and fill us with joy."[38]

As the Selective Service, the State Department, and the War Department continued to discuss the conscription of enemy aliens, mistakenly drafted immigrant soldiers were allowed to remain in the armed forces if they were deemed loyal by commanding officers. Ethnic leaders from the Czech and Slovak communities pressured the government to change the enemy alien status so that their people could help destroy the Central Powers. Once the United States officially recognized Czechoslovakia in September, 1918, officials lifted the enemy alien status for American Czechs and Slovaks, and the Selective Service reopened registration for these two groups. Despite the change in policy, some Selective Service boards continued to list Czechs and Slovaks as "enemy aliens." Ethnic organizations, such as the Czech National Alliance, worked to straighten out the confusion.[39]

While the United States was at war de facto with both Turkey and Bulgaria, official declarations of war never occurred. Therefore, the status of some 43,000 Selective Service registrants from these two countries was in question. During the debate over what to do with Turkish and Bulgarian immigrants, the United States drafted men from both nationalities. Eventually, the Provost Marshal General's Office mandated that subjects of both Turkey and Bulgaria should be considered enemy aliens until the State Department had time to further investigate the situation. Still, names of immigrants born in those nations appeared on the muster rolls, and discussions of enemy alien soldiers continued in War Department correspondence. By October, 1918, the State Department confirmed their alien enemy status; however, before instructions could be sent to local draft boards, the Armistice had taken effect.[40]

Military correspondence included many references that spoke to the need to respect "technical" enemy aliens who sincerely desired to fight for the United States. As with the German immigrants, the War Department mandated that instead of immediately discharging all soldiers with enemy alien status, commanding officers would review each case and make a decision based on the recommendation from the man's direct supervisor and the camp intelligence officer. Eventually, "a total of 5,637 enemy aliens were discharged from the Army between the period of April 6, 1917 and November 11, 1918." Considering the thousands of enemy aliens who waived their right to exemption, clearly, a significant number continued to serve in the American Army during the First World War. While the secretary of war deliberated over the question of enemy aliens, the adjutant general announced that until a policy was released, all "nationals of other countries in the draft should be treated as [were] other men in the Regular Army and draft."[41]

The War Department prepared its "Ethnic Bulletin" to educate commanding officers about the political status of Austrian-born soldiers serving in the U.S. Army. It stated that the majority of Austrian-born soldiers in the army spoke no German (or spoke the language imperfectly) and "often hate[d] the Austro-Hungarian government very bitterly." Slovens, Croatian, and Serbian draftees came from the "disaffected" southern provinces of the Austro-Hungarian Empire, which were "seething in half-suppressed revolt against the oppression and exploitation of the Central Powers." The War Department warned that Bohemians, or Czechs, although classified as Austrians, would be insulted and disgruntled if mistaken for Germans. According to the bulletin, this group was apt to be fully naturalized Americans, and it noted that a Czechoslovak division was fighting on the Italian front against the Austrian government. Polish immigrants were also considered loyal, and the report acknowledged the efforts of the renowned Polish patriot and pianist Ignace Paderewski, who raised money in the United States to help support the Allied cause. Ruthenians from the Russian Ukraine and Romanians from Transylvania were also considered loyal to the American cause. The bulletin concluded that each member of this group of technical enemy aliens was considered "thoroughly loyal and an enthusiastic soldier" who took hardship well and fought vigorously. It instructed "those who come in contact" with the Slovene, Croatian, and Serbian soldiers should inform them that "his people" and the Italians had "buried their old animosities" and were working together "for the liberation of the Yugoslav (or Serb-Croat-Slovene) districts of Austria."[42]

Most enemy aliens either remained in the army or were discharged. U.S. Attorney General Thomas W. Gregory insisted that soldiers whose loyalty was under question must be investigated or put under observation before internment was recommended. The chief of the Military Intelligence Division, Marlborough Churchill, in his correspondence to the adjutant general of the army, noted that the "responsibility for internment is lodged solely in the Department of Justice." He noted "that under the terms of the President's Proclamation, alien enemies are to be interned only when there is evidence tending to prove that, if at large, they would be dangerous to the country." Enemy aliens considered disloyal to the United States were sent to an internment camp under the supervision of the adjutant general of the army. Prisons were located in Georgia at Fort Oglethorpe and Fort McPherson and in Utah at Fort Douglas. Each facility had the capacity to hold 1,800 prisoners, which included enemy aliens, radicals, and German prisoners of war. For the most part, prisoners were treated well. Historian Mitchell Yockelson noted that the camp administrator at Fort Oglethorpe allowed prisoners to plant gardens, participate in sports (baseball, volleyball, basketball, tennis, boxing, and wrestling), perform plays, read books, play music and billiards, and watch motion pictures provided by the YMCA. At the war's end, enemy aliens who wished to stay in America "were transferred to the Department of Justice and granted permanent parole."[43]

Another solution to the issue of technical enemy alien status was the creation of a "Slavic Legion" of nonnaturalized immigrants attached to the United States Army. Congress approved this unit in July, 1918, to include noncitizen volunteers from among the Yugoslavs (Southern Slavic), Czechoslovaks, and Ruthenians (Ukrainians), the "oppressed races of the Austro-Hungarian or German Empire," living in the United States.

The South Slavic National Council of Washington, D.C., applauded the idea, noting that the "Slavic Legion would give the Slavs from Austro-Hungary, and especially the Jugoslavs, opportunity to fight against a State which is the greatest enemy and the only obstacle to the realization of their nationalistic aspirations." The plan called for immigrant volunteers considered loyal to their adopted country to be brought together in a special unit under the direction of the president. Adolph J. Sabath, a U.S. congressman from Chicago, estimated that the legion could be as large as 25,000 men (5,000 Yugoslavs, 12,000 Czechs and Slovaks, and 8,000 Ruthenians). A War Department report projected a legion of 15,000 Jugoslavs, 10,000 Czechoslovaks, and 20,000 Ruthenians that could be used effectively to "disrupt" Austrian troops behind enemy lines. It concluded, "in base of American operations on the Dalmatian or Serbian front, the Jugoslav element might be able to render military service of great value." The War Plans Division recommended that immigrants should not be recruited in the coal mining areas because "the services of men of theses races, employed in coal mining, is more valuable to the Government in that capacity than in the Army."[44]

However, despite the excitement over the idea of the Slavic Legion, organization moved slowly. In October, 1918, War Department General Order No. 90 announced the formation of the Slovak Legion made up of infantry regiments. Each company, "if practical," would consist of members of the same "race," Yugoslavs, Czechoslovaks, or Ruthenians. All officers had to speak English in addition to the language of their unit and, if possible, come from the same ethnic group. The War Department required all officers, except for field officers, to attend the Central Officers' Training School at Camp Lee, Virginia, to "furnish proof of their loyalty to the United States, and to sign a loyalty oath." The order forbade the drafting of immigrants in the nation's coal mining districts. By November, the Slavic Legion, located at Camp Wadsworth, South Carolina, consisted of only 114 men and sixteen officers. The officers, all first lieutenants, included five Bohemians, seven Poles, two Russian Jews, and two American doctors. The War Department noted that the failure to activate the legion earlier, especially after it was "extensively heralded" in July, was being used in enemy propaganda and could affect the morale of the immigrant soldiers. Eventually, the Armistice prevented the complete organization of the Slavic Legion.[45]

Another way to eliminate the confusion over the status of immigrants and to prevent diplomatic protests regarding proper or improper induction was to loosen the requirements for the naturalization of immigrant servicemen, making it easier for alien soldiers to become U.S. citizens. The provost marshal general hoped that these changes would help convert the "'Foreign Legion' of the army of the United States into a host of loyal American citizen-soldiers."[46]

On May 9, 1918, Congress approved several amendments to the naturalization laws making it easier for declarant, nondeclarant, and enemy alien immigrants serving in the American military forces to become United States citizens. The amendment also declared that during the war the collection of naturalization fees from immigrants in military service was forbidden unless state law required payment (and then only that portion of the fee going to the state could be collected). In May, 1918, the chief of staff informed commanding generals of the new law: "This Act entitles all aliens in the service (including enemy aliens) to citizenship whether they have their first papers or not. No fee will be charged. Before the application is presented, however, it should be understood that the application is wholly voluntary and is a privilege which can only be granted to those producing evidence of loyalty. No commanding officers should allow a petition to be presented unless he is convinced of the loyalty of the applicant. When the application is granted, the soldier will immediately become a citizen, with all privileges and immunities of citizenship." As satisfactory "evidence," soldiers had to bring a witness to personally "vouch for his loyalty."[47]

This act also allowed for the naturalization of soldiers of declarant, nondeclarant, and enemy birth in the American Expeditionary Force (AEF) who were considered loyal to the United States. The new law eliminated the requirement of filing the preliminary declaration of intention ("first papers") and disregarded the requirement of five years' United States residency. In addition, Congress made it easier for immigrant combatants stationed overseas to become citizens. Immigrant soldiers could file for citizenship without appearing in person in an authorized court and without taking the oath of allegiance in open court, provided that two credible citizen-witnesses verified the soldier's petition for naturalization. The Bureau of Naturalization simplified the forms to make it easier for foreign-born soldiers to secure citizenship and sent representatives to Europe to help AEF personnel who wished to become citizens. The War Department asked commanding officers to assist any interested applicant. However, the department ordered officers not to "use coercive or persuasive measures" to assure citizenship of the immigrants in their ranks.[48]

Although new naturalization laws made it easier for civilian immigrants to secure citizenship, these measures were clearly intended to end the confusion over conscription of aliens and to prevent further international protests from neutral and Allied nations. The provost marshal general considered naturalization "one test for the spirit of loyalty"—a test that the alien soldiers clearly passed. Army training camps held hundreds of naturalization ceremonies in which groups of immigrant soldiers officially became United States citizens. From May 8, 1918, through November 30, 1918, 155,246 immigrant soldiers became citizens of the United States along with an indeterminate number stationed overseas. This does not include over 32,510 foreign-born soldiers (6.67 percent) who were naturalized citizens prior to the draft. In addition, local boards referred some 53,346 immigrants to the Bureau of Naturalization.[49]

Some immigrant soldiers who did not want to serve in the U.S. Army asked for the assistance of the American Union Against Militarism (later called the American Civil Liberties Bureau) in New York. Roger N. Baldwin, director of the bureau, wrote to the War Department on behalf of these immigrants. Much of the confusion resulted from the drafting of noncitizen immigrants who had not filed their first citizenship papers, men from neutral countries, or conscientious objectors. Most misunderstandings came about because of language barriers. Baldwin personally contacted embassies of neutral counties to determine how to proceed in cases involving citizens from neutral territories. For example, Baldwin wrote to the Embassy of the Netherlands in Washington, D.C., citing a letter from a soldier who wanted to leave the army on the grounds that he was from a neutral country. The minister responded that "Netherlanders who have taken out their first papers, in the United States, are subject to draft. However, when once they are in the military service, I can take steps for their release with the State Department."[50]

The Civil Liberties Bureau also investigated complaints about the alleged mistreatment of immigrant soldiers. For instance, in early January, 1918, Morris Trasken from Camp Meade wrote to tell of the mistreatment of Esidore Ohilko (also written as Oeloo). Ohilko was a Russian-born laborer from Pennsylvania who "could hardly speak or understand English." He refused to put on an army uniform or to drill since he had been drafted despite being a nondeclarant. Ohilko explained, through an interpreter, that he was not eligible for the draft since he never filed for his first citizenship papers, and he wanted to return to Russia. The situation became more confusing when a friend sent Ohilko a newspaper clipping from his hometown saying that he and another immigrant soldier would be deported to Italy. Thinking that he would be sent to Italy when he really wanted to go to Russia, Ohilko left camp and went home to explain his situation to his local draft board. Returning to Pennsylvania, he was arrested by United States soldiers and put him in the guardhouse as a deserter. Baldwin also received a letter from William M. Kantor from Camp Meade, explaining that Ohilko was "a sincere C.O. and honestly wants to go back to Russia." Kantor noted, "it seems that the military authorities . . . are taking advantage of [Ohilko's] ignorance of military manners and customs and [his] inability to make himself understood in the English language and imprisoned him when he obviously had no intention of trying to desert or commit a crime." In response, Baldwin wrote to Assistant Secretary of War Frederick P. Keppel describing the soldier's treatment, noting his "exceedingly brutal treatment by the officer in charge, [such as] beatings and depravation of food and bedding." The War Department ordered the commanding general at Camp Meade to investigate the situation. On March 2, 1918, the Adjutant General's Office forwarded to Roger Baldwin a report by Maj. Martin C. Wise, Camp Meade's division inspector. The report explained that after Ohilko returned from his home, he was sent to the Conscientious Objectors' Detachment "pending the result of his claim for exemption." However, they determined that he was not a "C.O." since he had objected to serving in the military because he lost three brothers in Russia. Wise denied that the immigrant had been "brutally treated" and provided details of Ohilko's imprisonment along with names of people the major had interviewed. Baldwin thanked the War Department for the copy of the report of the "alleged conscientious objector."[51]

Baldwin also investigated the imprisonment of Russian immigrants from the "Molakans religious sect." In a letter asking for their release, he reminded Joseph P. Tumulty, secretary to President Wilson, of his (Baldwin's) previous visit with several Russian priests. At that time, Baldwin had explained that this group's religious beliefs "prevent their participation in war." Tumulty wrote Baldwin to assure him that the matter was "being taken care of as considerately and as successfully as possible."[52] Baldwin's efforts to help immigrants were halted when he was imprisoned for draft resistance in November, 1918.

Immigrants have served in the United States military since the Revolutionary War; however, their experience in the American Army during World War I represented a dramatic difference from previous military service. First, the Selective Service Act of 1917 affected an unprecedented number of men and quickly turned them from civilians to soldiers. Second, draftees who entered the U.S. Army in World War I served in a substantially more complex military organization than in any previous period in American history. Conscription in a multiethnic nation did not come without confusion and debate. Even though the Selective Service clearly spelled out the various categories for immigrant draft eligibility, mistakes occurred. The drafting of declarant immigrants took place with little fuss. However, neutral immigrants who did not want to serve turned to their embassies, which negotiated their release with the U.S. State Department. Some immigrants asked the Civil Liberties Bureau for assistance with their discharges. After gathering evidence against soldiers listed as disloyal, enemy aliens could be sent to an internment camp. However, tens of thousands of nondeclarants and enemy aliens wanted to remain in the army. Here, they could fight for both the freedom of their homeland and for their adopted country. The War Department instructed camp commanders to determine which of the enemy alien soldiers should remain in military service. Among other solutions to this confusion was the development of units such as the Slavic Legion for technical enemy aliens. However, delays and eventually the end of the war prevented the full mustering of these. Congress offered another solution by easing up the naturalization laws and expediting the process of becoming a United States citizen. In the end, though, the U.S. Army of World War I was an ethnically diverse force with almost one in every five soldiers born in a foreign country.

There are thousands and thousands of foreign-speaking soldiers in our army camps, and thousands more will arrive with the coming draft. We know what to do with them now, how to weed out the tares from the wheat, how to reach the best in the heart of the alien soldier and develop it, how to loosen his tongue and to teach him the principles of American citizenship. And we know, too, that he will respond to such treatment. We know that this so-called "Camp Gordon Plan" is the one which will add thousands and thousands of virile, efficient soldiers to our armies on the battle lines.

—Capt. Edward R. Padgett, October, 1918

CHAPTER 3

The Camp Gordon Plan

Organizing and Training Foreign-born Troops

When freshly recruited soldiers reported to army camps, the military was shocked to learn the extent of illiteracy among its new troops, including those with long American ancestries. The General Staff estimated that almost 25 percent of the drafted men tested "were unable to read the Constitution of the United States or an American newspaper, or to write a letter in English to the folks at home."[1] Many more soldiers were merely "technically literate," since they had mastered only the basics of reading at the elementary school level. Communication difficulties were complicated by thousands of immigrant soldiers from forty-six different nationalities who could not speak, read, write, or clearly understand the English language. The first draft alone brought in 76,545 immigrants. Capt. Edward R. Padgett of the General Staff reported, "not more than one in a hundred [foreign-born soldiers] knew the English language well enough to understand the instructions necessary to make them first-class fighting men."[2] Some army training camps claimed much higher numbers of non-English speaking soldiers. Camp Gordon, Georgia, an infantry replacement camp, reported that "75 percent [of new recruits] had neither learned English nor obtained even the most elementary knowledge of the art of war." Camp Gordon's 82nd "All-American" Division, drafted from many different areas of the nation, included a significant of foreign-born troops. In fact, almost half of its approximately 23,600 soldiers "were fairly fresh from Ellis Island, New York."[3] To exacerbate the situation, the military discovered that the morale of foreign-born soldiers had been badly shaken by the difficulty in communication and through the neglect and ignorance of some of the training-camp commanders. The military newspaper *Trench and Camp* reported that some of the ethnic groups "quarrel and bicker with one another: old scores from the pages of history were reopened . . . based on politics or region [and] began to spring up and disrupt the scant harmony that did exist."[4]

The War Department took great pains to evaluate and determine the best way to deal with the diverse cultures and languages found within their ranks. Much like the civilians who applied scientific-management techniques to reorder urban-industrial America, the military reformers used bureaucratic organizational skills that recognized environmental and situational factors as the roots of the immigrant soldiers' difficulties. Similar to civilian scientific-management reformers who utilized professional experts, set standards, streamlined systems, and conducted timesaving studies in order to reorganize the urban-industrial nation, the War Department assigned experts to study the difficulties of the foreign-born men. This group interviewed immigrant soldiers, compiled statistical data, implemented new management techniques, and developed rational, pragmatic solutions to the problems faced by immigrant soldiers. Their goal was to create an efficient fighting force and make "non-English-speaking soldiers . . . a permanent part of the camp machinery." Military leaders afterward set out to educate camp commanders and officers about the benefits found through the newly developed policies and assured them that "men of foreign races" generally were "ready pupils, capable of concentration and quick progress."[5]

In January, 1918, the War Department created of the Foreign-speaking Soldier Subsection (FSS) to assist in the training of immigrant soldiers. For the first five months thereafter, the FSS reported to the Military Intelligence Section under Maj. Ralph Van Deman. Van Deman graduated from Harvard in 1888 and received a medical degree from the Miami Medical School in Cincinnati, Ohio, in 1893. His career in the military began as an army sur-

geon, and in 1895 he attended Infantry and Cavalry School at Fort Leaven-
worth, Kansas. Van Deman became an intelligence officer in 1897 and served
in the Spanish-American War and the Philippine War. After attending the
Army War College in 1905, he went on a secret mission to China and supplied Pres. Theodore Roosevelt with intelligence reports during the Russo-
Japanese War. Major Van Deman reported to his new duty as head of the
Military Intelligence Section in early 1917.[6]

The depth and breadth of the work of the FSS was phenomenal considering it operated for only eleven months of the war and the demobilization
period. Through May, 1918, FSS was lead by D. Chauncy Brewer, a prominent Boston lawyer and president of the North American Civic League for
Immigrants (NACL). The War Department considered the Civic League a
"patriotic and philanthropic" organization that helped to assimilate and
Americanize the nation's immigrants with a "sympathetic personal approach and education in American ideals." Established in 1908, the NACL
included among its founders prominent industrialists, financiers, and a
number of famous social leaders such as Florence Kellor. This organization
combined humanitarian aid with propaganda methods to educate new ar-
rivals about employment, housing, and transportation opportunities. NACL
also Americanized the immigrants with patriotic lectures given in various
languages. The founders of the North American Civic League, "though not
unmoved by sympathy, were chiefly concerned with protecting the status
quo from the menace of ignorant, incendiary foreigners without resorting
to immigration restriction." NACL saw its role as helping to transform "unskilled, inefficient immigrants" into "skilled workers and efficient citizens."
Brewer brought this same ideology into the Foreign-speaking Soldier Subsection as he attempted to turn "unskilled" immigrants into skilled and efficient soldiers. Brewer focused the early efforts of FSS toward reorganizing
immigrant troops, establishing English education classes, and organizing
counterpropaganda material.[7]

Under Brewer's leadership, the newly created subsection began to investigate the crucial language and cultural barriers existing in the multiethnic
army. To head up this investigation, Brewer appointed Lt. Stanislaw A.
Gutowski to the FSS staff. Gutowski was a naturalized American citizen,
born in Russian Poland, "who spoke many languages and . . . specialized
on the problem of the foreigner." One FSS report described Gutowski as
"tall, fair-haired, boyish, despite his close-cropped mustache, slender, alert
of eye and mind."[8] In December, 1917, one month prior to the formation
of the FSS, the War Department sent Lieutenant Gutowski to investigate

conditions of Slavic soldiers with Company F, 303rd Infantry, in Camp Devens, Massachusetts. During the war, Camp Devens became the "mobilization and training" camp for the 76th Division, which drafted men from Maine, New Hampshire, Vermont, Massachusetts, Connecticut, and Rhode Island. Since the overwhelming majority of foreign-born soldiers did not speak English, Gutowski spoke to the soldiers in Russian and Polish and asked for the assistance of a Camp Devens officer, Major Rantlett, who "could manage practically all the Slavonic languages." Gutowski reported: "After I was through a very pathetic scene took place. The Poles, with tears in their eyes, with utmost confidence and sincerity, began to ask different questions and explain their hard position in the Army. They have had no chance to speak, to tell their troubles since the time they were put in the rank. Their officers could not understand their language, while the noncommissioned officers could understand neither their language nor their psychology; the result of which was that after three months' training, wasting time and energy, most of the men had learned absolutely nothing."[9]

Gutowski's report also noted that the immigrants' religious needs were not being met, so he asked for the assistance of Catholic priests, who held a Slavic Christmas service for the men. He concluded that the Slavic soldiers, "under proper influence," would develop "a magnificent fighting spirit which is fundamental for the success of our National Army."[10] In January, 1918, Gutowski reported to Washington, D.C., to begin his new duties with the Foreign-speaking Soldier Subsection.

Shortly afterward, the FSS sent the lieutenant to Camp Custer near Battle Creek, Michigan, where he found that the language and morale problems of the foreign soldiers in the 85th Division had gone unchecked. In response, Gutowski selected fifteen immigrant soldiers who had sufficient education and language skills and were cited as loyal and intelligent by army officials and outside organizations. Gutowski's newly organized, multilingual staff began to gather information and conduct individual interviews with the foreign-born soldiers. The division consisted of three brigades—the 160th Depot, 160th Artillery, and 169th Infantry—and each brigade was made up of four regiments. Each regiment included three battalions, and each battalion had four companies.[11]

The original FSS plan called for immigrants to be kept in ethnically mixed companies aided by translators. It quickly became clear that with forty-six different ethnic groups, this plan would require a large pool of multilingual interpreters for each unit. Recognizing the inefficiency of the plan, Gutowski instead reorganized the troops into ethnic-specific companies. In his reports to FSS, Gutowski justified the change and assured FSS that these companies were not designed to encourage immigrant "clannishness," but represented a necessary and temporary measure taken in an emergency situation.[12]

First, Gutowski appointed Lieutenant Swietlik as the assistant intelligence officer in charge of all foreigners in the division. Swietlik, a Polish immigrant, spoke Polish, Bohemian, French, and some German and Spanish. Considered a "first class man" in personality and intelligence, Swietlik had been a lawyer prior to his induction. Next, Gutowski selected the best and brightest of the foreign privates from the various nationalities to become interpreters within each brigade, regiment, battalion, and company. At the brigade level, Gutowski selected Private Chylinski, a lawyer in civilian life, to act as an interpreter and intermediary representing the Slavic troops in the 169th Infantry Brigade. Corporal Steiman, a Jewish soldier, represented the Jewish and German soldiers in the same brigade. Both men reported to the brigade commander. At the regimental level, Gutowski assigned foreign-born interpreters to the four regiments. The 337th Infantry Regiment included Polish and Russian soldiers; the 338th Infantry Regiment had Bohemian, Slav, and Bulgarian men; the 339th Infantry Regiment was made up of Germans and Jews; and the 340th Infantry Regiment comprised Hungarian and Rumanian soldiers. Within a few weeks, the staff reorganized all of the foreign-born units within the entire division.[13]

In a report to FSS dated February 1, 1918, Gutowski concluded that his reorganization was a complete success. The non-English speaking soldiers had been placed in the hands of loyal and competent bilingual comrades of the same nationality who translated orders and reported the needs of the foreign troops to the commanding officers. Gutowski assured the FSS that military authorities at Camp Custer were perfectly satisfied with the changes. Major Crawford, Camp Custer's division intelligence officer, praised Gutowski's "extremely important" work in a letter to Col. R. H. Van Deman, chief of the Military Intelligence Section. He assured Van Deman that Lieutenant Swietlik was admirably suited to continue and perfect the reorganization and training of the foreign-born soldiers.[14]

By the end of February, 1918, Gutowski had implemented a similar reorganization of the 86th Division at Camp Grant, Illinois. This camp, located four miles south of Rockford, opened its doors to its first group of draftees in September, 1917. Seven months later it became an infantry replacement training camp. Since a large number of the foreign troops in the 86th Division were Slavic, especially those drafted out of Chicago, the division commander asked that a Polish-speaking officer, Major Barzynski, be selected as division intelligence officer in charge of meeting the needs of the foreign-born troops. Barzynski was a regular officer of Polish ancestry and from one of the leading Polish families in the United States. The intelligence officer at Camp Grant noted how fortunate they were to have Barzynski's help, particularly since he was "in touch with the social strata which the Polish and other Slavonic peoples recognized, adhere[d] to and [did] not care to see disturbed . . . as they look[ed] up to and admire[d] persons distinguished for their culture."[15]

The original plan of the FSS called for bilingual soldiers to act as interpreters and representatives of the immigrant rank-and-file troops. However, within a month of its existence, the FSS began to rethink the role of immigrant interpreters and concluded that a more efficient system would be to train qualified foreign-born and foreign-speaking soldiers as commissioned and noncommissioned officers. This new plan would end the need for interpreters and improve the morale of the ethnic units by promoting from within the ranks. In February Brewer contacted Henry S. Drinker, president of Lehigh University in Bethlehem, Pennsylvania, and asked him to help in the search for foreign-born college men who could assist the FSS as commissioned officers in the ethnic units. Drinker recommended two Camp Meade, Maryland, soldiers, a Russian who spoke all the Slavic tongues as well as German and French and a Greek who "would be admirably qualified to deal with his countrymen." Gutowski's early efforts to secure officers for some companies was "handicapped" because officers thought that being assigned to a Development Battalion would "close their hope of going overseas." The FSS attempted to "correct that impression."[16]

Under Brewer, the FSS reorganized only the immigrant troops at Camps Custer and Grant. Additional establishments of new "foreign legions" and the promotion of ethnic officers would have to wait for new FSS leadership. In April, 1918, Brewer expressed his frustration with Van Deman, who he contended focused too much effort on espionage matters and counter-propaganda work and not enough on morale issues. Gutowski agreed that increasing the morale of the foreign-born soldiers was the most important part of military training: "One intelligent man well-grounded in human psychology, and the spirit of Democracy, of American Polish, Russian, or Bohemian descent can successfully get control of 1,000 enlisted foreigners and do more in the line of correct information in regard to them, than 100 secret service men."[17]

Brewer asked Raymond Fosdick for assistance in trying to convince the

War Department to change the mission of the FSS and allow the agency to focus more on morale than counterespionage matters. Fosdick in turn wrote a confidential memo to Assistant Secretary of War Keppel to request that the FSS be put under the Commission on Training Camp Activities. Fosdick explained that the Military Intelligence Division (MID) and FSS work under Van Deman "was largely of a detective nature" instead of focused on developing "constructive" methods of training the foreign-born soldiers. Early reports from FSS field agents (immigrants working in ethnic communities) demonstrate that Fosdick was correct (see chapter 5 for details). Keppel promised to hold a meeting to discuss the "whole question of morale." Although records do not reveal whether this meeting took place, it appears that the conflict between Brewer and Van Deman must have continued. In May, 1918, Brewer lamented to Fosdick that "like a troublesome child I am spanked, put into my cot and moved into a far corner, so that my howls will be unobjectionable." He warned: "What if the old time military methods of making a soldier out of a man . . . and damn what he is thinking about, demand some modification? What if a percentage of the soldiers who are going to follow our subaltern officers into battle, refuse to fight with vigor. What if these foreign-speaking men, taught to act in unison, return to industrial centers after the war with a grouch, because they have been manhandled? I leave the question to you."[18]

In June, 1918, Brewer resigned. At the time the War Department placed the Foreign-speaking Soldier Subsection under the newly created Military Morale Section (MMS) within the MID. Capt. George B. Perkins headed the MMS. Lt. Herbert A. Horgan, the new head of the FSS, reported directly to Perkins and both men signed much of the subsection's correspondence. Ironically, the FSS did change its mission, just as Brewer had suggested, and began concentrating most of its efforts on "stimulating and maintaining the morale of the army, not only as a whole but with special references to the various races." This included a major reorganizing of ethnic-specific companies, promoting and training immigrant officers, increasing efforts at English education, and improving the morale of the nonnative soldiers. A good deal of correspondence concerning immigrant soldiers came directly from the new chief of the MID, Brig. Gen. Marlborough Churchill.[19]

Churchill was born in Andover, Massachusetts. His father was a professor of sacred rhetoric at Andover Theological Seminary. Marlborough Churchill graduated from Harvard in 1900 and the following year began his military career as a second lieutenant in the coast artillery at Fort McHenry and Fort Howard. Later service came in various forts in Kansas,

Texas, Oklahoma, and the Philippine Islands. In 1907 he became the aide-de-camp to Brig. Gen. Albert L. Myer. After being promoted to captain in 1912, Churchill became field artillery instructor at Fort Sill and the editor of the *Field Artillery Journal*. From January, 1916, to June, 1917, Churchill was first an observer with the French Army and then later assigned to Maj. Gen. John J. Pershing's staff. From February to May, 1918, the then Colonel Churchill became acting chief of staff for the First Army. He returned to the United States in June, 1918, to replace Van Deman and was temporarily promoted to the rank of brigadier general. Churchill remained with the MID until September, 1920.[20]

Perkins and Horgan also came from Massachusetts, the former from Salem and the latter from Brookline. Both received commissions as second lieutenants in the Aviation Section of the Signal Corp at Camp Kelly Field, San Antonio, Texas, on the same day, November 27, 1917. Perkins became a first lieutenant on April 15, 1918, his commission papers sent care of the Army War College, Washington, D.C. In June, 1918, Captain Perkins was promoted to the chief of the Military Intelligence Branch, Executive Division, Office of the Chief of Staff in Washington, D.C. Although Horgan signed FSS correspondence beginning in June, army paperwork notes that he was promoted and transferred to "Intelligence duty" on August 8, 1918. Perkins received a promotion to major on November 11, 1918, and was honorably discharged in October, 1919. Horgan received his honorable discharge in early 1920.[21]

A month prior to the FSS reorganization, the secretary of war issued a general order requiring the transfer into special development battalions any soldiers who were physically, mentally, or morally incapable of performing their duties. To the War Department, this was an efficient way of either getting rid of or reclaiming "unfit men." The plan for development battalions also included the creation of special training battalions for illiterates and foreign-speaking servicemen, within which immigrants would be given intensive instruction in the reading and writing of English before joining regular units. These training battalions were to be geographically separated from other untrained units for the "unfit and venereal" soldiers. The training plan proved immediately successful for illiterate native-born soldiers and foreign-born soldiers who could speak some English. However, discourse with non-English-speaking soldiers, who together spoke dozens of different languages, continued to prove difficult.[22]

The War Department sent in the new FSS leaders to assist with the foreign-born troops. After investigating the situation, the FSS officers discovered that communications problems were greatly exacerbated because the army had mixed the immigrants in conglomerate masses within the development battalions. (Brewer's FSS had solved the situation by the reorganization of immigrants at Camps Custer and Grant.) Placed in companies with soldiers from various nationalities, many of the non-English-speaking men could not even communicate with members of their own units. Initially, the army compounded the problem by leaving most of the immigrant soldiers to themselves or by giving them "kitchen police" duties and menial tasks around the camp. Despite policies to keep immigrant training development battalions separate from those for the physically or mentally unfit, many army camps mixed the foreign-born soldiers indiscriminately in companies containing the "sick" and "cripple." Understandably, these practices resulted in a growing discontent among the ethnic troops, and subsequently the *Infantry Journal* reported that their morale had been "shattered to pieces." A confidential War Department bulletin concluded that the morale of foreign-born soldiers "had been utterly broken down."[23]

Many immigrant soldiers were anxious to fight to free their homeland from the "hated" Central Powers. "Others were out-and-out adherents of bolsheviki principles. Many were discontented because of their enforced isolation from spiritual and religious stimulus, believing that services at the Knights of Columbus huts were not Catholic because they were not Polish or Italian. Still others were real yellow dogs of the pacifist breed."[24]

Within a few weeks of its reorganization, the FSS began initiating its new mission when it responded to a request from Capt. Eugene C. Bryan, intelligence officer at Camp Gordon, Georgia, for assistance with a "distressing problem" involving non-English-speaking soldiers. Camp Gordon, an infantry replacement center, was designed to provide a three-month intensive training course before shipping its soldiers overseas at the rate of 10,000 a month. This process was severely delayed while training immigrant soldiers, of whom a substantial amount (up to 75 percent) could not effectively speak, read, or write English. In addition, Captain Bryan was concerned with the spiritual life of the soldiers, which had been neglected for months. The situation was made even worse for the Catholics, who did not have an opportunity to attend confession and therefore felt they would be condemned to hell if killed in action. The morale of the soldiers had degenerated even further due to the communication handicap being virtually ignored since the fall of 1917. During this time, immigrants had been indiscriminately assigned to "pick and shovel" work to keep them active. An FSS officer later reported that this created resentment among the nonnative troops, especially in those who had previous military experience in their native country: "Many of them already were trained soldiers, who had served in the armies of their native lands and, more to the point, they had answered the call to the colors with enthusiasm because they saw in it a chance to fight not only the battles of their adopted country but likewise opportunity to avenge some of the wrongs perpetrated upon their own countrymen in the past by the unholy Hun, the treacherous Austrian and the 'unspeakable Turk.' They had come into camp ready to fight, not to lie around and grow discontented and lazy as part of a badly discipline rabble."[25]

With thousands of non-English-speaking soldiers, Camp Gordon was a great place to "experiment" with foreign legions on "a big scale." The FSS once again turned to its experts. The subsection immediately deployed Lieutenant Gutowski to investigate the situation and develop solutions. This time, Lt. Eugene C. Weisz, an Italian-born officer who was fluent in seven different languages, joined Gutowski. A number of other experienced line officers assisted in the reorganization. The FSS staff began with the 5th Training Battalion, Depot Brigade. With the help of translators, the staff interviewed some 976 immigrant soldiers and noted their complaints concerning the army's treatment so that steps could be taken to solve morale problems. Gutowski and his staff classified all non-English-speaking men according to their language, nationality, education, military experience, and willingness to fight for the United States. The lieutenant then placed the immigrants into three groups—development battalions, labor battalions, and noncombatant battalions. "Really disloyal" and enemy alien soldiers went into a labor battalion. Those deemed physically unfit but proficient in a trade went into the noncombatant battalion. Crippled and diseased soldiers were sent to the hospital for treatment or discharged. The FSS placed all other immigrants in the development battalion.[26]

Eventually, 7,000 physically fit non-English-speaking soldiers were placed into Camp Gordon's development battalion. FSS officers began to organize the companies according to the immigrants' native tongues. The first two units formed included a company of Slavic soldiers (primarily Poles) and a company of Italians. The FSS then selected three Polish officers and a native Russian to head the Slavic company and two Italian officers to command the Italian company. In this manner the immigrant soldiers could easily communicate with their officers while being trained as troop replacements. Greek, Russian, Jewish, and other "Foreign Legion" companies soon followed. The FSS staff also selected a foreign-born or second-generation officer to head each company. The foreign-speaking officers immediately began to train and drill their soldiers and lecture them about military discipline and the Articles of War. The FSS team also coordinated English classes, social activities, and special religious services. The ethnic companies competed with each other in drill proficiency, and the units were soon able to match their skills with any company in the camp.[27]

Camp Gordon intelligence officer Captain Bryan praised the work of Gutowski and his staff, noting that the morale of the immigrant soldiers had changed dramatically from discontentment to enthusiasm and self-satisfaction and was "excellent." In fact, Bryan reported that just one month prior to the arrival of the FSS personnel, all of the foreign-speaking soldiers had refused to go overseas. However, after the "Camp Gordon Plan" was implemented, 85 percent expressed their willingness "in no uncertain terms" to fight in Europe. Later, this number increased to 92 percent. (According to Bryan, the men who continued to refuse overseas service did so to avoid possibly fighting their relatives in Germany.) The commanding officer at Camp Gordon and Major Hunt of the General Staff also expressed their "entire satisfaction" with the reorganization.[28]

After Camp Gordon's successful reorganization, a number of immigrant soldiers asked to become citizens of the United States. By July 22, 1918, some 1,470 aliens from thirty-six different countries became naturalized citizens; the Italian and Russian soldiers represented the largest number. Camp Gordon handled naturalization in a "workmen-like [sic] manner" consistent with military policy, which forbade pressuring immigrants to become citizens.[29]

The Camp Gordon Plan called for each ethnic company to be led by the best qualified foreign-speaking immigrant or second-generation officer. Therefore, the FSS began an intensive search for bilingual and multilingual soldiers. Recommendations for immigrant officers also came from the General Staff. For instance, Capt. E. R. Padgett recommended Mishel George Daavid from the Supply Company, 138th Field Artillery, Camp Shelby, Mississippi, for Officers' Training Camp. Padgett personally knew the family of the young Syrian immigrant for many years and reported that Daavid was "splendidly educated, a young man of fine appearance, a man of utmost refinement and [was] thoroughly Americanized . . . who spoke English with the fluency of a native American."[30]

To assist in its quest for ethnic officers, the War Department ordered the immediate transfer of existing foreign-speaking officers to development battalions to assist with the program. In addition, they transferred the most

qualified rank-and-file men to Officers' Training School to become commissioned and noncommissioned officers. Men were chosen for their education, business experience, previous military training, leadership qualities,
and linguistic skills. The FSS preferred officers of foreign "blood" who had
"grown up with the language" and understood the psychology of their
people rather than officers who learned languages through study or travel.
However, the military accepted both native-born and foreign-born men to
lead the ethnic units. To stem tensions, the military warned native-born
officers to avoid prejudice against or stereotyping officers with "accents" by
reminding them that many of these nonnative men had been "successful
in civilian life as members of the professions or in business."[31]

The FSS arranged to have foreign-speaking graduates of Officers' Training School transferred directly to development battalions. It concluded that
sending immigrant candidates to Officers' Training School and their sub-
sequent commissioning also had "a most excellent effect" on the larger foreign-speaking communities in the country. In addition, "commissioned and
non-commissioned officers of similar race knowing the habits, language
and psychology of their respective companies, [had] drilled and turned out
splendid Polish, Greek, Italian, etc. companies, . . . [and] thousands of foreign-born fighters [had] been added to the army and sent to the front."[32]

Since the Camp Gordon plan proved so successful, the FSS increased
Gutowski's staff and began to address troop reorganization in other army
training camps. In August, Churchill informed the chief of staff that "an
officer was urgently needed" to create ethnic platoons at Camp Meade and
assist in the "upbuilding of the morale" of foreign-speaking soldiers, sending Gutowski to do the job. Due to his "excellent" assistance at Camp Gordon, the FSS transferred Lieutenant Weisz to help reorganize the Italian
soldiers at Camp Meade. The MID considered Weisz to be an able and efficient officer and an asset to the subsection because of his "correct" military manner and his ability to work through military channels. The FSS
also selected Lieutenant Walczynski because of his "considerable experience" with immigrant soldiers at Camp Custer. First Lts. M. A. Viracola,
Louis Zara, I. Prylinski, and Walter S. Przybyszewski along with 2nd Lt.
Frank J. Kracha also joined the FSS staff at Camp Meade. Walczynski had
been born in Russia, where he attended Military Cadet School (1884–91)
before emigrating to the United States. The lieutenant's skills included command of the Russian, Polish, and Lithuanian languages. His military experiences in the United States included service in the 32nd Regiment of the
New York National Guard (as corporal, 1891–94), The Polish Uhlans of New

York State (part of the National Guard, 1891–93), the 4th U.S. Cavalry (1894–97), and the U.S. infantry (second lieutenant, 1908–9). In 1917 Walczynski attended Officers' Training School before becoming part of the FSS staff.[33]

Lieutenant Przybyszewski, son of Polish immigrants and a former postal clerk and law student, enlisted in the army in 1915 and served with the Mexican Expedition in 1916. The following year Przybyszewski acted as an instructor in "Army Paper Work" at Camp Lee, Virginia, and served in the 317th Infantry unit before his transfer to the MID in August, 1918. Przybyszewski had begun as a private in December, 1915, but rose in rank to first lieutenant by June, 1918. The officer's mastery of Russian and Polish made him particularly qualified for work with the FSS. Lt. Louis Zara, native-born son of a Philadelphia minister, graduated from the University of Pennsylvania and began studying law at Temple University before being commissioned as a second lieutenant in the United States Army in August, 1917. Zara was assigned to infantry units in the 79th, 27th, and 80th Divisions before his transfer to military intelligence. Although Zara had the ability to communicate in French and Spanish, it was his fluency in Italian that attracted MID. These men were assigned to implement the Camp Gordon Plan in army camps throughout the United States.[34]

Secretary of War Baker expedited the "Camp Gordon Plan" by directing commanding officers at thirty-five training camps to classify ethnic troops for reorganization. The order issued by the War Department's chief of staff requested a list of the number of foreign-born soldiers (classified by mother tongue) along with the name, rank, organization, and language of all foreign-speaking line officers. Horgan's staff quickly designed and distributed written instructions for the development of "Foreign Legion" training companies so that the plan could be easily duplicated in camps throughout the United States.[35]

First, the instructions recommended that all camp commanders form training companies organized by native tongue, noting the principal languages as Italian, Polish, Russian, Ukrainian (including Ruthenian), Czechoslovak (Bohemian), Greek (including Albanian), Scandinavian, Armenian, Yugoslav (South Slav), and Syrian. Second, Horgan suggested that qualified foreign-speaking soldiers be selected and trained as commissioned and noncommissioned officers to drill the foreign companies as infantry units. Third, the FSS recommended the formation of a board of foreign-speaking officers who could investigate actions of "supposed disloyalty" among immigrant soldiers. Fourth, Horgan's plan called for an intensive study program in conversational English and military terms to be conducted in the morning and afternoon, since the men would be too tired after drill for evening classes. Finally, FSS suggested that the camps provide ethnic entertainment and host prominent ethnic speakers to help raise the spirit of the foreign troops. Other ideas included moving pictures that would interest specific groups (such as Italian war movies) and providing reading material in the soldiers' native languages. Horgan continued to cite the success of the Camp Gordon Plan when he strongly recommended it to other commanders at camps throughout the United States.[36]

The FSS leader assured training-camp officials that the immigrants came from "sturdy fighting stock," which made them good soldiers. Under the plan, the foreign-born troops became trained combatants within six weeks and learned English well enough to make them "valuable fighting units." In correspondence with camps throughout the United States, Horgan provided numerous examples of the success of the Camp Gordon Plan and reminded commanders of the special qualifications of many of the foreign-born soldiers who were veterans of past European wars. In addition, since most had been engaged in hard work in civilian life, Horgan continually assured military officials that immigrants made good soldiers.[37]

During the next several months, the FSS began to implement the Camp Gordon Plan in fifteen army cantonments including Camp Meade (Maryland), Camp Devens (Massachusetts), Camp Upton (New York), Camp Dix (New Jersey), Camp Lee (Virginia), Camp Custer (Michigan), Camp Grant (Illinois), Camp Dodge (Iowa), Camp Cody (New Mexico), Camp McClellan (Alabama), Camp Sherman (Ohio), Camp Taylor (Kentucky), and Camps Wadsworth, Sevier, and Jackson (South Carolina).[38]

Camp Meade, Maryland, was the first to utilize the Camp Gordon Plan when, in order to promote the efficiency of development battalions, Brig. Gen. Henry Jervey, assistant chief of staff and director of operations, ordered its implementation. Jervey created a model development battalion to test the efficiency of the program before implementing it in other Meade units. Recognizing the importance of the reorganization effort, the secretary of war ordered thirty-four foreign-speaking officers from various camps to go to Meade to observe the program and help coordinate the activities. A number of representatives from the Military Morale Section also studied general morale problems and introduced morale-boosting ideas.

The reorganization at Camp Meade marked FSS's second success with the Camp Gordon Plan, and authorization was quickly given for the formation of other "Foreign Legion" companies. The War Department directed

Lieutenant Kracha to stay behind to continue the work at Meade, while Przybyszewski and Zara received special orders for Camp Devens, Massachusetts, where they assisted Gutowski's next reorganization effort. Eight months had passed since Gutowski's original visit to that camp.[39]

At Camp Devens, Massachusetts, the FSS officers reorganized the immigrant soldiers into groups according to their "race" and language. Companies included Slavic (chiefly Russians and Poles), Italian, Greek/Albanian, and Syrian/Armenian units. Initial reports from Camp Devens indicated that 4,735 of its 17,932 troops (26 percent) were born in foreign countries. The MID recommended that some of the foreign-speaking soldiers at Camp Devens be considered for commissions to assist as officers with the growing percentage of immigrant draftees. In the meantime, Churchill arranged for the rapid transfer of two Italian and two Slavic officers to Camp Devens and continued to search for two Armenians and two Greeks for similar duty. Eventually, each company at Devens had its own officers who spoke the soldiers' language. Out of the eighty officers there who spoke foreign languages (Bohemian, French, German, Hebrew, Italian, Norwegian, Polish, Portuguese, Spanish, Swedish, and Yiddish), twenty-one were listed as being of foreign extraction; most were second-generation Americans.[40]

Eventually, Lieutenant Gutowski reported that he and his staff reorganized about 10,000 ethnic soldiers at Camp Devens into "Foreign Legion Companies." The dramatic increase in immigrant trainees (from 4,735 to some 10,000) was no doubt the result of new conscripts being inducted after the second national registration held in June, 1918. The reorganization of foreign-speaking soldiers at Camp Devens also proved to be a complete success. According to the FSS, foreign troops were in "excellent shape" within ten days, and the morale of the soldiers had improved "100%." In August, Gutowski headed to Camp Upton, New York, to "install" the Camp Gordon Plan there. Camp Upton housed the 77th Division, about 23,000 soldiers drafted out of New York City and surrounding counties. At the time, New York City housed the largest immigrant population in the United States. Reorganizations continued throughout the summer of 1918.[41]

In September, 1918, Gutowski and Col. K. C. Masteller of the General Staff delivered a speech to intelligence officers from various camps in an effort to encourage the expansion of the Camp Gordon Plan. The lieutenant reported that there remained some 100,000 ethnic soldiers who still could not speak English. Although the foreign servicemen came from forty-six different nationalities, 80 percent were Italians, Slavs, Jews (mostly Russian), Greeks, or Armenians. Gutowski outlined the problems faced by these

men and made suggestions to facilitate the implementation of the reorganization plan. The next month, Gutowski and Lt. M. A. Viracola reported to
Camp Dix, New Jersey, to begin the development of foreign-speaking companies. Once there, the FSS team began to concentrate on the 3rd Battalion,
153rd Depot Brigade, temporarily renamed the "Camp Gordon Battalion."
As in the other camps, the officers met with success. In a letter to the director of Military Intelligence, Capt. J. Joseph Lilly, the Camp Dix intelligence
officer, reported that Gutowski had been of immense assistance in "clearing
up the foreign soldier situation."[42]

In October, 1918, the War Department placed the Foreign-speaking Soldier Subsection (with Horgan still as leader) directly under the new head of
the Military Intelligence Division, Brig. Gen. Marlborough Churchill. Implementing the Camp Gordon Plan continued when 1st Lts. Eugene Weisz and
Ignatius Prylinski reorganized ethnic soldiers at Camp Lee, Virginia. The
two were particularly well qualified since between them the officers spoke
Italian, Magyar, Serbo-Croation, Russian, Polish, and several other languages. The FSS selected Joseph Girdzeunis, a "bright soldier" from Company F, 17th Training Battalion, to assist Weisz and Prylinski with their
work. The Camp Lee Situation Survey, which appraised the FSS reorganization, reported a vast improvement in the morale of foreign-born troops:
"The men go to their work . . . with a song on their lips." The soldiers' drill
was "exceptionally good and the execution of their movements [was] very
precise."[43]

November proved a busy month for the FSS team as they continued reorganizing camps throughout the United States. Camp intelligence officers
supplied the War Department with needed information on immigrant soldiers. For example, Camp Sherman, Ohio, had 509 Italians, 371 Russians,
152 Greeks, 126 Turks, 56 Austrians, 55 Austrian Poles, 37 Bulgarians, and
19 Hungarians, all "handicapped in their training in purely English-speaking companies." Camp Taylor, Kentucky, reported 1,492 Germans, 581 Italians, 331 Russians, 138 Norwegians, 333 French, 210 Swedes, 194 Poles,
and 187 Polish Russians.[44]

The FSS detailed Capt. J. Mott Dahlgren to Camp Cody, New Mexico, to
reorganize Spanish-speaking soldiers into training companies. The subsection arranged for the transfer of five Spanish-speaking officers to work with
the over six hundred Mexican soldiers. It also assigned two of its staff personnel, Lt. Frank Kracha and Capt. W. J. Semerad, to Camps Wadsworth,
Sevier, and Jackson in South Carolina for the formation of foreign-speaking training battalions. After completing their work at Camp Lee, Weisz

and Prylinski moved on to Camp Custer, Michigan; Camp Grant, Illinois; and Camp Dodge, Iowa, to continue their work with non-English-speaking soldiers at each site. Lieutenant Walczynski reported to Camp Sherman, Ohio, and Camp Taylor, Kentucky. The FSS obtained permission from the commanding officer at Camp Gordon, Georgia, to reassign Lt. Felix Mateia as an FSS officer to assist the reorganization of foreign-born troops at Camp Sherman, Ohio, and Camp McClellan, Alabama. Mateia was selected due to his excellent work with the Slavic-speaking soldiers in the first FSS reorganization program at Camp Gordon.[45]

In the autumn of 1918, Churchill asked the intelligence officer at Camp Gordon to report on the number of foreign-born soldiers currently undergoing training through the Camp Gordon Plan. That officer's report of October, 1918, divided the soldiers into four categories: alien enemies (including the names of thirty-five German and Austrian soldiers), Allied enemy aliens (including the names of ninety-five Turkish, Syrian, and Bulgarian soldiers), Allies (including the names of 692 Italians, English, Canadians, Greeks, Montenegrins, Portuguese, Scots, Armenians, Irish, Lithuanians, French, Persians, Polish Russians, Poles, and Russians), and neutrals (including the names of thirty Mexicans, Swedes, Norwegians, Romanians, Dutch, Swiss, and Danes). Italians and Russians made up the two largest groups of immigrants.[46]

The leaders of the Military Intelligence Division had an excellent relationship with their FSS officers. Lieutenant Gutowski received continual compliments from his superiors and obtained a promotion to captain in the fall of 1918. In January, 1919, both Col. John M. Dunn of the General Staff and Horgan praised Przybyszewski for his work with the FSS and recommended him for Officers' Training School and a commission in the regular army. Other FSS officers also received career support due to their work with the MID. After obtaining a "strong" recommendation for Kracha from Maj. A. P. Deering, commanding officer of the development battalions at Camp Meade, Horgan asked Churchill to promote the officer to first lieutenant. Kracha displayed "the greatest keenness, zeal, and energy" in assisting in the development of foreign-legion companies. Unfortunately, Kracha's recommendations coincided with the Armistice and the temporary freezing of all promotions by the War Department. Not all FSS officers received commendations. Horgan considered Zara's work unsatisfactory, and he was not recommended for a commission in the regular army. Horgan also found fault with Walczynski's work at Camp Sherman, Ohio, and had to send Gutowski to "clean up the Walczynski fiasco." Early that year, on November 13, 1918,

Brig. Gen. M. Churchill reprimanded Walczynski for his failure to follow orders in organizing ethnic soldiers at Camp Sherman; two days later Churchill transferred him to the Mail Censor's Office. Many of the reorganizations continued even after the Armistice was declared. The MID intended to institute the Camp Gordon Plan in every cantonment in the United States with a sufficient number of foreign-born soldiers.[47]

The War Department raved about the success of the Camp Gordon Plan in various military journals, army newspapers, and the mainstream press. While negative ethnic stereotypes filled the pages of the wartime popular press in association with the "100 percent Americanization" movement and anti-German propaganda, the War Department promoted positive images of foreign-born soldiers. Popular civilian war songs reminded immigrants not to "Bite the Hand that Feeds Them." Even the song "When Tony Goes Over the Top," which applauded immigrant soldiers fighting for the Stars and Stripes, was riddled with negative stereotyping:

> *Hey! You know Tony the Barber who shaves and cuts-a the hair.*
> *He said ska-booch, to his mariooch. He's gonna fight "Over There."*
> *Hey! You know Tony could shave you. He'd cut you from ear to ear—*
> *I just got a letter from Tony and this is what I hear.*
> *When Tony goes over the top.*
> *He no think of the barber shop, he grab-a-da gun and chas-a-da hun.*
>   *And make-em all run like a long-of-a-gun.*
> *You can bet your life he'll never stop.*
> *When Tony goes over the top.*
> *Keep your eyes on the fighting wop. . . .*
> *With a rope of spa-gett and a big a-sti-lette. He'll make-a the German*
>   *sweat.*
> *When Tony goes over the top.*[48]

In contrast, the War Department purposely created a positive public image of immigrant soldiers in storybook tales of instant loyalty and rapid assimilation. Their press releases, hailing the Camp Gordon Plan, claimed that once the immigrants donned military uniforms and attended a few weeks of English and civil lessons, they became ready-made Americans. The military news releases provided positive images of the immigrant soldier, but many stories nevertheless had stereotypical overtones. For instance, military writers described ethnic soldiers as "sturdy stock" Europeans, "splendid physical specimens" with a "quick ability to learn." Positive stories told of foreign-born troops who rapidly grasped the "principles of America" and immediately displayed a "burning desire" to become naturalized citizens. Military writers called the immigrants "eager and loyal . . . friends, fellow-citizens, and brother."[49]

In thousands of pieces of correspondence, the Foreign-speaking Soldier Subsection consistently demonstrated a clear respect for the immigrant soldier. Only a few memos stereotyped foreign-born troops. In one, Horgan concluded that European men greatly "respected discipline" and made rapid progress when the army required "strict and immediate compliance" to military orders. Horgan occasionally made reference to the immigrants as being from "sturdy fighting stock." Yet, Horgan also told military officials not to use "guinea," "bohunk," "wop," or other stereotypical terms when addressing these soldiers since it would hurt their feelings.[50]

Capt. Edward R. Padgett of the General Staff applauded the Camp Gordon Plan, which he believed completely and quickly solved the tremendous problem of the ethnic soldiers: "One should observe him at work in the camp, see him covered with the dust of the parade ground, smell the very sweat of him! He drills—the best type, that is with a snap and a go that bespeak the foreign-born soldiers. Big of frame and strong of muscle, he is truly a glutton for work. Once he fully understands why he is there, why we are at war and what we (including himself) are fighting for, he tackles the job of become [sic] a soldier with determination."[51]

In a report on the success completion of the Camp Gordon Plan, the FSS bragged that it was able in only three months' time to make efficient soldiers of these nonnatives when "it seemed that from this melting pot could be poured only a conglomerate mass of humanity, confused by a babel of tongues." However, with the effective reorganization of soldiers into ethnic-specific companies under command of bilingual officers, the military discovered that "out of the melting pot of America's admixture of races is being poured a new American trained and ready to make the world safe for Democracy, to tear the bloody hand of the Hun from the throat of civilization."[52]

The War Department applauded the "extraordinary" efficiency of the Camp Gordon Plan and noted the amazing increase in the morale of foreign-born troops that resulted. An article in the *Infantry Journal* agreed, citing a recent fitness examination that found the Slavic and Italian soldiers and their officers to be the best companies in the camp. Originally left behind as "unfit" when their division went overseas, the newly reorganized ethnic companies quickly improved within a few weeks under the Camp Gordon Plan. Shortly afterward, the companies were broken up into platoons and sent overseas as replacement troops. Clearly, the United States military rejected prevailing negative attitudes about the foreign born. To the FSS, the question was not one of ability, but organization; that is, its personnel never doubted that foreign-born recruits had the ability to be effective soldiers if they were organized in units where they could receive training in their own language. A MID bulletin best summarized the military search for order: "Instead of distributing the non-English speaking men among the English speaking and thus creating confusion and misunderstanding, they can be grouped, handled and controlled together, and the wastage which has existed of time, money and foreign human material can be brought to an end." Lieutenant Horgan concluded that "sympathetic and understanding compliance" with the Camp Gordon Plan would save the military "great numbers of soldiers of proved fighting stock and capability." In his report, Horgan quoted Napoleon: "No stimulus is more potent than the pride of men who have a common bond, either of race, nationality, color, or even affliction. Men thus put together, in a regiment, battalion, or company, want to show the rest of the army their extreme capability."[53]

The chief of the Military Intelligence Division, General Churchill, along with Major Lentz of the Operations Division and Colonel Fleming and Major Brown of the Training Committee of the War Plans Division all agreed that the Camp Gordon Plan prepared "many thousand loyal fighting men ready for service overseas . . . in the shortest possible time." Churchill actually calculated the value of the FSS plan in dollar savings. He estimated that the direct financial loss of an untrained man was $1,000 (including pay, clothing, food, and the effort in training). Therefore, Churchill claimed that the government was financially bettered by $1,000,000 for each 1,000 immigrant men "saved" and turned into efficient soldiers.[54]

Efficiency was not just an issue in the training of the foreign born, but it was also a primary concern when the immigrants were transferred out of the development battalions as replacement troops. A final report analyzing the success of the Camp Gordon Plan by Lt. E. G. Moyer, the camp's intelligence officer, emphasized efficiency as a motivating factor of the program. The report is significant since the MID used Camp Gordon as a training prototype for other army cantonments. Although development battalions were sometimes kept together as companies in overseas units, Camp Gordon officials preferred to transfer immigrant soldiers in smaller platoon-sized units, preferably accompanied by their foreign-speaking officers whenever possible. It was believed that transferring immigrants in larger units would encourage them to associate only with members of their own nationality and result in their loss of newly acquired English-language skills. The final report also objected to the transfer of individual immigrant soldiers into nonethnic companies, since it could subject them "to the baneful conditions that prevail[ed] where a single foreign-speaking soldier [was] thrown with English-speaking soldiers." However, transferring immigrants in small platoons proved beneficial, since the immigrants could converse in their native language and still be in contact with English-speaking soldiers in the larger companies. The report associated the platoon with a little immigrant "colony" and the company with the "melting pot." In this way, an ethnic platoon within an English-speaking company could provide a "foundation" for "Americanization" while it could also "keep up [the immigrants'] morale much better than if put among people of entirely different customs."[55]

The United States military faced a serious challenge when almost a half-million immigrants reported to army training camps. While both the 82nd and 77th Divisions had substantial numbers of immigrant soldiers, foreign-born troops could be found throughout other units of the army. Language barriers complicated the situation, and a lack of communication had left the foreign-born men frustrated and confused. The War Department set out to create an effective fighting force and increase the morale of the soldiers. Efficiency drove military policies. Military reorganization efforts matched ideas of civilian scientific-management techniques including psychological and statistical studies, new managerial methods, and a reliance on professional experts. Military reformers studied the problems affecting the soldiers' attitudes and sought solutions. In many ways, the military's immigrant reorganization efforts reflect a rational pragmatic approach consistent with that of professional urban reformers who "developed the new values of 'continuity and regularity, functionality and rationality, administration and management' in order to cope with twentieth-century problems." Likewise, military reformers "worked day and night to bring some sort of order out of the chaos" associated with foreign-born troops. In this case, "order" translated into reorganizing foreign-speaking men into ethnic companies, promoting immigrant and second-generation soldiers to commissioned and noncommissioned officers, and providing for the specific needs of the immigrant combatants. The War Department justifiably bragged about the efficiency and success of the Camp Gordon Plan in memos, journals, and national newspapers.[56]

Life in a U.S. Army Cantonment. This YMCA social room was one way of implementing the military's "moral-uplifting" program, designed to keep soldiers away from unhealthy influences such as drinking, gambling, and prostitution.

YMCA Auditorium, Camp Merritt, New Jersey. This structure had a seating capacity of over 2,500. The Foreign-speaking Soldier Subsection used the YMCA facilities for ethnic programs and cultural celebrations, and the Jewish Welfare Board organized and held religious services in these buildings for practicing Jews in the army.

Baseball Game, Camp Lee, Virginia. The Commission on Training Camp Activities offered sports as an alternative to "negative" influences.

Reading in the Camp Library, American Library Association, Camp Sherman, Ohio. The Foreign-speaking Soldier Subsection arranged to have newspapers and books in various languages available for the immigrant soldiers.

Interior of a Camp Library, Camp Hancock, Georgia. Along with books on American history and civics, camp libraries included both English and foreign-language literature.

Italian American Soldiers Learning English at Camp Kearny, California. "'The Palestine Chart, made from the Geographic, was a joy to make and a joy to teach.' Often, though not always, the teacher of the same nationality as the class finds a readier response from the pupils. The young Italian in this photograph welded his Italian class at the base hospital into a friendly unit of which he was very definitely the center." *(From* National Geographic Magazine, *August, 1918; photo by Christina Krysto)*

Foreign-born Soldiers Reading National Geographic Magazine, *Camp Kearny, California. Teaching English to foreign-born soldiers became a joint effort of the War Department, social welfare agencies, and ethnic leaders. Bilingual immigrant soldiers also helped train their comrades. (From* National Geographic Magazine, *August, 1918; photo by Christina Krysto)*

Foreign-born Soldiers Using National Geographic Magazine *as Their Text, Camp Kearny, California. Camp instructors also taught English through the use of "universal language charts—pictures." At Camp Kearny, soldiers completed "a six weeks' normal school course in three days and then put their knowledge into practice with the aid of picture text-books made from copies of the* National Geographic Magazine." *(From* National Geographic Magazine, *August, 1918; photo by Christina Krysto)*

REGIMENTAL BAND
CAMP LEE, VA.

Regimental Band, Camp Lee, Virgina. Music was another way of keeping soldiers out of trouble while both encouraging pride through ethnic songs and promoting benign "Americanization" through patriotic works. Camp music programs included Foreign Legion bands designed to improve the morale of immigrant soldiers.

Knights of Columbus Building, Camp Hancock, Georgia. The Knights of Columbus provided recreational activities for the Catholic soldiers, including thousands of immigrants.

Soldiers Attending Mass, Knights of Columbus Building, Camp Hancock, Georgia. Native- and foreign-born Catholic recruits attended services in Knights of Columbus "Hostess Huts" at training camps throughout the United States.

Postcard Provided to Returning Jewish Servicemen. Cards such as this one, made available to soldiers and sailors by the Jewish Welfare Board, allowed the men to notify family and friends that they had returned to the United States after the Armistice.

The Commission's aim to surround the men in service with an environment which is not only clean and wholesome but positively inspiring—the kind of environment which a democracy owes to those who fight on its behalf.

—Raymond B. Fosdick, Commission on Training Camp Activities

CHAPTER 4

Military Moral Uplifting

Socializing Native-born and Foreign-born Soldiers

The War Department needed to turn millions of civilians into productive soldiers in a rapid, efficient, and systemic manner. Yet at the same time, military leaders recognized that the same social problems that plagued civilian Progressives challenged them as well. Furthermore, these social ills— alcohol, prostitution, gambling, and poor health conditions—translated into inefficient troops. The War Department's ultimate goal was "to prevent as far as humanly possible, inefficiency in [the] fighting forces endangered by drunkenness and disease" and other social evils by "civilian moral-uplift[ing] work." Shortly after the United States entered the war, Secretary of War Newton D. Baker created the Commission on Training Camp Activities (CTCA). Baker selected Progressive reformer Raymond Fosdick to head the new agency and charged him with "the responsibility of cultivating and conserving the manhood and manpower of America's fighting forces" by providing a "clean and wholesome" environment. The commission accepted the difficult task of morally uplifting troops in order to create a productive force, but its members acknowledged the difficulty of taking on a "task never before faced and deliberately undertaken by any nation." The military socialized immigrant soldiers with the same "moral uplifting" methods used on the native born. In addition to socialization, ethnic soldiers underwent educational classes in English, civics, and citizenship with undertones of Americanization.[1]

Fosdick, in his former position as New York's commissioner of accounts, had worked diligently to break up the corrupt Tammany Hall political machine, investigated fraudulent actions of city employees, and pushed for safety and sanitary regulations for New York's businesses. It was Fosdick's excellent reputation as a municipal reformer that first attracted the attention of the secretary of war. Both men came from a new generation of reformers who sought to end the nation's problems with urban social engineering and attempted to reorder society in the "virtuous" image of the middle-class value system. In a letter to Fosdick, Baker wrote: "We will accept as the fundamental concept of our work, the fact which every social worker knows to be true, that young men spontaneously prefer to be decent, and that opportunities for wholesome recreation are the best possible cure for irregularities in conduct which arise from idleness and the baser temptations." This became the philosophy of the CTCA. Fosdick had high praise for the secretary of war and noted that due to Baker's "lifetime of work with social agencies he had a sympathetic understanding of the problems of youth."[2]

Baker's mayoral experiences in Cleveland had taught him a great lesson. In his first few years leading the city, Baker had desperately attempted to end crime and vice by means of legal punishment and watched in frustration as his police force's effort proved futile at fighting popular depravity. Finally, the mayor adopted methods of many social welfare agencies that offered alternative recreation to "immoral" activities. The city of Cleveland soon hosted successful alcohol-free dance halls and pavilions, municipal amusement parks, civil pageants, city art shows, and other city-planning efforts. From this experience, Baker had quickly learned that "the most promising long-range strategy of urban moral control was not repression, but a more subtle and complex process of influencing behavior and molding character through a transformed, consciously planned urban environment."[3] Baker brought these lessons to his position with the United States military.

The secretary of war worked diligently to create a planned wholesome environment in his military training camps.

Soldiers typically engaged in an intense sixteen-week (forty hours per week) training program. During this time the men were trained in military combat, discipline, packing and tent pitching, close order drill, trench and open warfare, fire control, signaling, anti-gas protection, "bombing" (hand-grenade throwing), target shooting, and other key skills needed to be an efficient soldier. Wednesday and Saturday afternoons and most evenings were kept free for recreation or for additional drill for "backward men." Other evenings found solders learning about trench construction, scouting, patrolling, and night relief for troops in the trenches. Training, however, went beyond the typical focus on military matters. Soldiers also attended patriotic lectures to learn why they were fighting the Great War, and much effort was put into socializing soldiers in "proper moral behavior."[4]

The War Department's Commission on Training Camp Activities had several divisions including Social Hygiene, Law Enforcement, Athletics, Music, Theaters, Education, and Publicity. The commission also worked in conjunction with a number of organizations that could trace their roots, leadership, and philosophy to the ideology of Progressivism. Officially affiliated organizations included the Young Men's and Young Women's Christian Associations, American Social Hygiene Association, Playground Recreation Association, American Library Association, Knights of Columbus, and the Jewish Welfare Board. A number of other social welfare organizations also cooperated with the CTCA including the American Red Cross and the Salvation Army. Support also came from a significant number of ethnic organizations and prominent ethnic leaders nationwide.

The social welfare and ethnic organizations joined forces to educate soldiers about social diseases and offer alternatives to vice, alcohol, and gambling. To this end, the CTCA attempted a two-front attack on social evils. The "negative or repressive" approach educated troops to the immorality and dangers of prostitution, alcohol, and gambling, while the "positive" strategy provided "wholesome" alternatives to social immorality.[5]

Venereal disease spread rapidly during the Great War. In October, 1917, VD incidences in the American Expeditionary Forces at one port (St. Nazaiare, France) shot up from its usual rate of "forty per thousand" to "two hundred per thousand" when soldiers found themselves with a lot of free time waiting for transportation to arrive. American troops were not the only ones plagued with these problems. The CTCA claimed that the Central Powers had lost many divisions because of men who became "incapacitated" by venereal disease, and the British reported losing some 70,495,000 "soldier-days" per year. "One British division reputedly lost 25 percent of its strength through such diseases. Infection required evacuating the sick to a rear hospital, where they remained almost two months, and meant a sharp decline in military effectiveness."[6]

Prior to the United States entrance in World War I, the disease rate among American soldiers in Mexico in 1916 had been "extraordinarily high." Fosdick testified before the House Committee on Military Affairs that he hoped to prevent a repetition of problems faced during the Mexican conflict of 1916–17, when "out of sheer boredom [soldiers] went to the only places where they were welcomed which were the saloon and the house of prostitution." A contradictory account of the Mexican Punitive Expedition tells of the American military creation of a "Remount Station," where soldiers could visit "regularly inspected" prostitutes and be provided with a prophylactic ointment. The reported result was no new cases of VD. However, during World War I, this method was not an option. With several million "citizen-soldiers" in the military, Maj. Gen. Leonard Wood concluded, "I don't think that the mothers . . . would want their sons to go to death from the arms of a prostitute."[7]

Molding and controlling sexual behavior was not an easy task, especially since it contradicted old ideas still existing among many seasoned officers who believed that sexual activities were necessary to keep soldiers content. Newton D. Baker's biographer, Frederick Palmer, summed up the prevailing attitude: "Men would be men. 'Sissies' were no use on the firing line. Soldiers must have women. They made poor soldiers if they did not have women." In order to change this attitude, World War I Progressive leaders found it necessary to reeducate the older officers and their rank-and-file soldiers to new moral standards. In the case of prostitution, the reformers chose to reshape values, remove temptation, and offer alternative recreation. In fact, since providing soldiers with prophylaxes (to prevent venereal infection) "ran afoul of inherited Anglo-Saxon compunction" (because it encouraged sex-license and promiscuity), military reformers emphasized the importance of changing the environmental atmosphere of the young soldiers.[8]

The CTCA and its affiliated organizations divided the socialization duties among various representatives including district directors, law enforcement representatives, social hygiene representatives, physical-training officers and athletic directors, song leaders, theater mangers, and dramatic directors. Fosdick appointed the district directors, who under the authority of the secretary of war oversaw the activities of the various camps in their territory.

Law enforcement representatives protected soldiers "from the evils of prostitution and alcoholism," and the Social Hygiene Division combated "venereal disease through education." Athletic directors and physical-training
officers designed sporting activities while song leaders, theater mangers,
and dramatic directors promoted choirs, sing-alongs, bands, and plays as
alternatives to negative temptations. All these activities were tied to "military efficiency" and "promoted morale."[9]

Baker and Fosdick secured the help of the American Social Hygiene Association (ASHA) to help them in their vice cleanup programs. ASHA was
formed in 1913 when a number of other social welfare organizations such
as the Anti-Saloon League and the American Society of Sanitary and Moral
Prophylaxis joined forces. The goals of the ASHA reflected those of other
highly organized Progressive associations concerned with molding "the
interests, activities, and organized volition of youth, that [would] put the
brothel out of business through lack of patronage." In its civilian efforts,
the association offered alternative urban recreational opportunities, provided informative publications, lobbied for state laws supporting prohibition and antiprostitution, and pressured local and state officials to support
their moral cause. ASHA reformers recruited by the government would use
these ideas. Working throughout the United States in the military training
camps, the Social Hygiene Division spent a considerable amount of time
educating troops to the nature and prevention of venereal diseases. This
was attempted through the use of movies, exhibits, informative pamphlets,
and lectures accompanied by a graphic slide presentation. In civilian communities, the CTCA conducted social-hygiene education through the distribution of pamphlets and lectures by both men and women. Local and
state health departments also assisted in health education.[10]

Baker and Fosdick selected Bascon Johnson, a lawyer for the American
Social Hygiene Association, to head the CTCA's Division of Law Enforcement, which included the Bureau of Vice and Liquor Control, the Section
on Women and Girls Work, and the Section on Reformatories. His division
was in charge of "protecting the men in all branches of the service." Johnson
(commissioned as a major) selected forty men, mostly attorneys, to help in
the vice cleanup effort. Each member of this team of lawyers was commissioned as a lieutenant in the Social Hygiene Division of the Sanitary Corps
of the Surgeon General's Office. Their duties included assisting the Law
Enforcement Division in pressuring local and state officials to campaign
against vice and rallying public opinion for removal of such "sordid places."
The lieutenants were helped by a "vigorous" letter from Secretary Baker

addressed to all governors, which threatened to move training camps from any area deemed unhealthy.[11]

The Law Enforcement Division patrolled dance halls, moving pictures and burlesque theaters, parks, and amusement centers as a way of deterring vice. Fosdick claimed (although there is no definitive proof of this) that with the help of the local police and the Social Hygiene Division, "every red light district in the United States had [eventually] been closed." Fosdick recommended that every effort be made to take temptation out of the way of the young troops and return "the soldier to his home a better man than when he left it." In addition, Fosdick urged the establishment of rules that required soldiers who could still not stay away from wayward women to "use the prophylaxis or suffer punishment."[12]

The division's Section on Women and Girls' Work established reformatories for the rehabilitation of prostitutes. The section attempted to educate local communities on the need to rehabilitate delinquent women and to influence courts to sentence wayward girls to "suitable institutions." Fosdick was also concerned with "baby vamps," hundreds of young girls between eleven and eighteen years old who suffered "uniformities." Although in most cases the flirtation by the girls was innocent of immoral intentions, Fosdick worried that things could get out of hand and ordered the rigid supervision of city recreation areas.[13]

The "cleanup" was assisted by the Military Draft Act, which outlawed prostitution and the sale of liquor in broad zones around military camps and prohibited the sale of alcohol to soldiers in uniform. A Sanitary Corps officer, attached to the commission and the office of the Surgeon General, was stationed in towns and cities near training camps and aided in enforcing liquor laws. The corps used military police to investigate violations and enforce laws and reported infractions to the local, state, and federal authorities. The CTCA kept the secretary of war abreast of conditions concerning both liquor control and vice.[14]

The success of the military's efforts to keep temptation out of the way of soldiers is noted in the *History of the Seventy-Seventh Division,* written in the "Field of France" during the war. Recalling the division's training at Camp Upton, the author records that "camp-followers of yore, the harlot, the beggar, the thief, had disappeared" from the training areas. In a report to Frederick P. Keppel, the third assistant secretary of war, Fosdick concluded that the venereal rate was low, cases of intoxicated soldiers in the camps were "exceedingly small," and almost no instances of "drunkenness or rowdyism" occurred in the camp welfare clubs.[15]

In addition to cleaning up vice areas, the Commission on Training Camp Activities offered alternative "positive" recreation activities designed to keep soldiers away from "evil" influences. Military reformers "fill[ed] every moment of [the soldiers'] leisure time" with exercise, sports, books, and singing as ways of molding and controlling moral behavior. In the spring of 1917, Baker and Fosdick selected Joseph Lee, an environmental Progressive reformer, to head the War Camp Community Service, a derivative of the Playground and Recreation Association of America. Lee was the founder and champion of the nationwide playground movement, which sought to regulate urban behavior by controlling environmental conditions. This group of Progressives attempted to reshape the urban area by creating city play areas with swimming pools, sandboxes, sports fields, slides, and swings. By restructuring the urban atmosphere, the Playground Association supporters hoped to build a new "urban citizenry" who would be "moral, industrious, and socially responsible."[16]

Lee carried this ideology with him in his military work as a member of the CTCA. Lee and Howard S. Braucher, executive secretary of the Playground Association, headed the War Camp Community Service (WCCS). Similar to other cooperating social welfare associations, the WCCS worked diligently to provide the soldiers with the "right kind" of leisure-time activities. As in their civilian effort, Lee and Braucher sought to clean up the "immoral" environments surrounding army-training camps and to offer positive alternatives to prostitution, alcohol, gambling, and other vices.[17]

The War Camp Community Service was put in charge of ensuring that the training camps and the areas surrounding the cantonments would be filled with well-organized social, recreational, and athletic activities. Lee, Braucher, and over one hundred Playground Association representatives worked with area chambers of commerce, churches, clubs, and fraternal organizations to create a friendly and safe atmosphere for soldiers to feel at home in the nearby towns. By March, 1919, the WCCS had organized moral activities in 615 towns and cities with the help of approximately 2,700 WCCS workers. The WCCS established 342 clubs for soldiers, sailors, and marines; many complete with kitchens, cafeterias, canteens, dormitories, shower baths, reading rooms, pianos, victrolas, billiard and pool tables, and cigar and candy stands. WCCS also helped equip 180 additional clubs affiliated with their organization in what the service claimed was a successful effort to make the clubs the "centers of social life for solders and civilians."[18]

Other WCCS activities included community dinners, dances, banquets, pageants, festivals, and parades. According to WCCS officials, their most significant program opened civilian homes to soldiers. The "Take a Soldier or Sailor Home to Dinner" campaigns included special holiday events as well as receptions, dances, lawn parties, automobile rides, picnics, musicals, concerts, organ recitals, and other civilian-soldier programs. Communities also invited soldiers to athletic fields, swimming pools, gymnasiums, skating rinks, tennis courts, bowling alleys, and playgrounds. The WCCS worked with local boards of trade and chambers of commerce in a continuing effort to prevent local merchants from profiteering by overcharging or taking advantages of soldiers.[19]

The War Department's Commission on Training Camp Activities also asked the Young Men's Christian Association (YMCA) for assistance. The YMCA developed from a mid-nineteenth-century evangelical reform movement. Its roots can be traced to the anxieties surrounding the migration of young men from rural areas to large cities. The belief that urban areas were immoral bastions of crime and vice underlined the concerns of the YMCA founders. Young men far away from "mothers' watchful eyes, fathers' warning voices, and neighbors' tell-tale tongues" had the opportunity to engage in "every degree of wickedness, from the slightest excesses to the foulest villainies."[20]

With this threat supposedly looming on the horizon, YMCAs quickly spread throughout the United States. The association hoped to replace the influences of the family and church left behind by rural migrants, thus protecting the morality of those young men. The late-nineteenth-century urban-industrial expansion greatly increased the concern about the evil influences of the nation's cities. Not surprisingly, the YMCA movement expanded rapidly during the Progressive Era.

The YMCA recognized the profound changes faced by men who suddenly left a civilian life for a soldier's world. Social welfare workers maintained that men hastily severed from their close association with women and children tended toward "excessive profanity and vulgarity." Therefore, the YMCA attempted to re-create as much as possible "an actual link with the home community" by providing "a program of athletic, entertainment, social, educational, and religious" programs for the soldiers. YMCA welfare workers also sought to combat the "age-old passions of mankind" that traditionally "appeared with white-hot intensity in the fighting forces[,] . . . gambling, alcoholic intoxication, and sex license."[21] Just as the prewar YMCAs attempted to recreate a familial and virtuous atmosphere in the urban environment, these same organizations attempted to do the same in the military training camps.

YMCA recreational and social facilities were quickly constructed in all U.S. Army cantonments and National Guard camps. Here, soldiers could participate in numerous activities free of charge. YMCA huts provided pianos, motion picture machines, phonographs, stationery, and reading materials. The organization also sponsored concerts, lectures, mass singing events, and amateur theaters. Between eight and ten million feet of film were shown to soldiers each week. Each army cantonment included a large YMCA auditorium that seated three thousand soldiers. Thousands of religious services took place in these auditoriums, along with hundreds of guest-speaker programs. The YMCA provided public health and sex education classes that included lecturers, films, posters, exhibits, pamphlets, and books focusing on public health issues.[22]

By the end of the war, the YMCA had completed construction of over four hundred buildings. Over three thousand secretaries assisted the soldiers and coordinated activities. The YMCA also distributed its newspaper, *Trench and Camp*, to the soldiers. Although the organization technically represented Protestant denominations, all of the YMCA's activities were nonsectarian.[23]

The War Department also worked in close cooperation with the Young Women's Christian Association (YWCA). The roots of the YWCA can also be found in the religious revival movement in the late 1850s. Similar to the YMCA, the women's organization focused much of its early work on protecting migrating rural Protestant women from the wickedness of the nation's cities. The YWCA offered inexpensive rooms, religious services, Bible studies, educational classes, and recreational programs, all designed to safeguard the women from immoral forces. During the Progressive Era, the YWCA expanded into a worldwide effort. During the mobilization of United States troops along the Mexican border in 1916, the women's organization sent representatives to nearby communities to "investigate the amount and kind of [moral] constructive work among the local girls which should be undertaken" by the YWCA.[24]

Once the First World War began, the National War Work Council of the Young Women's Christian Association implemented its urban moral reform efforts in military training camps, in the surrounding communities, and in industrial areas nationwide. Some 1,052 women staffed the National War Work Council of the YWCA. Drawing from its 1916 investigation, the women began making plans for moral uplifting among local girls including social, recreational, and educational activities and creating the "right kind of meeting place" for soldiers and women to mingle.[25]

In communities near army training camps and in industrial areas, the YWCA war work included guiding the "moral standards" of girls and women and informing them of their responsibility during the war. Ultimately, the YWCA hoped to reshape a woman into a "happier, better and more well-rounded patriotic citizen . . . [of] high morale and also self respect and backbone." In addition to making better citizens, the YWCA clearly hoped to keep local women from "immoral" activities with soldiers from the local training camps. To this end, the YWCA worked closely with the Playground and Recreation Association of America.[26]

The YWCA's Social Morality Bureau attempted to clean up areas around the army training camps by the "promotion of education in social morality among girls and women." The Social Morality Bureau included a lecture bureau subsection that provided talks on social hygiene. Seventy-five women physicians served as speakers for the bureau. The doctors worked in conjunction with local committees of women who assisted with the programs. The women provided some 3,220 lectures to over 276 communities in forty-one states; the reformers estimated that they eventually reached some one million women and girls. The lecture bureau particularly targeted women in community groups, department stores, normal schools, colleges, universities, and industries with a large number of women employees.[27]

The lecture bureau became an official agency of the federal government under the administration of Dr. Katharine B. David, the director of the Section on Women's Work in the Social Hygiene Division of the War Department Commission on Training Camp Activities. In a speech at the National Conference of Social Work, David emphasized that women have been "safeguarded" from discussions on sex for generations, but that the time had come to educate women to the "evils resulting from irregular sex relations." According to David, the U.S. government was taking a stand that "illicit indulgences [were] not necessary for health or for physical or moral vigor," therefore, the public needed to be reeducated as well. David stressed that the greatest possible service contributed by women would be to educate themselves and the public to issues of vice and disease. Otherwise, soldiers "who brave[d] the dangers of bullets in the trenches," would return to equally dangerous conditions in the nation's communities. In the army training camps, the YWCA constructed 102 hostess houses/huts staffed with 306 women. Overseas, YWCA activities included 18 hostess houses and outreach programs to over forty base hospitals and twenty-four nurses clubs. Staff positions included director-hostess, receiving-hostess, cafeteria-hostess, business-hostess, and information-emergency-hostess. The hostess huts provided a wholesome place where soldiers could visit with their wives, mothers, or sweethearts in a respectable homelike atmosphere maintained by qualified YWCA workers.[28]

On the home front and in overseas hostess huts and canteens, the YWCA helped the army's effort in acting as moral guardians of America's youth. Thousands of women staffed the huts, which each included a cafeteria, a children's nursery, and a traveler's aid station, and chaperoned soldiers who met with outside visitors.[29]

Other "unofficial" organizations also assisted the Commission on Training Camp Activities. The American Library Association provided small libraries in various social welfare buildings. The association also tried to procure books that soldiers made by special request whenever possible. The Military Intelligence Division provided the Library Association with a list of books that were "not desirable" for camp libraries, since the books either did not put the Allies in the best light or provided a pro-German perspective. The Military Morale Section requested that the libraries' book selections should include items that discuss American "war aims" to reinforce why soldiers were fighting. With so many social welfare agencies meeting the needs of soldiers in training camps, the Salvation Army focused its efforts "outside" of the camps and overseas. Under Comdr. Evangeline Booth, the Salvation Army provided homelike hostels in training camps and near French battlefields at which soldiers could be comforted and morally and spiritually fortified. The organization's newspaper, *The War Cry*, dramatically portrayed stories of Salvationists in the battlefields of France preparing tea and donuts as shells exploded overhead. The staff faithfully conducted religious services for men of all denominations, and all were welcome to partake in refreshments and music. The Salvationists also held services in and near front-line trenches.[30]

In addition to soliciting the help of well-known social welfare organizations, the Commission on Training Camp Activities appointed sports directors, athletic instructors, song coaches, bandleaders, and dramatic entertainment directors. The Training Committee of the War Plans Division of the General Staff trained athletic directors at the Camp Gordon Athletic School. After satisfactorily completing the course and examination, directors received a captain's commission and reported to their duty assignment.[31]

The CTCA sponsored baseball, rugby, football, volleyball, basketball, boxing, and other sports activities. In addition to providing alternative leisure activities, CTCA officials believed that competitive sports brought out the fighting instinct in the troops. Boxing was especially emphasized due to its "war-like" quality that emulated bayonet fighting. Capt. Frank Glick sent word to the *New York Evening World* to publicize the Camp Upton (New York) Boxing Championship, "the biggest athletic event of the season" for the 77th Division. Baseball also became a favorite in camps. In addition, soldiers played in intramural games between various camps. The Camp Gordon baseball team played against Camp Jessup at Ponce de Leon Park in Atlanta, Georgia, to some four thousand spectators. Capt. Eugene C. Bryan, intelligence officer at Camp Gordon, noted that baseball represented "healthy competition" and developed "espirt de corps."[32]

The CTCA divided the Music Division into two sections: singing and military bands. The commission considered singing not only as a recreational activity but also claimed that "the power of song [would be] a constructive social force" designed to raise spirits. Song leaders sought to instill the "spirit of service" that would "bring to bear and make effective the best elements in democratic society" and instill in soldiers citizenship, self-respect, loyalty, and enthusiasm.[33]

Liberty Theaters, established in the training camps, produced professional entertainment and motion pictures at reasonable prices; the cost of production was supplemented by War Department funds. Plays and entertainment were carefully selected and censored by the Military Entertainment Committee of the CTCA. Soldiers also put on short amateur shows under the direction of the camp dramatic director. The commission selected experienced producers and actors, often selected from enlisted soldiers with special theatrical talents. Various companies and regiments put on frequent amateur performances. Larger shows included a cooperative effort of several units or entire camps. Since the War Department funded the productions, soldiers could attend free of charge.[34]

Foreign-born soldiers received the same socialization opportunities as did their American-born counterparts. The CTCA added two additional social welfare organizations, the Knights of Columbus and the Jewish Welfare Board, to attend to the spiritual and religious needs of non-Protestant servicemen. Since many of the foreign-born soldiers were Catholic or Jewish, both agencies dealt extensively with the immigrants. The CTCA worked closely with the Foreign-speaking Soldier Subsection, Progressive social welfare organizations, and ethnic community leaders in their effort to socialize foreign-born troops.

Immigrant community leaders, ethnic organizations, and immigrant MID agents translated most of the socialization materials into various languages. These national leaders championed ethnic pride, pushed the retention of immigrant traditions, and demanded fair and just treatment of foreign-born soldiers. At the same time, they also assisted with the socialization of immigrant troops and inspired American patriotism. In this way, ethnic leaders acted as "agents of change" for the immigrant troops and helped reshape their ethnic identity. This was not an unusual role for these men, who often straddled the line between their ethnic community and the outside world. Leaders of ethnic organizations protected their communities from the harsh encroachment of the dominant culture and helped preserve important Old World traditions and values. Concurrently, ethnic leaders also worked to help their fellow immigrants adjust to the dominant culture. In his work on ethnic leadership in America, Victor Green found that "on the one hand, [ethnic leaders] could have been agencies of ethnic persistence, created to segregate their groups' members from the society of the larger majority outside, that is, Anglo-America, and to inhibit assimilation and isolate members from alien influences and values. On the other hand, they may have been agents of change, associations organized to provide badly needed social services or education to enable members to function and participate advantageously in the total American Milieu."[35]

Ethnic community leaders and immigrant MID agents provided multilingual social-hygiene literature and translations of movies on proper moral behavior. The American Social Hygiene Association prepared the *Keeping Fit to Fight* pamphlet on VD at the request of the Surgeon General of the Army. The pamphlet began with a strong introduction that cleverly combined health concerns with patriotic messages: "This is a man-to-man talk, straight from the shoulder without gloves. It calls a spade a spade without camouflage. Read it because you are a soldier of the United States. Read it because you are loyal to the flag and because you want the respect of love of your comrades and those you have left at home." The pamphlet makes clear that a soldier in the hospital with venereal disease dishonored his family and the United States government. It warned that "booze" contributed to soldiers making bad decisions. The pamphlet claimed that 90 percent of prostitutes (also referred to as "whores" throughout the publication) had both gonorrhea and syphilis: "Women who solicit soldiers for immoral purposes are usually diseased spreaders and friends of the enemy. No matter how thirsty or hungry you were, you wouldn't eat or drink anything that you knew in advance would weaken your vitality, poison your blood, cripple your limbs, rot your flesh, blind you and destroy your brain. Then why take the same chance with a prostitute?"[36]

Keeping Fit to Fight also challenged the belief that "sex organs" had to be used to remain "healthy" by calling it a "lie." "Sex power is not lost by laying off . . . ; on the other hand, over-exercise or excitement of the sex glands, may exhaust them and weaken a man." A discussion on masturbation concluded that men should put their energy into athletics and "quit the habit." Very graphic details of how each venereal disease would attack the body followed. The CTCA distributed *Keeping Fit to Fit* to native-born soldiers and immigrants who could read English. The FSS turned to ethnic leaders to translate the pamphlet into various languages and distributed some 78,000 copies of a social-hygiene VD pamphlet that ethnic leaders had translated into Polish, Russian, Italian, Bohemian, Hungarian, and Spanish. The Jewish Welfare Board provided copies of these in both Yiddish and Russian, and the FSS provided translations in other "principle languages represented" in the army. The American Association of Foreign Language Newspapers published articles such as "Soldiers and Sailors on Leave" in order to protect immigrant servicemen from social evils. Located in New York City, this organization worked in conjunction with the FSS and the CTCA to educate immigrants in ethnic enclaves about social-hygiene issues.[37]

The film version of *Keeping Fit to Fight* also emphasized proper social and moral behavior. The English-language version of the film was shown to both native- and foreign-born troops in the American camps. Many of the immigrant soldiers were unable to understand the anti–venereal disease message provided in English and misunderstood the intention of the film, construing it as "a smutty exhibition." The film had the "opposite effect of that intended."[38] The FSS quickly intervened and arranged for bilingual officers to interpret the film to foreign-born troops in Russian, Polish, Bohemian, Serbian, Italian, Spanish, German, and Magyar. In future showings to non-English-speaking troops, the film was stopped several times to allow these officers to translate and elaborate. The FSS explained to one intelligence officer, "We are very much interested in the success of this moving picture foreign language experiment . . . and feel confident of the excellent effect it will have on the morale and morals of the foreign-speaking soldiers."[39]

FSS leaders also pushed the War Department to station foreign-speaking medical officers in depot brigades to assist immigrant soldiers. The War Department responded by transferring many such doctors to the Surgeon General's office to work with the "Combating Venereal Disease" program.[40] The *Soldier's Bulletin*, which provided social, recreational, and military information to servicemen, was distributed in nine languages. One edition included a letter from Capt. Spiro Sargentich, an officer with the Medical

Reserve Corp, Army War College, who emphasized that the immigrants should keep their surroundings clean and safe to ward off diseases. Sargentich, a trained physician, spoke a number of Slavonic languages and was assigned to work with the foreign born concerning their medical needs. Other foreign-speaking medical officers provided social-hygiene lectures to the immigrant troops. The FSS worked with the Medical Section of the Council of National Defense and the Social Hygiene Instruction Division of the Commission on Training Camp Activities to translate information on venereal-disease prevention into various foreign languages.[41]

The CTCA (with the help of ethnic leaders) provided translations of the pamphlet *The Girl You Leave behind You* to immigrant soldiers when they departed overseas. The publication explained that the men were fighting to defend European women from being "raped and ravished" by the Hun and reminded them to keep their "bodies clean" and their "hearts pure" by staying away from prostitutes. "It would never do for the avengers of women's wrongs to profit by the degradation and debasement of womanhood. . . . [E]very hardened prostitute who offers herself to you was a young girl once till some man ruined her. . . . If you accept her, you are shaming all girlhood." A Polish immigrant artist painted the young girl on the cover of the pamphlet, which the CTCA suggested should be place in the soldiers' knapsacks to remind them of girls, similar to their sisters, who were suffering in the war. FSS officials asked ethnic MID agents Joseph Spano and Erich Bernhard to translate another social-hygiene pamphlet, *Before You Go*, noting that they needed the "best translation" and knew the agents would do a good job.[42]

Although immigrant leaders translated most of the socialization material, the Illinois Vigilance Association translated and made 173,000 copies of another pamphlet, *Sexual Hygiene for Young Men*. This association was organized in 1908 and consisted of some four hundred ministers and social welfare workers who sought to suppress "vice, venereal disease and those conditions that make vice possible." They distributed tens of thousands of copies translated into several languages: 35,000 copies in German, 25,000 in Italian, 30,000 in Polish, 35,000 in Hebrew, 22,000 in Bohemian Slovak, 8,000 in Hungarian, 7,000 in Russian, 6,000 in Serbo-Croatian, and 5,000 in Greek. The division distributed the material along with copies of the English version for native-born soldiers.[43]

Prior to World War I, the Young Women's Christian Association worked with the nation's native-born and foreign-born women. The Committee on Work for Foreign-Born Women and Americanization Work grew out of the

YWCA's Committee on Immigration and Foreign Community Work, which had assisted foreign-born women and girls for seven years prior to the war. This committee trained staff from different nationalities for the "delicate work of international service in the United States," focusing on issues like the history of immigration, the problems of foreign countries, and "nationalistic psychology" in the economic and religious backgrounds of Europe. Two other wartime branches of the YWCA, the Division on Foreign-Community Organizing Work and the Division of International Information and Service Bureau, concentrated their efforts on women in America's ethnic enclaves. Much of their work consisted of socializing and Americanizing foreign-born women by teaching them English and explaining "all manner of things American." The Social Morality Committee also lectured in immigrant communities.[44]

During the war, the YWCA established the Division on Work for Foreign-born Women under the direction of Edith Terry Bremer. In June, 1917, the YWCA included foreign-born soldiers in its activities and worked closely with the Commission on Training Camp Activities and the Foreign-Speaking Soldier Subsection.[45]

In training camps, the YWCA provided special services for the foreign-born solders by employing "international hostesses" to assist "American" secretaries in the hostess huts. These international secretaries included "foreign-speaking women [who] could administer to the wants of and counsel foreign-speaking soldiers." Foreign hostesses were thought to help the ethnic servicemen with specific problems and to "reach the foreign soldiers and . . . link him with his home." FSS officials requested that the YWCA women advise them of specific difficulties faced by the immigrants so that they could take "corrective measures" to improve the morale of the foreign troops. The YWCA complied by sending clippings from Polish and Russian newspapers that made special reference to army "matters and conditions" affecting foreign-born soldiers.[46]

The FSS and the YWCA's Division on Work for Foreign-born Women continued to set up hostess huts in camps throughout the United States that had a large concentration of immigrants. In rapid succession from August 12 through October 2, the FSS arranged for international secretaries (foreign-speaking hostesses) at Camps Kearney, Lewis, Meade, Upton, Dix, Grant, Sherman, and Custer. After reading a newspaper article stating that the Slovak League had been mobilized in Camp Wadsworth, South Carolina, Mrs. Abby Stauton Shafroth, field secretary of the Camp and Community Service of the YWCA, immediately contacted Lieutenant Horgan to see if he wanted a foreign hostess sent to the camp. Throughout the war years, the FSS and the YWCA continued working together with "the interest of the foreign-speaking soldiers in the army at heart."[47]

After the war, the YWCA's Refugee-Locating Bureau directed immigrants to proper government agencies in an effort to locate lost relatives. In addition, the association selected foreign-born women with leadership abilities for special training to continue YWCA work in eighty-nine ethnic enclaves throughout the United States. The first group of Polish trainees established the Polish Grey Samaritans in 1919, and the YWCA reported that Czechoslovak, Serbian, Italian, and Greek women had asked for similar training.[48]

Although all social welfare huts were open to immigrant soldiers, the facilities did not always provide for the social needs of the foreign born. In a letter to Fosdick dated July 16, 1918, Capt. George B. Perkins, Military Morale Section (MMS), complained that the YMCA lacked reading material for non-English-speaking soldiers. He requested that the social welfare organizations provide newspapers, books, magazines, and helpful posters in various languages in camp huts.[49] Three days later, the YMCA announced that a foreign-speaking secretary would be located in each YMCA hut to care for the needs of the immigrant soldiers. John Mott also discussed creating a foreign-speaking bureau of the YMCA to assist the immigrant troops. The YMCA began their new program in eight select camps, which trained the largest number of foreign-born soldiers: Camps Devens, Upton, Meade, Gordon, Sherman, Grant, Custer, and Lewis. Immigrant soldiers in these locations came from large ethnic enclaves, primarily Italian, Pole, Russian, and Russian Jew. The FSS suggested that secretaries should be drawn from these four groups but opened up the positions to all ethnicities.

Applications soon arrived from immigrant communities. After conferring with a prominent Syrian American leader, Perkins and Horgan sent Mott the names of several Syrian Americans interesting in becoming YMCA secretaries, among them three New Yorkers, Rasheed Simon, N. Kalaf, and Nadra Haddad. Simon, a naturalized citizen, was "well-known" in the community and "well informed." Kalaf had taken out his first papers and was eagerly waiting to become a citizen. His work as a Four-Minute Man and his service for the Committee on Public Information was considered "excellent." Haddad, a prominent ethnic leader, was active in a number of Syrian clubs and societies. The FSS noted that the three came from different religions: Simon was Catholic, Kalaf was Protestant, and Haddad was an

Orthodox Greek. By October, 1918, the YMCA had appointed Italian-speaking secretaries in various camps. Other immigrant secretaries joined the YMCA that fall.[50]

The Knights of Columbus (K of C) represented Roman Catholics, who were estimated to be about 35 percent of American servicemen, a large number of them probably from among the immigrants who arrived in the United States during the late nineteenth and early twentieth centuries. Camp Gordon, Georgia, for instance, reported that 41.9 percent of their immigrant troops were Catholic. The K of C provided meeting halls in army camps and naval training stations, complete with phonographs, player pianos, moving pictures, athletic equipment, reading materials stationery, and other entertainment-related items. The huts were designed to ensure a "high moral tone": "Literature of an interesting, clean, and instructive characters . . . should be plentiful, as this is one of the very best ways for bringing our Catholic boys in touch with their separated brethren whom they can edify; both by work and example."[51]

Although all activities were open to all soldiers regardless of creed, the K of C buildings also provided a place for the Catholic troops to hold their religious services. In fact, the K of C designed hostess huts "symbolic of the dual character of the center: the altar, sacristy, and confessional were located on the stage, while the gallery was a recreation hall suitable for motion pictures and general entertainment." By September, 1917, the Knights had constructed some forty-eight buildings in twenty-four training camps throughout the United States and hired some 375 secretaries to assist the servicemen. The National Catholic War Council estimated that "during the comparatively short period these houses were open approximately one million five hundred thousand guests were received within the home-like halls of the Catholic visitor's houses and that more than half a million meals were furnished to the men in the service." When the American troops went to France, the K of C followed and established nearly 150 clubs and hostess huts with over 1,000 Knight secretaries.[52]

FSS officials informed the Knights that their help was urgently needed to work with the large immigrant population in army training camps. They ask the K of C to arrange for Catholic clergyman to care for the men's "spiritual needs"; provide foreign-language books, literature, magazines, and newspapers; and hire foreign-speaking secretaries to help the immigrant soldiers adjust to army life. They also asked the K of C and the YMCA to work together in sponsoring events for ethnic servicemen. Ever politic, FSS officials suggested that when the majority of soldiers were Catholic, a K of C person should be in charge of the event, and when a majority of soldiers were Protestant, a YMCA spokesman should direct the events. John Mott promised K of C secretaries and chaplains that when the Catholic immigrants attended YMCA programs or went to YMCA foreign-speaking huts, no "proselytizing" would take place. In October, 1918, the National Catholic War Council requested permission to build a visitor house at Camp Wadsworth for the newly created Slavic Legion to assist the immigrants with their religious and social needs.[53]

The Jewish Welfare Board (JWB), headed by Col. Harry Cutler, chairman, and Dr. Cyrus Adler, vice chairman, was another organization that aided the U.S. Army with the needs of its ethnic soldiers. The board developed from twenty-two different national Jewish organizations that joined forces in September, 1917, "for the purpose of serving the religious and morale needs of Jewish service personnel in the Armed Forces." JWB rabbis came from the Orthodox, Conservative, and Reform branches and received official government permission to become Jewish military chaplains. The JWB estimated that a quarter of a million Jews served in the United States military during World War I, and its volunteers worked tirelessly to assist in meeting the needs of the Jewish soldiers. The board constructed sixteen buildings in the larger training cantonments, and employees provided soldiers with Jewish periodicals, newspapers, and religious publications as well as Yiddish translations of government pamphlets. In addition, the JWB furnished stationery, games, books, and other activities for all soldiers regardless of religious background.[54] Both the Foreign-speaking Soldier Subsection and the Commission on Training Camp Activities worked closely with ethnic religious organizations—the Young Men's Christian Association, the Knights of Columbus, and the Jewish Welfare Board—to provide for the specific spiritual needs of the immigrant servicemen.

The American Library Association provided some camps with a selection of books in various languages. Mr. Frank L. Tolman, camp librarian at Camp Upton, reported that his library held "a few hundred select titles in Yiddish, Russian, Italian, Romanian, Spanish and Polish." His selection included "purely literary material" along with books that would educate the immigrants about the American government and history.[55] FSS administrators investigated the possibility of constructing similar foreign-language reading huts in all training camps. Perkins and Horgan asked ethnic community leaders to recommend good Polish, German, Greek, Swedish, and

Lithuanian newspapers. They also asked ethnic MID agents to provide them with the names of "three or four good Italian newspaper and two Italian magazines which [he] would recommend as being good reading for the Italian soldiers in camp."[56] Prof. Ernest H. Wilkins, associate executive secretary and director of education for the YMCA, also coordinated a project that would supply camp huts with foreign-language newspapers. Ethnic MID agents reported on periodicals to avoid, recommending, for example, that *Novy Mir* should be restricted because the paper reported to Russian-American soldiers that the U.S. government had "no right to draft him" into the army. Brigadier General Churchill contacted Russian leaders to counter the propaganda, and Perkins and Horgan passed the information on to Wilkins.[57]

The War Camp Community Service Division of the American Playground Association coordinated with ethnic organizations to provide the "right kind" of social, recreational, and educational activities for immigrant soldiers. The Jewish community in Rockford, Illinois, opened a "splendidly equipped" clubroom for their servicemen and other soldiers stationed at Camp Grant. The Jewish community at Macon, Georgia, sponsored home hospitality activities for Jewish soldiers from Camp Wheeler. In addition, some five hundred Greek soldiers from Camp Gordon and Camp McPherson attended a Christmas dinner in Atlanta, Georgia.[58]

Combined with this socialization of foreign-born troops, the military also engaged in some effort at Americanization. This included providing classes in the English language, civics, and citizenship. In a letter dated June 12, 1918, explaining the role of the FSS, Brewer wrote that he "personally regret[ted] the use of the word 'Americanization,'" while fully understanding the patriotic object of those who use it." Brewer concluded that the foreign-born did not like to be "patronized" and were "more readily assimilated through classes in English and American history and also in the teaching of the fundamental things which lie at the base of American citizenship." Brewer's successors, Perkins and Horgan, understood that the time spent in the development battalions was far too limited to Americanize the foreign born fully, so instead, the FSS strove to give the immigrants "a foundation upon which to build." Civilian organizations also assisted in this effort. The YMCA, in its manual of 1918, noted that "the native population" had neglected to "train" immigrants to American "standards," but also acknowledged that the native born "have not appreciate[d] sufficiently [the immigrants] standards." They, along with the CTCA, sought to assist the military and FSS with their "Americanization work" through education.

So, in addition to the typical forty-hours of military drill each week, the foreign-born also received special training.[59]

The War Department knew that knowledge of the English language was imperative for the foreign-speaking soldier to communicate and understand military orders. This would lessen confusion on the battlefield and create a more efficient system by "saving time and labor." Initially, training-camp commanders selected an officer to head each camp school, but as thousands of immigrants poured into the training centers, the War Department asked for the assistance of a number of educational agencies. In July, 1918, Assistant Secretary of War Frederick Keppel directed the implementation of new English instruction programs for non-English-speaking soldiers. He was assisted by the Bureau of Education, the YMCA, the Jewish Welfare Board, national educational organizations, universities, bilingual soldiers, and native-born and foreign-born civilian volunteer instructors. English-language education became standardized when the War Department provided detailed instructions on the development of training-camp English schools. Immigrant soldiers attended three hours per day of English classes as part of their mandatory military duties. This instruction normally lasted four months, although some programs were shorter.[60]

The War Department provided a "vocabulary and phrase book" entitled *Topics for Instruction in Enlisted Men Schools* based on the teaching methods designed by Capt. Emery Bryan, intelligence officer at Camp Upton, New York. This lesson plan included military-related vocabulary words that taught English while giving particular military instruction such as reveille, inspection, drilling, marching, saluting, double time, officer recognition, and other necessary information. The National War Work Council of the YMCA provided school supplies and publications such as the *Spelling Book for Soldiers.* The military also utilized methods developed by the Reverend Dr. Peter Roberts of the Industrial Department of the International Young Men's Christian Association and special textbooks such as *The Soldier's Text-Book,* by Mrs. Cora Wilson Stewart, and the *Camp Reader,* by J. Duncan Spaeth (educational director at Camp Wheeler). The YWCA's National War Work Council recommended Robert's *English Reader* for more advanced students and scheduled classroom space in huts and auditoriums. The Department of the Interior's Bureau of Education circulated its pamphlet *Teaching English to Foreigners* to aid camp educators. The War Department instructed teachers to impress upon immigrant soldiers in development battalions that they were not "segregated for any fault, but only to give them a deserved opportunity." Also, teachers were directed to relate English-language instruction to military life so soldiers could adjust "to the new surroundings and to the new national ideal and purpose."[61]

Trained teachers, chaplains, and foreign-speaking first- and second-generation immigrants assisted in the classes. New York State Commissioner of Education John H. Finley recounted a training session he observed in a camp mess hall in which Italian and Slavic soldiers practiced sentry duty in English. Finley noted that the immigrant soldiers responded to their teacher "in as yet unintelligible English (the voices of innumerable ancestors struggling in their throats to pronounce it) the words, 'Advance and give the countersign.' So are those confused tongues learning to speak the language of the land they have been summoned to defend."[62]

The War Department noted the one of the "most successful" programs was that of Miss Christine Krysto, who supervised at Camp Kearny, California. Krysto, who worked for the Bureau of Immigrant Education, and Miss Ruby Baughman, superintendent of immigrant education in Los Angeles, trained bilingual "sergeants, corporals, and privates" to become English-language teachers. Most of their teachers were from the same nationality as the army pupils. Krysto noted that new teachers "took from the camp classes the taint of the 'Mex' and the 'Wop' and the 'Squarehead' and made them all plain fellow-men—Americans." In addition to basic English reading and writing skills, students learned a number of key military terms: "tent," "rifle," "guard," "bayonet," "gun," "shoot," "soldiers," "officer," "march," "drill," "eat," and "run." Teachers also explained more complex terms including "tank," "submarine," "howitzer," "aeroplane," "transport," "destroyers," and "Red Cross." Teachers used the *National Geographic Magazine* to show the geographic location of France and to teach English by using the "universal language" of pictures. Krysto also noted the "cultural differences" among some of the immigrant soldiers: "It is customary to believe that the Mexican is indifferent to learning English and the Italians eager for the opportunity, yet some of the finest pupils in Camp Kearny are Mexican. The difference lies chiefly in the method of attack. The Mexican, quite unconsciously, plays at indifference, yet is disappointed if the lesson is not thrust upon him. The Italian reaches out for information. A Mexican, in studying a chart, will answer stolidly and reluctantly, and then, after class, will stand long and thoughtfully before it. An Italian begins to talk before the chart is really in place, and given a chart of Italy and an Italian class, the passers-by out in the street will stop to listen to the result."[63]

Classes in civics and citizenship often accompanied the English lessons and focused on the country's democratic objectives. The army asked various ethnic organizations to translate bulletins into the soldiers' languages so that the servicemen could be kept abreast of vital war information while learning English. In addition to foreign-language books of a "purely literary" nature, the American Library Association also provided camps with Americanization books that introduced immigrants to the government and history of the United States. The YMCA also provided classes in history, geography, elementary science, English, and conversational French to interested native-born and foreign-born soldiers. In addition, the YWCA's Division on Home Information Service for Foreign Families of Enlisted Men provided information to immigrant families about soldiers and to soldiers about their homes in America. The division also encouraged soldiers to "urge their women-folk to learn English and to seek acquaintance with American customs, ideals and people." However, civic and citizenship classes not only taught the history of the United States, but they also made "some references to the countries from which groups have come."[64]

The MID applauded the success of the Foreign Legion band, which was of "vital importance in improving morale" of the immigrant soldiers. The FSS suggested to camp intelligence officers that Polish singing organizations would improve morale, officials noting that Polish Americans were "very musical." Song leaders encouraged immigrants to sing of their homeland, and music officers put English lyrics to "foreign songs" to help teach the men English. Americanization efforts also came through music. The Camp Music Division instilled patriotic spirit and American loyalty to foreign-born soldiers with such songs as "The Star Spangled Banner," "America," and "The Battle Hymn of the Republic." Music directors concluded that by "slowly repeating the words and interjecting a plea for loyalty," the foreign born "fully sensed the meaning of true patriotism, . . . making them true Americans though song."[65]

The War Department enlisted the talents of thousands of social welfare workers during World War I. One magazine concluded that the efforts of the lead agency, the Commission on Training Camp Activities, represented "the most stupendous piece of social work in modern times."[66] The philosophy of the Progressive reformers in the military reflected that of prewar civilian social welfare reformers who vigilantly crusaded against prostitution, alcohol, social diseases, and poor sanitary conditions in the nation's major cities. Army Progressives fought relentlessly to end these problems within the military, and at the same time, they sought to socialize the native-born and foreign-born recruits to the standards of the dominant middle-class value system. Ethnic community leaders assisted in the socialization process by translating much of the social welfare literature into various languages, helping teach English to immigrant troops. These leaders often straddled the line between assimilation and cultural retention. However, they also successfully pushed the War Department to support important Old World values and traditions and to provide for the cultural needs of foreign-born troops.

Soldier after soldier is turned out fit and eager to fight for liberty under the Stars and Stripes, mindful of the traditions of his race and the land of his nativity and conscious of the principles for which he [was] fighting.

—Capt. Edward R. Padgett, October, 1918

CHAPTER 5

"Mindful of the Traditions of His Race"

Respecting the Culture of the Foreign-born Draftees

The War Department understood the vital link between maintaining a high level of troop morale and creating an effective fighting force. Although ethnic leaders willingly assisted the military, they also saw morale in terms of retaining important cultural traditions and ensuring fair and just treatment for immigrant soldiers. As advisers to and partners with the War Department, ethnic leaders were in a position to make cultural demands. They educated the military leaders about the religious traditions of the soldiers, explained key cultural needs, and reported specific cultural problems faced by foreign-born troops. Through the help of these men, the War Department began to understand the various immigrant groups within their ranks, and many military policies demonstrated cultural respect.

Ethnic leaders also did their part to instill an esprit de corps among non-native soldiers. They translated the same war propaganda materials that native-born soldiers received and gave inspirational speeches; immigrant soldiers who had been decorated for bravery made public-speaking appearances as well. In addition, ethnic leaders served as MID intelligence agents and assisted the War Department in reporting on the morale of foreign-born soldiers, countered enemy propaganda, and helped with patriotic and ethnic celebrations. The War Department not only depended on prominent community leaders but also developed a mutual respect with them. Officials warned camp commanders to avoid stereotyping and name-calling. They also worked to provide cultural and social activities, satisfy ethnic spiritual life, and generally address the "human needs" of the foreign-born troops.[1] Ultimately, ethnic leaders affected new military policies that did not simply mirror the harsh conformity of "100 percent Americanism" encountered in the civilian society but instead included a more attenuated attempt at instilling patriotism with a demonstrated sensitivity and respect for the immigrants' cultures.

The War Department concluded that the "upbuilding of morale should begin with the first arrival of a new draftee. . . . Anything that can be done to make the new man feel reasonably at home and glad to be in the Army . . . will be of the first importance." Morale officers served in thirty-eight different army training camps throughout the United States. The War Department created the position at the rank of major or captain with "no duties other than those relating to the stimulation of military morale." The morale officer staff included a sergeant to act as an office assistant and two noncommissioned officers within each company. The War Department instructed morale officers to keep the camp commanders informed on the "state of morale in each unit" and to organize and participate in various uplifting activities. The department also instructed these men to educate all camp officers on the importance and "value of morale work" and to report any circumstances that "tend to depress morale." In addition to native-born men, foreign-speaking soldiers also served as morale officers and helped "improve the morale of the foreign-speaking soldiers by loyalty meetings, and talks in their own languages on pertinent subjects."[2]

The War Department's Military Intelligence Division (MID) investigated America's cities, neighborhoods, and army camps to counter pro-German propaganda, assess the loyalty of Americans, and report on the spirit of immigrant soldiers. Ethnic agents also made key suggestions on how to increase morale. The MID's association with civilian ethnic agents went through two distinct periods, one under civilian and the second under military leadership. D. Chauncy Brewer, the original civilian head of the MID, agents assisted with the very early stages of reorganization efforts and studied questions of morale. "Inside camp" agents investigated the loyalty of soldiers and interpreters, ascertained whether soldiers understood their purpose in fighting, and reported on the general condition of foreign born troops. Brewer asked agents, "what is the racial psychology [and] temperament . . . which would not readily occur to the military authorities, but which on the other hand [would] make the soldiers a fair mark for enemy intrigue."[3] Most of the immigrant agents' early work, however, was concentrated in ethnic communities. The agents generally applauded the loyalty of these enclaves, but some reports that raised questions were forwarded to the MID. Even though Brewer thought counterintelligence work was important, he wanted to refocus the mission of division's Foreign-speaking Soldier Subsection (FSS) toward increasing morale-related activities. After he failed to convince Maj. Gen. Ralph Van Deman, chief of the MID, of this change, Brewer quit in frustration.

The new leadership, which brought in military officers Capt. G. B. Perkins and Lt. H. A. Horgan under Brig. Gen. Marlborough Churchill, had a more direct link to the War Department. With the reorganization of the FSS, the agency refocused most of its attention on issues of soldier morale, and "its primary purpose" was to "improvement of the conditions" of foreign-born soldiers in the U.S. Army. The new military approach reflected a more pragmatic method of training immigrant soldiers as MID recognized the vital link between creating an effective fighting force and the need for a high level of morale. In June, 1918, Perkins and Horgan "released most" of the ethnic agents from the service except for twenty men. The FSS continued to work in the ethnic communities, but the main job of these agents was to assist in the training camps. Ethnic agents investigated morale issues concerning their fellow immigrants, helped translate social-hygiene literature into various foreign languages, and organized patriotic programs that also celebrated ethnic cultures.

Horgan and Perkins de-emphasized the investigation of "suspicious persons" as a *"bi-product"* of the agents' work. While reports under Brewer's command contained vague accusations, Perkins and Horgan took a much more professional approach as they repeatedly warned agents not to report "rumors" about foreign-born soldiers or the immigrant community. They explained to the agents, "we cannot take as quick action on matters in the absence of definite proof." The main reason that the new FSS kept agents in urban areas was to understand the soldiers' home life. "Agents must not lose sight" that information gained in ethnic enclaves was so that FSS could "more intelligently handle the problem of the foreign-speaking solders in the Army."[4]

Ethnic agents came from the upper classes, and they tended to be well-educated, multilingual, professional men: doctors, lawyers, professors, and newspaper editors. Croatian-born Francis (Frank) L. Kerzie of Tacoma, Washington, was a former editor of a Slavic newspaper shutdown by the Austrian government (because of its strongly opposed government policies). As an FSS intelligence agent, Kerzie frequently visited Camp Lewis, Washington, and mingled with Slovak, Russian, Italian, German, and Polish troops. Italian-born Joseph Spano graduated from the American International College and attended the Massachusetts Institute of Technology for one year before he began work with the North American Civic League for Immigrants (NACL) in Boston. The NACL provided aid to new immigrants while introducing "American" values and ideals. The MID assigned Spano, who spoke Italian, French, and English, to Camp Devens, Massachusetts, to work with Italian-born soldiers there. Erich Bernard, who was born in Petrograd, Russia, received his Ph.D., *summa cum laude,* from the University of Erlangen-Germany, migrated to the United States in 1915, and worked with the NACL. He was the son of the late official government delegate from Imperial Russia to the Chicago World Exhibition. Bernhard worked as an agent in the Russian community in Philadelphia and with Russian soldiers at Camp Humphrey, Virginia. Baker Douros Bairman (formally Bairamian), born in Greece, received his law degree from the University of Michigan and began as an FSS agent in the Greek community in Detroit, Michigan.[5]

Rev. Sarkis M. Albarian graduated from Tarsus College in Tarsus, Asia Minor. He studied English and Greek at the American International College, earned a degree from the Hartford Theological Seminary, and received his M.A. in philosophy from Yale University and his law degree from Boston University. Reverend Albarian worked as a social services pastor before he joined the FSS as an undercover agent assigned to the Armenian community in New York; after the war, Albarian became a pastor of the Armenian Presbyterian Church in Troy, New York. Prof. H. A. Miller of Oberlin University, Ohio, trained German soldiers at Camp Grant, Illinois. Vince Schultz, a lawyer from Russian Poland, worked in Newark, New Jersey. John A. Stalinski, a Polish immigrant who graduated from Moscow University with a degree in diplomacy in March, 1916, worked as an interpreter in the American Embassy in Petrograd before becoming an FSS agent. Stalinski's loyalty came into question when an informant accused him of being pro-German. However, after a War Department investigation, the MID concluded that Stalinski was indeed loyal to the Allies. In all, the MID employed some forty-seven agents between January and November, 1918, and their individual employment lasted anywhere from two to eleven months.[6]

In addition to full-time paid agents, the Military Intelligence Division asked ethnic community leaders to inform them about activities in their enclaves. Names of the "volunteer cooperating" agents—doctors, clergyman, businessmen, and editors of ethnic papers—often came from mayors of the various ethnic communities. The American Medical Association also provided the MID with a list of "prominent physicians" serving in the "foreign neighborhoods." MID officials sent out more than a hundred letters to foreign-born and native-born doctors asking them to recommend loyal soldiers from their communities who could assist them or be commissioned as officers to lead foreign-born troops. In addition, the division asked the doctors to watch for any signs of disloyalty in their ethnic communities.[7]

FSS and Military Morale Section (MSS) officers worked with prominent immigrant community leaders and ethnic organizations. Many of these citizens assisted the War Department in meeting the needs of the immigrant troops directly. In addition, leaders representing various ethnic organizations worked with the military: the Czechoslovak National Alliance, the Bohemian National Alliance, the South Slavic National Council, the Slav Press Bureau of New York, the Polish National Department of Washington, D.C., the Bohemian Alliance of Chicago, the Slovak League, the American-Hungarian Loyalty League, the Russian-American Bureau of Chicago, the Russian-American Economic Association, the Russian-American Association, the National Romanian Society, and the Lithuanian National Council. Other groups included the American Scandinavian Foundation, the Italian Bureau of Information, the Greek Orthodox Church, the Central Conference of American Rabbis, the Union of Hebrew Congregations, the Union of Orthodox Jewish Congregation, the Jewish Publication Society, the United Synagogue of America, the Association of Orthodox Rabbis, and the Rabbinical College of America.

Immigrant organizations had their roots in Old World village leadership or in New World mutual aid societies and fraternities; some developed from World War I patriotic associations. The role of ethnic leaders during the First World War was similar to their prewar role. "Urging segregation *and* integration at the same time, these men of influence supplied a rationale for their people . . . as to how they could carry over and reestablish their Old

World culture and still be considered American." In their work with the United States military, ethnic group leaders assisted the War Department in the training of immigrant troops by promoting aspects of the dominant culture and by pressuring to keep important Old World cultural traditions and values. This dual method ultimately improved morale. The FSS understood the value of foreign-born troops and concluded: "this Section believes the need is urgent, and that the improvement of the morale of such an important element of our cosmopolitan army will be an important factor in the final victory."[8]

Immigrant soldiers who were members of the patriotic society, the Order and Liberty Association, helped to "build up a loyal spirit in the army" by distributing patriotic literature to fellow immigrants. They also interpreted the needs of their brothers-in-arms to military officials, helped improve the morale of their comrades, explained war issues to the ethnic troops, and reported on the sentiments of the soldiers and their old neighborhoods. Brewer hoped that the Order and Liberty members would "first, by their example, second, by their expressed devotion to the great cause, and third, by such helpful words as they may find it convenient to speak, they will do what they can to improve the morale of their friends and comrades." Although little information is available about their activities, Brewer bragged about the success of the Order and Liberty Association and the success of the soldiers in promoting a patriotic atmosphere.[9]

Ethnic leaders lobbied the military to meet special religious needs, which included worship services provided by spiritual leaders from specific ethnic groups, observances of different holy days, and religious readings from specific religious groups. The military investigated psychological issues of war, especially the critical concern over troop morale. Many understood that "morale [was] as important as ammunition in winning a conflict." The War Department considered religion key to "foster[ing] a feeling of satisfaction and higher morale among both the men and their families," and they therefore worked in conjunction with ethnic organizations to meet the spiritual needs of foreign-born troops. Social welfare agencies also helped out in the process. The many different nationalities and religious groups found among the ethnic soldiers complicated the religious situation in the army training camps.[10]

Even prior to the creation of MID's Military Morale Section and the Foreign-speaking Soldier Subsection, the military was concerned about the religious needs of its ethnic soldiers. Prior to January, 1918, when the FSS was established, each camp dealt individually with religious questions as they arose. In early September, 1917, Maj. Gen. J. Bell, commanding officer at Camp Upton in Yaphank (Long Island), New York, forwarded a letter from the Union of Orthodox Rabbis to Secretary of War Newton Baker asking for leave for soldiers on the Jewish Day of Atonement, "the most important Jewish holiday of the entire year." The letter, signed by the president, executive member, and secretary of the Association of Orthodox Rabbi of the United States and Canada, the president of the Association of Orthodox Rabbis of New York City, and a professor at the Rabbinical College of America, requested a furlough for all Jewish soldiers at Camp Upton for September 26, the date of the holiday. The rabbis estimated that about 25 percent of the soldiers at Camp Upton were Jewish and suggested these soldiers make up the time on Christmas Day. Bell noted the "constitutional principles against religious discrimination" and noted that although this option was "a little inconvenient," he had "no special objection to granting the petition." The secretary of war responded through a letter from the adjutant general to the commanding general of the 77th Division. In it, he granted leave to soldiers of the Jewish faith for both the Jewish New Year (September 16) and the Day of Atonement (September 26) as long as it did not "interfere with the public service."[11]

For the Jewish Day of Atonement, Lt. Col. E. E. Booth of the General Staff arranged a special train to accommodate the 3,000 Jewish soldiers who wanted to go to services in New York City. In his letter to the general manager of the Long Island Railroad Company, Booth noted that this leave was "in compliance with the request of the Association of Orthodox Rabbis of New York City." He also told the railroad manager what time the soldiers should be picked up at Camp Upton and when to return them from the city. He even suggested a price for the train ride of sixty cents per passenger. Jewish leaders also requested that services be held at Camp Upton for the Jewish New Year for soldiers who could not "take advantage of the furlough privileges," who were in the camp hospital, or who were passing through on their way overseas. Bell arranged for rabbis to use the YMCA auditorium and the camp chapel. Bell also worked with Dr. G. Bacarat from the Rabbinical College of America to coordinate the shipment of three barrels of kosher food. In September of 1917, the commander of the 27th Division at Camp Wadsworth, South Carolina, issued an order granting members of the Jewish faith a four-day furlough to celebrate the Jewish New Year and a three-day furlough for the Jewish Day of Atonement.[12]

In December of 1917, the military reprinted a letter in the 27th Division's bulletin from Toakeim Georges, archimandrites and rector of the Greek

Orthodox Church. The letter requested that all soldiers of the Greek Orthodox religion be excused from drills for the Feast of St. Nicholas, an important celebration in which the members renewed their vows to the church. Division officers were instructed to abide by this request.[13]

Not all leaves were granted. Maj. John Richardson, assistant to the chief of staff, denied Rev. Nicholas Lazaris's leave request for Greek Christmas, January 7, 1918. Richardson noted that Camp Upton's soldiers had already lost ten days of training during the Christmas and New Year holidays, and he could not spare the time and disrupt his mission to prepare solders to "serve on the fighting line."[14]

The quartermaster general also refused the Jewish communities request for kosher rations for Jewish soldiers, since it was "not feasible to establish or provide a special rations for men of different faiths." It must be remembered that supplying rations to the troops was a major undertaking, especially in the field. Breakfast often consisted of bread, bacon, molasses, and coffee, and a corned beef stew called "slum" was a common meal.[15]

With the development of the Foreign-speaking Soldier Subsection in January, 1918, the military began to look into uniformed policies concerning religious needs. Adjutant General of the Army John H. Gregory Jr. instructed camp commanding generals to take a religious census of the troops. The resulting general report noted sixty-seven different religious groups among the men. For example, the Camp Gordon report showed that the religious composition of the 82nd Division was 41.9 percent Catholic, 14.2 percent Methodist, 11.1 percent Baptist, 7.3 percent Jewish, 5.5 percent Presbyterian, 4.4 percent Lutheran, 4.7 percent Protestant Episcopalian, 1.4 percent Congregational, 1.2 percent Greek Orthodox, and 1 percent Christian Church; less than 1 percent of the men professed other religions, twenty-four soldiers were listed as atheists, and six as pagans. The report also noted particular ethnic religious groups including the Serbian Church, the Church of Scotland, the Greek Church, the Dunkards, the Mennonites, the Moravians, the Dutch Reform, the Mormons, the Russian Orthodox, the German Reform, the Jewish Reform, and the Jewish Orthodox. Divisions recruiting out of heavily ethnic areas naturally had more Catholic and Jewish soldiers. Since most of the nation's new immigrants were Catholic and Jewish, not surprisingly both religions were represented in large numbers among these ethnic soldiers: for example, the Jewish Welfare Board estimated that a quarter of a million Jewish soldiers served in the American military during World War I. At Camp Upton, New York, General Bell reported that between eight to ten thousand Jews were undergoing training with the 77th

Division. Raymond Fosdick estimated that 35 percent of all solders were Catholic.[16]

The FSS worked closely with the Commission on Training Camp Activities (CTCA) and various ethnic religious organizations to provide for the spiritual needs of the immigrant servicemen. Subsection officials noted the importance of the church's influence in improving morale and preparing each soldier for the possible "supreme sacrifice." One issue concerned army chaplains who were overwhelmingly from the Protestant denominations. With a growing Catholic segment in the ranks, the military decided to increase the ratio of Roman Catholic chaplains by 25 percent. Since the YMCA and YWCA represented the Protestant religions, FSS administrators asked the Knights of Columbus (K of C) to help the Catholic soldiers and the Jewish Welfare Board (JWB) to assist the Jewish troops.[17]

Religious needs often had cultural overtones. Polish soldiers requested Catholic masses conducted by Polish priests and expressed an earnest concern about dying in battle before confessing their sins. The FSS began to solve this problem at Camp Gordon by asking Polish clergy to conduct masses for the 1,000 Polish immigrant soldiers who preferred to hear the sermons in their own language and were "especially concerned about missing confession."[18] FSS personnel continued their efforts to secure ethnic priests to meet the needs of immigrant soldiers. They were assisted by the K of C, which provided Catholic priests to hear confession and conduct masses in foreign languages at other army training camps throughout the United States. The K of C began their service with the War Department under a cloud of controversy, since other Catholic fraternal organizations protested the selection of the Knights to represent the entire Catholic faith. Baker eventually interceded and explained that the group was "a kind of Catholic Y.W.C.A." and that all fraternal societies were welcome to use the building and participate in all the programs. The K of C offered Catholic chaplains accommodations in their hostess huts. As one of the Knight commissions put it, "We all saw the great need of our religion to preserve the morals, build up the morale, and intensify the patriotism of the soldier, which made it necessary for us to utilize more and more K-C chaplains."[19] A Polish American intelligence agent (who had formerly studied for the priesthood) assigned to Camp Sheridan, Alabama, reported to the FSS that there was a crucial need for a priest who could speak Slavic languages, noting that "religion is the great factor to stimulate energy in man." The agency set out to comply with the request. In another search for Greek Orthodox priests, FSS administrators contacted the editor of the *New York Greek National Herald.*

Brewer explained that Greek American soldiers would welcome this type of religious service, and he later applauded the paper for its loyalty to the United States and its support for the war. Despite the War Department's efforts to bring in specific religious leaders, it became clear that in the heat of battle, "the Protestant, Roman Catholic, and Jewish chaplains had to learn how to minister to a dying soldier of a different faith." For example, in the 82nd Division, Jewish chaplains carried a crucifix "in order to minister to a dying Catholic," and Protestant and Roman Catholic chaplains "learned the proper Hebrew prayers."[20]

The Jewish community organized with the Jewish Welfare Board to serve the cultural and religious needs of Jewish soldiers in the U.S. Army during the First World War, and the JWB constantly lobbied the War Department to allow them to meet the needs of Hebrew servicemen. Congressman Isaac Siegel assisted Jewish community leaders by sending a series of letters educating the Adjutant General's Office, the Navy Department, the U.S. Military Intelligence Division, and the Office of the Chief of Staff to the specific needs of Jewish troops. Both the JWB and Siegel enlightened the War Department on the importance of Jewish religious observances and the need for unleavened bread (matzoh) during Passover. They were successful in their educational efforts. The War Department officially acknowledged the Jewish Welfare Board for its assistance and issued a general order directing all commanding officers to cooperate with representatives of the organization. The War Department also issued a bulletin stating that all training camps had to provide each enlisted man of the Jewish faith with one pound of matzos or other unleavened bread during Passover and to approve of furloughs for Jewish soldiers on important holidays including Rosh Hashanah, Yom Kippur, and Passover. The JWB provided the training camps with daily services, Friday night Sabbath, High Holiday observances, and celebrations of Jewish festivals.[21]

Various Jewish religious organizations ministered to the Jewish soldiers. The JWB representatives, known as the "Star of David" men, acted as a "source of solace, friendship and counsel to the new recruits coming from civilian pursuits, especially to those of foreign birth, who in many instances found it difficult to adjust themselves to military life."[22] In addition, other groups ministered to soldiers: the Central Conference of American Rabbis, the Union of American Hebrew Congregations, the Union of Orthodox Jewish Congregation, the Council of Young Men's Hebrew and Kindred Associations, the Jewish Publication Society of America, the Agudath ha-Rabbonim, and the United Synagogue of America. Many of these organizations also worked with the Jewish Publication Society of America and the Jewish Welfare Board to supply religious material to Jewish soldiers including over 145,000 prayer books and 80,000 Bibles in Yiddish, Hebrew, and English. They also distributed the *Prayer Book for Jews in the Army and Navy of the United States*. Among the eighteen religious prayers provided, the prayer book included patriotic prayers for the American government and words to three patriotic songs: "America," "The Star Spangled Banner," and "Hail! Columbia." Jewish organizations successfully pressured the War Department and the U.S. Congress to replace the Christian cross on the grave markings of Jewish soldiers with the Star of David and sent representatives to France to assist with the task.[23]

Most Jewish religious services took place in the same buildings that were used by the Young Men's Christian Association and the Knights of Columbus for their Protestant and Catholic Church services (respectively). One exception took place in Camp Upton, New York, which housed the largest group of Jewish solders. Here, the commanding general "thought that some special consideration was due to the members" of the Jewish faith and granted them "permission to erect a synagogue. The head of the Military Morale Section, Captain Perkins, and representatives of the Jewish community also discussed the possibility of "establishing a store for the sale of Kosher food to member of the Orthodox Jewish faith" at Camp Upton. Also discussed was the building of a kosher restaurant to serve the large number of Jewish visitors to the camp. Not everyone agreed with these ideas. In September, 1918, Raymond Fosdick sent a heated memo to Secretary Keppel calling for "something" to "be done about Captain Perkins right away." Fosdick objected to the letter the captain wrote to the Jewish Welfare Board asking for the "establishment" of a restaurant for "Jewish soldiers at Camp Upton." The director of the CTCA noted that Baker had previously turned down a similar request to serve kosher food in army camps, which created some backlash from the Jewish community. Fosdick complained: "along comes this young Captain and over-rules the Secretary. . . . I tremble for what he may do this next week." It is not clear whether Camp Upton eventually built the restaurant.[24]

Even on the European front, the military attempted to meet the religious needs of the ethnic soldiers. As long as it did not interfere with "military operations" in France, the War Department mandated that "soldiers of the Jewish faith serving in the American Expeditionary Forces will be excused from all duty, and where deemed practicable, granted passes, to enable them to observe in their customary manner" Jewish religious holidays. The

YMCA, the YWCA, the Salvation Army, and the Knights of Columbus also set up facilities near the front.[25]

The War Department understood the direct connection between respecting the culture of their immigrant soldiers and increasing the men's morale. In response to a letter from Dr. Antonio Grasso of Springfield, Massachusetts, expressing concern that officers at Camp Meade, Maryland, were not patient enough with non-English-speaking draftees, the FSS contacted the camp's intelligence officer asking him to investigate the situation since it was "of a nature likely to affect their morale." After Camp Sheridan's foreign-speaking agent reported that Sfc. P. Lucas was creating discontent among the foreign soldiers by using "ethnic slurs" and treating them in an abusive manner, the FSS reported the incident and drew attention to a general order forbidding the practice of name calling. Perkins assured the camp intelligence office that all of the foreign soldiers were "faithful to their superiors and ready to sacrifice their lives" but noted that they were "sensitive."[26]

FSS agent Budrewicz from Camp Lee, Virginia, reported that immigrants were not getting a "square deal" by some commissioned officers who treated them as "an inferior class of people" and called them "wops." Chief of MID Churchill sent a copy of Budrewicz's report to the intelligence officer at Camp Lee so that the situation would be "brought promptly" to the attention of the "proper authorities." After receiving various other complaints by immigrant soldiers about the use of derogatory ethnic terms such as "wop" and "dago," the FSS circulated a copy of a War Department general order forbidding the use of these names since they created discontent among immigrant soldiers and hurt their "national feelings." The War Department followed through on the policy by reprimanding officers and enlisted men who violated the order. The directive received high praise from immigrant soldiers. After a captain publicly reprimanded soldiers for using ethnic slurs when referring to Italian servicemen, one immigrant remarked, "I felt like hugging and kissing the Captain as he was telling the company that we Italians were as good men as they were, and that we should be respected as brothers."[27]

After receiving various complaints from Italian soldiers and national Italian American organizations that the Italian flag was not regularly displayed along side of other Allied flags in all army camps and on buildings throughout the United States, the Italian Bureau of Information in New York complained to the War Department. The bureau pressured the War Department to have the flag displayed along with those of other American allies, pointing out that millions of loyal American citizens of Italian descent were serving in the U.S. Army and tens of thousands were working in war-related industries. The War Department responded immediately, citing Italy's contributions and concluding that the oversight could have a detrimental effect on both first- and second-generation Italian soldiers in the American Army. Furthermore, the FSS contacted the War Work Council of the YMCA, the Knights of Columbus, and other social welfare agencies and asked them to display the Italian flag prominently with the flags of England and France on all buildings. The War Department communicated with the Committee on Public Information and suggested that they alert editors of magazines and newspapers of the need to increase the attention paid to Italy's important role in the war. They also asked the Commission on Training Camp Activities to use their influence "through proper channels" for a "more general display" of the Italian flag. Captain Perkins noted, "Our soldiers of Italian descent are particularly responsive to little courtesies which tend to draw out their many splendid qualities, which is of course of the greatest importance from the standpoint of morale."[28] In addition, Perkins and Lieutenant Horgan wrote to the chairman of the Kansas City July 4th Celebration Committee to note the omission of Italy when acknowledging America's allies in the holiday speech. The FSS maintained that the lack of recognition had a "very depressing effect on the Italian Colony, which had been so enthusiastically represented in the Celebration."[29]

Perkins distributed copies of a *Life* magazine cartoon, entitled "Now Italy," that he thought would help improve the morale of Italian troops and "give credit to their race." The FSS requested one hundred copies of the cartoon, which depicts a strong, powerful-looking Italian soldier with his bayonet pointed at two huddled and frightened Germans (smaller figures representing "Militarism" and "Autocracy"). Since many of the Italian soldiers could not read English, it was believed that the picture would help them realize that they were appreciated for their "importance in the present struggle." FSS officials also suggested that moving pictures showing the "wonderful work being accomplished by the Italian Army" would "awaken the national spirit" and build morale of the Italian troops in the American Army.[30]

After receiving a letter from a Philadelphia resident, John Kliniewski, concerning alleged mistreatment of Polish soldiers in the army, administrators wrote to Kliniewski asking for specific details (facts, names, military addresses, and regiments) of the incidents. The letter assured him that if the reports were true, conditions would "immediately improve." The letter went on to describe the work being done by Polish-born Lieutenant Gutowski and the successes at the various camps with the reorganization of ethnic troops. Officials praised the Camp Gordon Polish Company and considered it the best-drilled unit in the camp, a "credit to all Americans of Polish ancestry in the United States."[31]

When a prominent Russian American from the Russian-American Economic Association wrote a letter to the State Department concerning possible mistreatment of Russian soldiers in the American Army, the military administration took immediate action. The allegations originated in a conversation with a Pvt. M. Bagnuk from Camp Upton that took place in a New York City restaurant and somehow made their way to the Russian Association. Bagnuk claimed that Russian soldiers were "persecuted" by Jewish American officers, "bullied and badly treated" by noncoms and officers, discriminated against in cases of leave, and punished for not speaking English. Perkins and Horgan contacted the intelligence officer at Camp Upton and asked him to select a non-Jewish Russian to act as a "tactful operative" to investigate and report on the situation. In addition, the operative was instructed to contact Pvt. M. Bagnuk and tell him that the Russian-American Economic Association wished to know if his remarks were true.[32]

On another occasion, the Bohemian National Alliance in America and the Czecho-Slovak National Council sent a protest letter to the War Department concerning a local judge in the Camp Meade area who was preventing Czech soldiers, born in Austria, from becoming United States citizens—without citizenship, "technical enemy aliens" could not be sent overseas to fight with the U.S. Army. Mr. J. J. Toula, treasurer of the alliance, and Dr. Jaroslav F. Smetanka, a member of the council, complained that nonnaturalized Czech soldiers at Camp Meade were anxious to fight against the Central Powers but were "denied that privilege" because Judge Rose of Baltimore would not approve the Czechs' naturalization requests. Perkins and Horgan contacted the Camp Meade intelligence officer and asked him to investigate the situation, noting the "valiant work" of the Czechoslovak forces in Russia fighting against the Central Powers. Captain Perkins told the Meade officer to meet with local authorities and have the soldiers reclassified from "Austrians" to "Czechs," which would expedite naturalization of the soldiers. He also took the opportunity to remind the intelligence officer that just because a soldier had been born in Austria did not make him an enemy, especially since Czechs "hate[d] the Magyars and Germans" and wanted to free their homeland from Austrian rule.[33]

The National Romanian Society and Romanian American newspapers successfully challenged Camp Gordon reorganization policies that inadvertently put together Romanian soldiers with Hungarians of Magyar stock, two groups that held "one of the most intense and deep-rooted of the many race hatreds" found in southeastern Europe. Leaders from the Romanian Society and Romanian American editors protested this situation to the War Department claiming that the two groups had recent altercations at Camps Sherman, Lee, and Sheridan. In addition, Dr. Moldovan, the leading official of the National Romanian Society, contacted Maj. Stephen Bonsal of the War Department staff and asked that the situation be changed immediately. Bonsal, who had lived in Romania and neighboring countries, responded with an informative memo to Col. R. H. Van Deman, the new chief of the Military Intelligence Division, explaining the hatred that divided the Romanians and Hungarians of Magyar stock. Bonsal's report included a history of ancient conflicts that were renewed and increased with the invasion of Transylvania by the Romanian Army in 1916. According to the major, tension had recently escalated when the Austro-Hungarian Army occupied Transylvania and inflicted severe punishment on the Romanians. Bonsal strongly advised the War Department to follow the Romanian Society's recommendation to immediately separate the men from unfriendly nationalities into separate companies. Van Deman concluded that Bonsal's opinion carried "a great deal of weight" since the major had "a very intimate knowledge of conditions, in connection with these races." Subsequently, the War Department ordered the separation of the two ethnic groups.[34]

Even after the Armistice was declared, the War Department remained concerned over the morale of the immigrant soldiers. On November 26, 1918, the Department of the Interior received complaints from Armenian soldiers at Camp Del Rio, Texas. Orders from the acting director of military intelligence, Col. John M. Dunn, instructed the MSS and FSS to investigate the complaints and take whatever action was necessary to remedy the situation. Dunn feared that dissatisfaction among the foreign soldiers would be "magnified" in the ethnic communities and cause "grave social unrest in industrial centers." The MID had difficulty locating the Armenian soldiers since their units had been split up for demobilization. However, they did learn the nature of the complaint from soldiers who had transferred to Fort Sam Houston. The incident involved a native-born soldier in the mess hall who shouted: "The whole d—— bunch of wops step out for a fight." Lieutenant Horgan of the FSS pointed out that "wop" was only applied to Italian soldiers and was probably not directed at the Armenians. Furthermore, "many of the non-coms in the army are rough and ready types, who [did] not use the King's English on all occasions, and use[d] the same sort of language that hurt the feelings of those foreign-born soldiers in talking to soldiers of American birth." Horgan concluded that he did not believe the incident reflected the general experience of the foreign-born soldiers in the American Army.[35]

Another way of increasing the morale of nonnative soldiers was to settle conflicts or solve the problems of these men, especially as they related to their cultural needs. The military quickly recognized the self-evident truth that a positive attitude produced a high level of morale. Prior to the reorganization of the immigrant troops into ethnic-specific companies, most of them had been assigned to menial labor duties. Understanding the dispiriting effect that this prolonged duty had on the immigrants, the War Department issued a general order prohibiting members of foreign-speaking companies from being used as menial "fatigue" laborers. The MID agreed that foreign-speaking soldiers had already "borne a reasonable share" of the army's fatigue duties, and Lieutenant Horgan worked to ensure that the morale of the immigrant conscripts would not be "shattered by being detailed for menial work."[36]

At Camp Devens, Massachusetts, some 15,000 soldiers gathered to hear men of their own "races in their own tongue" discuss why they were called to join the native-born Americans in putting an end to the Kaisers. FSS agent Alfanso Lambiase reported that Mr. F. H. Clark, head of the Knights of Columbus hut on base, refused to allow him to put up signs in Italian informing soldiers about the Italian entertainment evening. Lambiase concluded that although the incident did not affect attendance (2,000 soldiers showed up), it "had quite a blow to the morale of the Italian soldiers." FSS officials reported the incident to the camp's commanding officer and wrote a letter to Mr. Denis McCarthy, head of the Knights of Columbus in Washington, D.C., expressing their "surprise" at this action. Captain Perkins noted, "excellent results in improving the morale of the foreign-speaking soldiers had been obtained by arranging for Greek, Italian and Polish evenings at Y.M.C.A. huts."[37]

Ethnic agents reported that immigrant soldiers at several camps also displayed "considerable unrest" over missing or delayed allotment checks for their relatives in the United States and Europe. Most of the delays were caused by the incorrect spelling of "long, strange and difficult names and addresses" and because of checks mailed to remote rural areas in Europe.[38] An FSS circular later instructed all camp authorities and draft boards to be especially careful when recording the names of immigrant soldiers. The MID suggested that the Operations Division of the General Staff hire "competent interpreters" for camp personal offices to avoid future mistakes and eliminate the "cause of dissatisfaction among our non-English speaking draftees and their families."[39] FSS administrators also arranged for the Red Cross Home Services to act as a liaison between the men and their relatives. When delayed and lost allotment checks placed families of foreign-born soldiers in destitute circumstances, Lieutenant Horgan assured the soldiers that the Red Cross would furnish their families with emergency funds and medical care. The MID, ethnic agents, and the Treasury Department worked together in an effort to educate the soldiers and their ethnic communities about soldiers' War Risk Insurance and allotment checks. Perkins's office provided translations of the insurance and allotment information in various languages. The War Department considered it the duty of every solider to buy the inexpensive government insurance to safeguard his family if the solider was killed. Allotments provided family members with a portion of the soldiers' pay.[40]

Other problems arose when many of the Italian-born servicemen in the American Army expressed concern because they were listed as deserters in Italy when they did not report for duty in the Italian Army. This practice created hardship for the families in the soldiers' native country, who were subject to heavy military taxes due to an immigrant's alleged desertion. In General Order No. 33, the War Department requested that commanding officers promptly provide information on the Italian soldiers so the situation could be corrected. The department then negotiated with Italian officials and provided the government of Italy with a list of all Italian-born soldiers (naturalized and alien) serving in the U.S. Army. At the Camp Lee patriotic and ethnic celebration evening, Italian soldiers applauded enthusiastically when the camp's ethnic agent announced their exemptions from the Italian Army.[41]

The Foreign-speaking Soldier Subsection worked in conjunction with the New York City Bar Association to provide free legal advice to foreign-born soldiers as a way of demonstrating the nation's gratitude for their war efforts. The YWCA Foreign Division produced posters in Polish, Italian, and Armenian giving details of the free legal services. The chief of the Military Morale Branch contacted intelligence officers at various camps to ask their assistance in advertising this program. He included posters in several languages to be displayed in key areas. Working in coordination with MID's FSS, YWCA social worker Dr. Justine Klotz also looked into the possibility of expanding these services to other bar associations throughout the nation.[42]

The War Department's concern over the morale of the immigrant soldiers extended into other areas as well. The Military Morale Section grew out of MID's apprehension that the troops did not understand why they were fighting. Division administrators felt that enemy propaganda undermined the morale of these soldiers. Immigrant FSS agents combated rumors that circulated among the troops and worked to keep disloyal material out of reach of the men. Agents countered the claim that immigrant soldiers who became U.S. citizens could never return to their native country for even a visit. Other "hearsay" incorrectly warned immigrants that once they became citizens, their foreign property would be confiscated and families in the old country punished. In addition, widespread antinaturalization propaganda claimed that the United States deliberately held up the naturalization process in times of peace but was willing to expedite it for soldiers as a way of sending them to the front. Antinaturalization supporters in Syrian communities encouraged their fellows to retain their nationality in order to rebuild their homeland after the war. The FSS considered this action "un-American" and asked prominent Syrian leaders to use their influence to counter the argument and encourage every Syrian American to "give his All for the Cause."[43]

The South-Slavic Council and the Polish National Department, both based in Washington, D.C.; the Bohemian Alliance of Chicago; and the Slav Press Bureau of New York offered to send volunteers to work in the YMCA huts in order to protect "men of different nationalities . . . from unreliable men" who may pass on German propaganda in the U.S. Army. The military attempted to clarify all rumors and counter all anti-American material with their own pro-war propaganda. Although FSS officers worked closely with ethnic leaders, it did not welcome all organizations into army training camps. In September, 1918, the Polish National Committee volunteered to assist with Polish soldiers in what they said were "frequent misunderstandings" with government officials. Brig. Gen. Lytle Brown of the War Plans Division recommended against this involvement since the Polish National Committee also wanted to discuss transferring Polish Americans from the U.S. Army to the Polish Army of France, and Brown feared they would act as "recruiting officers" if allowed in the training camps. Acting Secretary of War Benedict Crowell agreed and sent a letter to Col. James Martin of the French Military Mission explaining the decision.[44]

A number of ethnic newspaper editors contacted the FSS about "enemy propaganda" entering their immigrant communities, and the office sent out immigrant agents to investigate. Most of the agents' reports applauded the loyalty of ethnic presses, and many editors assisted the Military Intelligence

Division in its work with foreign-born soldiers. The Bohemian newspaper *Denni Hlasatel* fought rumors that the United States government would confiscate the immigrants' bank savings to pay for the war. The editor assured his readers that federal law protected their personal property and that America was "different from Austria." The editor concluded, "we cannot warn our countrymen enough not to lend an ear to the seditious talk of the German and Magyar agitators." The Lithuanian newspaper *Lietuva* feared that the "poison of German lies [was] being injected into the minds of Lithuanians . . . and every national group." The editor pleaded with readers to combat German propaganda by refusing to "listen to such lies." The editor of the Hungarian paper *Szabad Sajt* notified the MID that he would "be glad to print any matter affecting the Hungarians," especially letters from Hungarian soldiers that could help curtail rumors circulating through the community. The editor of *Free Russia*, volunteer agent J. Spolansky, reported that his paper was going to organize a permanent society of loyal and patriotic American citizens of Russian descent.[45]

A few FSS immigrant agents reported on possible disloyalty among some of the ethnic press, and others expressed concern over the expansion of radical newspapers. A Russian priest (volunteer agent) with a Carpatho-Russian congregation reported that his people were more loyal to America's democratic ideas than other Russian immigrants. The priest found Carpatho-Russian newspapers to be loyal except for an anarchistic semimonthly publication known as *New Russia*. Another agent warned MID offices about the Croatian daily paper *Narodni List* and its pro-Austrian "leanings" and showed concern over a Solvenian daily paper, *Glas Naroda*, calling it more Austrian than American. An agent from Newark passed on data from an informant that accused the editor of *Telegram Codzienny* of being an Austrian Army officer with an "antagonistic attitude toward the government and its policies." Another agent reported that *Novy Mir* had changed from an "anti-Bolsheviki" to a "Bolsheviki" paper. In addition, the report maintained that a former employee of the paper (a man named Brailovski) left the staff of *Novy Mir* to edit his own Bolshevik paper, *Krist Yunin I Rabotchi*. MID agent Broel-Plater visited Chicago's I.W.W. headquarters and reported that the organization was preparing to publish a new organ in Russian, *Novoye Obshchestwe (The New Society)*.[46]

Volunteer agents also commented on the loyalty of ethnic communities. Dr. Bina Seymour from Springfield, Massachusetts, concluded that the immigrants in his area were sympathetic with America's war aims. According to Seymour, the Greeks, who had lived in Turkey, as well as the Syrians had not yet grasped the importance of the war for "human liberty" since "to them government means autocracy—without regard for the rights of the individual." Dr. F. D. LaRochelle of Springfield, Massachusetts, informed the War Department that there was "not, nor has there been any pro-German sentiment or tendency to so-called radicalism" in his community. The doctor concluded that the Springfield immigrants he met, especially the French, were well informed and understood the issues of the war. LaRochelle promised to send the names of soldiers who were drafted from his area. The doctor also provided advice on how to facilitate the acculturation of immigrants. Dr. Bernard Klein of Joliet, Illinois, reported that he "very seldom [heard] disloyal remarks" by immigrants and concluded that "a great majority of them [were] loyal and frequently express[ed] their appreciation for the opportunities" given in their new country. However, Klein was concerned that the foreign born were ignorant of national matters and did not fully understand the issues of the war. Klein advised that a campaign was needed to educate Joliet immigrants with the reasons for the war. He suggested that John Martin, a justice of the peace and "prominent among the Slovaks," and Stephan Reshan, a Hungarian leader, could assist in this matter. Dr. F. J. Lepak of Duluth, Minnesota, told MID officials that the foreign-speaking community in his area understood the war issues as thoroughly as the Americans did. The few Germans who were outspoken were kept under control after being told to "keep still or they might be tarred and feathered." Although the volunteer agents did report what they believed to be disloyal behavior of some immigrants and newspaper editors, their reports generally applauded the loyalty of the ethnic communities.[47]

The Russian-American Bureau, located in Chicago, Illinois, assisted the MID with its investigation of ethnic communities in Chicago. MID agents asked the bureau to find out whether foreigners in their area understood the issues of the war and whether they were in any way influenced by pro-German or radical forces. Division personnel also asked the Russian-American Bureau for the names of Russian soldiers in the American Army who may have had an influence over their neighborhoods and could assist with the distribution of counterpropaganda matters. The Lithuanian National Council investigated a prominent ethnic leader and president of the society "Palangos Juju" who refused to participate in the Fourth of July Parade and was considered disloyal. The council then advised the MID on how to take "steps to curb his activities and to encourage loyalty among this group." The Lithuanian National Council also supplied division officials with a list of prominent Lithuanian leaders and organizations representing the

"Catholics, Liberals, and Socialists" so that the greatest number of Lithuanians could be reached in counterpropaganda efforts.[48]

To help the foreign-born soldiers fully understand the causes of the war, the FSS began to organize patriotic programs designed to educate the troops about the conflict. Many programs featured ethnic leaders or immigrant officers. Lieutenant Gutowski, the Polish immigrant who headed the Camp Gordon reorganization plan, listed the teaching of patriotism and loyalty as an important objective. He considered it the duty of all commanding officers to instruct both native- and foreign-born soldiers about the rules of war and discipline in the army and to provide lectures on making "the world safe for Democracy." Many civilian ethnic leaders also expressed similar concerns and contacted the War Department with suggestions for improving the fighting spirit among their people. An article in a New York Polish daily newspaper suggested that soldiers should receive "translations of pamphlets similar to the *Red, White, and Blue Series* published by the Committee on Public Information, *The President's Flag Address, How the War Came to America, A Nation in Arms,* and *War Measures and Facts.* . . . This method would enable them to understand clearly why the United States is waging war against Germany."[49]

FSS officials focused their patriotic programs in three areas: the ethnic press, personal appearances by ethnic leaders, and cultural celebrations. Captain Perkins and Lieutenant Horgan asked various ethnic presses to publish patriotic letters from soldiers of foreign extraction and to distribute editorials that declared the "noble" principles of democracy. The Institute for Public Service worked with Assistant Secretary of War Frederick P. Keppel by supplying literature that helped soldiers understand the current conflict. The War Department also worked diligently bolster the esprit de corps of immigrant troops through inspirational meetings and war propaganda, and the FSS designed entertainment programs to increase morale. The patriotic programs, however, cannot be viewed as purely Americanization efforts. Ethnic groups participated in the patriotic demonstrations on their own terms, and the focus of these events was often on speeches about the war contributions of their native countries and the important service of immigrant soldiers. Organizers also often combined lectures with ethnic entertainers and Old World music. FSS officials recognized the need to applaud the foreign born for their war efforts, showed respect for various ethnic groups in the ranks, and planned specific ethnic celebration programs.[50]

Ethnic leaders translated inspirational writings and war propaganda into various languages that often celebrated both American greatness and ethnic pride. The MID circulated copies of a speech by the Polish patriot Ignace Paderewski among Polish American troops in all training camps. Paderewski's speech traced the contribution of Poles in art, science, politics, and literature. It also discussed the contribution of Polish soldiers in the American Army, noting the dedication of Poles who made up only 4 percent of the population in America and yet constituted as much as 12.5 percent of the death casualties by August, 1918. Colonel Van Deman requested copies of Rev. Alex Syaki's editorial on Wilson's peace conditions in the *Polish Daily News (Kruyer Bostonski)*. Van Deman noted that this "excellent" editorial "proves loyalty and love to the noble principles of Democracy and humanity," and he wanted it "read to Poles in the National Army."[51] The FSS requested 3,000 copies of a speech by a Syrian American leader, Ameen Rihani. Captain Perkins wrote to Rabbi William Rosenau of the Eutaw Palace Temple in Baltimore, Maryland, requesting an article with special inspirational materials for Jewish soldiers. He also requested suggestions for "Gentile" camp morale officers so they could meet the "special needs of the Jewish soldiers."[52]

Perkins distributed copies of a series of articles in Baltimore's *Sun* that discussed efforts of the city's foreign born to help win the Great War. His office also utilized copies of a *Boston Globe* article that detailed the "assimilation" of immigrants drafted at Camp Devens in August, 1918. The article emphasized the efforts of prominent ethnic leaders from the various races who had helped the war effort. FSS officers also distributed translations of the *Soldiers' Bulletin*, a periodical collection of inspirational and patriotic messages in nine languages from President Wilson, James Cardinal Gibbons, and Union leader Samuel Gompers. The cardinal reminded soldiers of the honor they were receiving by serving with the army from the "grandest land in the world" and told them to pray to God and be obedient to military officers. Gompers assured the servicemen that the war was not a capitalistic conflict but a people's war.[53]

Prominent ethnic civilians made personal appearances in camps throughout the United States to promote "loyalty among soldiers of foreign extraction."[54] Perkins and his agents found that these patriotic speeches had a tremendous effect on increasing the morale and the fighting spirit of the foreign-born troops. He asked the Italian Embassy in Washington, D.C., to arrange for Capt. Bruno Rosselli, a soldier in the Italian Army, to talk to the Italian American soldiers about the "issues of war." Later, Perkins applauded Rosselli, noting that his lecture was "quite effective." Horgan worked with the Conference on Publicity Methods in Washington, D.C., to arrange for twenty bilingual returning ethnic soldiers to discuss the reasons why the United States was at war and why the immigrant soldiers should help in the conflict. Horgan was particularly interested in soldiers who were decorated for bravery, had public-speaking experience, and who spoke Russian, Polish, Italian, Greek, or Armenian. After Capt. Ernest J. Hall of Camp Devens, Massachusetts, learned that his foreign-born soldiers were "very willing to serve and are loyal, but [do] not understand what they were fighting for and why," he arranged weekly meetings with Italian, Greek, French, and troops of other nationalities for discussions on these topics. After learning of these programs, Perkins asked for full details of Hall's activities, being "keenly interest[ed]" in work that "touche[d] upon morale."[55] The FSS sought the assistance of Pvt. Shucri Baccash of Company F, 2nd Development Battalion, at Camp Upton, New York, who had formerly been an editor of *Al Fatata*, an influential Syrian weekly paper. Baccash assisted the FSS in understanding the needs of the Syrian soldiers and provided inspiring speeches to his fellow Syrian servicemen that encouraged "loyalty to American principles."[56]

Camp Devens hosted a number of patriotic lectures in early August, 1918. Two hundred Armenian soldiers listened to Dr. A. Dermargossian talk about the war effort and to Mrs. Dermargossian as she sang "The Star-Spangled Banner." About three hundred Greek soldiers heard a stirring "patriotic talk in their own tongue" provided by Dr. John K. Catsopoulos of Lowell, Massachusetts. He compared the war to a "crusade" and the men to "soldiers of God, doing His will and privileged to fight for the flag of the country in which they lived."[57]

Many leaders combined ethnic pride with American nationalism. In May, 1918, Lieutenant Orlandini of the Italian Army addressed all Italian-speaking soldiers of the 76th Division at Camp Devens, Massachusetts, in which he praised Italy's role in the war. Later, a speech by Rev. Fan S. Noli was shared with soldiers of Albanian descent, and a Polish speaker from the Massachusetts Immigration Bureau spoke to Polish soldiers in the division. After such programs, mess sergeants prepared special ethnic foods for the soldiers. Arrangements were also made to have Greek, Swedish, and Russian speakers address their ethnic countrymen in arms. A secret report on these activities at Camp Devens was sent to all camp intelligence officers and prompted Capt. A. W. O'Leary of the 17th Infantry, stationed at Fort McPherson, Georgia, to request that arrangements be made for loyal foreign-born speakers to address the German and Austrian troops in his camp. At Camp Lee, Virginia, civilian ethnic leaders lectured to some two thousand immigrant soldiers about the causes of the war and about Italy's war contributions. The FSS arranged for five Italian soldiers, all former prisoners of war, to address Italian American servicemen at Camp Dix, New Jersey, and made plans for them to speak at other camps.[58]

In addition to relying on outside entertainment, the FSS also recruited rank-and-file talent. Perkins introduced Pvt. Frank Della Lana of Company 31, Depot Brigade, Camp Dix, New Jersey, to the camp intelligence officer. The subsection suggested that Lana, "a most loyal Italian-American" and former tenor soloist for his church, could entertain the Italian troops at that cantonment. The MID also distributed articles and cartoons to acknowledge the contributions of the various nationalities toward the war effort. Perkins credited much of the success at Camps Devens and Meade with ethnic agents who arranged Polish, Italian, and Greek evenings at YMCA huts. Officials wrote to the presidents of universities and intelligence officers at training camps to arrange for Austrian, German, Polish, Hungarian, and Bohemian soldiers to act as guest speakers. The FSS promised to "leave no stone unturned that would aid [the immigrants] in becoming good, loyal, American soldiers."[59]

Cultural festivals included the Italian Gala Night, the Italian "Fall of Rome" Celebration, and the Syrian activity night. Perkins issued telegrams to all camps with Italian soldiers requesting that the "Fall of Rome" celebration take place in the army cantonments. The holiday, a widely held national event in Italy celebrating the fall of Rome to the Kingdom of Italy, was equated in importance with France's Bastille Day celebration. Camp intelligence officers made arrangements for Italian speakers to help celebrate the occasion. The FSS suggested that Italian soldiers be given the courtesy of a half-day leave since "it [was] believed that the morale effect of the recognition of this day on the Italians would be worthwhile."[60] Camp Devens's intelligence officer for the foreign companies also arranged for an "Italian Day" celebration and issued invitations to the Italian consul and vice consul in Boston, Italian officers in the American Army, and prominent Italian civilians in the Boston area. Camp Meade, Maryland, organized a massive "Gala Day Celebration" with the help of the Bureau of Foreign Language Organizations in Washington, D.C. The festivities marked the end of training for many immigrant soldiers who were ready for active service and included an array of ethnic speakers. The FSS also located a Syrian speaker to address the soldiers at Camp Upton, New York, for any future "Syrian nights" held at the cantonment.[61]

The War Department's concern with morale continued during the demobilization period following the Armistice, granting soldiers from the 82nd Division, who had recently served in a number of battles, short leaves "to relax and sightsee before returning to the United States." However, Italian American soldiers from the division asked for an extended absence in order to travel to Italy to visit their family and relatives. After being inundated with requests, the War Department helped organize the "Italian Leave Train" and take more than 1,200 Italian American servicemen to visit their homeland. Each soldier had to supply their commanding officer with family names and the specific city or village of destination. The military took care of every detail, stocking the train with rations, supplying six cooks and helpers to prepare meals during the trip, and instructing soldiers what to pack. The War Department was concerned about the "morale" and "spirit" of the troops, but it also "warned [the ethnic soldiers] that those contracting venereal disease will not be permitted to return to the U.S. with their organization."[62]

Far from harshly implementing "Anglo-conformity" or automatically forcing the foreign-born soldier into an "American mold," the United States military showed a remarkable sensitivity and respect for its immigrant troops. Military policies indicated a clear understanding of the connection between efficiency and high morale. While expecting loyalty from their soldiers, the military remained "mindful of the traditions" of the foreign born. War Department policies also were the result of a complex alliance with leaders from the immigrant communities and the power and strength of America's ethnic organizations. Ethnic leaders assisted in training immigrant soldiers and instilling American patriotism within their communities and servicemen, but they also championed ethnic pride and pushed for fair and just treatment of the foreign born soldiers. In addition, these leaders put pressure on the military to meet the cultural needs of the troops. The resulting military policies created an atmosphere that made dual identity and dual pride acceptable and the nonnative soldiers' duty personally easier.

The recruit detachment which is to illustrate both the benefits of this new system of training and the social value of the War Department's new work will probably be known as the "Americans All" detachment. No happier name could be chosen. It is a fortunate augury of the day when the War Department will be permitted to bring to every young man of the country, under a system of universal training, the advantages which are accruing to these men who are fortunate enough to be chosen for this new and liberal experiment in Americanization.

—*New York Herald*, September 16, 1919

Conclusion

"Americans All!"

During the First World War, the United States government drafted nearly a half million immigrants, and thousands of second-generation immigrants, into the American Army. The war took place on the heels of the Progressive Era, when middle-class reformers worked relentlessly to reorder the industrial society, socialize and morally uplift the working classes through new social welfare agencies, and restructure the urban environment with the use of scientific-management theories. Public war hysteria created an atmosphere of mindless fervor and a crusade for moral righteousness that knew no bounds, and immigrants faced harassment, discrimination, and even violence. Newspaper articles, cartoons, posters, and speeches fostered ethnic distrust and continued to depict immigrants in a negative and stereotypical manner, repeating the need for 100 percent conformity.

Many of the nation's new immigrants originally came from areas controlled by the Central Powers and had long felt the oppression of those authoritarian governments. Once in the United States, these ethnic groups worked tirelessly for the freedom of their homelands. Even before America's entrance into the war, they continually attempted to draw the public's attention to the problems that faced the "Old Country" through fundraisers, speeches, and political activity. Once the United States declared war against the Central Powers, many of these immigrants were labeled "technical" enemy aliens because of their birth. They immediately began to fight against this label so they could join ethnic legions attached to foreign armies or serve in the United States military to help defeat the Central Powers.

Eventually, almost one in five draftees in the U.S. military were foreign born. The War Department took a unique approach to training immigrant soldiers that had many similarities to the social welfare and scientific-management movements of its day. Progressive philosophy was not unknown to leading military officers. By the First World War, the military had dramatically expanded the officer corps to include many non–West Point graduates. Many of these new leaders came from the nation's universities and businesses and from an environment that was struggling with Progressive challenges and solutions. In fact, Secretary of War Newton D. Baker referred to the military leaders who designed and implemented new military policies as "Progressive officers."[1]

The War Department created the Foreign-speaking Soldier Subsection and worked with social welfare reformers and prominent ethnic leaders. The FSS took direction from the Military Morale Section and the director of the Military Intelligence Division. The result was a systematic and efficient manner of organizing and training foreign-born soldiers and an active campaign to both socialize and Americanize these immigrant troops. The military encouraged Americanism through English-language classes and foreign-language translations of war propaganda, inspirational speeches by ethnic leaders, and public-speaking appearances by immigrant soldiers who had been decorated for bravery. Ethnic organizations provided translations of socialization and Americanization materials, and immigrants became intelligence agents for the War Department.

However, immigrant leaders helped formulate military policy as they educated the military about the various ethnicities in the camps, pressured for observation of important religious traditions, and fought for fair and just treatment of foreign-born servicemen. Ethnic leaders also worked in conjunction with the War Department to meet the cultural, educational, and social needs of foreign-born soldiers. The military celebrated ethnic traditions, promoted immigrant officers, applauded the war efforts of various nationalities, and demanded that native-born soldiers respect their foreign-born counterparts.

The fact that ethnic leaders assisted in both celebrating ethnicity and instilling American patriotism was not unusual for men from the professional classes of the ethnic communities, who often "synthesize[d] their Old and New World cultures."[2] In this way, they engaged in an active negotiation of ethnic identity and often appropriated the "language of patriotism" to this end. New War Department policies created an atmosphere wherein dual pride and dual identity became acceptable.

Although there is an abundance of correspondence between the War Department, the Foreign-speaking Soldier Subsection, Progressive reformers, and ethnic leaders that provide details of military policies, it is much more difficult to reconstruct the "voices" of the rank-and-file soldiers who served in the American Army. From available military records and postwar questionnaires, we can glimpse how foreign-born soldiers viewed their war experience. Like other soldiers who served during the First World War, the immigrant experience was a mixture of bewilderment, resentment, loyalty, heroism, and complaining. Most immigrants made positive statements about their treatment from the United States military. Their comments indicate that the foreign born did not generally have problems with native-born soldiers, often referring to their fellow servicemen as "buddies." The war experience of some included heroic stories, and a number of foreign-born soldiers received citations for bravery. Finally, soldiers expressed pride in both their ethnic group and in being "American."

Knowledge of foreign languages helped immigrants bond with native-born soldiers and also saved lives. Italian-born John Greco, who came through Ellis Island at the age of eleven, worked as a commercial clerk in Jamaica, New York, prior to the war. Drafted into the army in October, 1917, Private Greco served in the 152nd Field Artillery Brigade, 77th Division, and trained in signal code, morse code, and horseback riding in formation. In addition to clerical work, guard duty, K.P., and duties with the cavalry, the private also cleaned horses and spent time watching out for the mules, which "were vicious." In France, Greco's language skills came in handy, and he often acted as an interpreter for his fellow servicemen. The private recalled with some humor the difficulty the Americans had communicating with the French people without his help. Unable to ask for eggs in French, men would make the motions of a chicken. As another example, one of

Greco's "buddies" could not get help to put out a fire in his room because he could not speak French. Running into the street yelling "foo, foo, foo," the French responded by asking why the "crazy Americans called [themselves] fools?"[3]

Louis Van Iersel, one of the most highly decorated veterans of World War I, was born in the Netherlands.[4] The day he arrived in the United States, Van Iersel declared his intention of becoming an American citizen, registered for the draft, and enlisted in the army. There was only one problem: Van Iersel did not speak English. Initially, he served on kitchen duty while he learned English from a YMCA hostess. Within a few months, Van Iersel received a promotion to corporal in Company M, 9th Infantry, 2nd Division. Fluent in both French and German, Van Iersel was soon placed in charge of five noncommissioned corporals on the front lines in France. The young immigrant and a fellow combatant rescued seventeen wounded soldiers during a heavy barrage of German gunfire. Van Iersel also led a reconnaissance mission that successfully captured sixty enemy soldiers. Fluent in German, the corporal was able to infiltrate the German trenches and persuade German officers to surrender. For his bravery, Van Iersel received two Croix de Guerre.

Van Iersel also received America's highest military award, the Medal of Honor, for crossing the icy Seine River under heavy bombardment and spying on the Germans. He was able to warn his battalion of a planned heavy artillery bombardment directed at their position. Gen. John Pershing presented the medal, thought to be the first given to a noncitizen. Accredited with saving the lives of a thousand men during the First World War, Van Iersel eventually received fourteen American and French decorations for heroism.[5]

Some soldiers had to wait for their honors for bravery. Jack Guarracino, originally from Naples, Italy, was drafted into the American Army and wounded in Aisne, France, when his right foot was "ripped out by a piece of shrapnel." Guarracino, who had recently become an American citizen, had not yet mastered the English language and misspelled his name to the medical officers. Consequently, the immigrant soldier did not receive his Purple Heart and Silver Star medals until August 22, 1980, at the age of eighty-five years old. When he learned of his honors over dinner with his daughter, Guarracino "stopped eating and tears came to his eyes."[6]

Most ethnic servicemen did not have problems with their commanding officers and many became friends with their fellow soldiers. Pvt. Salvatore Campanelli came from Italy when he was fifteen years old and was drafted into the 306th Infantry, 77th Division in July, 1918, at the age of twenty-seven. Prior to his induction, Campanelli lived in Bellingham, Washington, and worked as a logging-camp foreman. The Italian immigrant described his reaction to the war as a "terrible experience . . . [with] his life in danger every second." In the trenches in France, Campanelli remembers being covered with lice, seeing the wounded and dead, and growing anxious to return home. However, he reported that the captains and lieutenants treated the men "very well" and found the French people helpful to American soldiers.[7]

John L. DiFonzo, a foundry worker from Jersey City, New Jersey, became a private in the Company C, 9th Infantry Regiment, 2nd Division, in September, 1917, at the age of twenty-one. The immigrant's overall evaluation of his war experience was good. DiFonzo found his training adequate, his weapons "pretty good," leadership acceptable ("some good, some not so good, one exceptional"), discipline "good," morale "good," and military justice "fair and just." His first taste of war left DiFonzo frightened and sick, but the private soon recovered from his first battle experience. However, the war affected DiFonzo's health for the rest of his life.[8]

George Dongarra worked in a number of occupations—railroad worker, laborer, shoe repairman, farmer, and road construction worker—before his enlistment; he later claimed to have joined the army because "all his friends had gone off to war." Private Dongarra served with the 2nd Ammunition Train, 2nd Division. There he hauled ammunition and other equipment and filled in as a relief truck driver. Dongarra found both good and bad leadership in the army. In Germany, his new company commander, a Cuban, made it clear that he did not like Italians. When Dongarra decided to reenlist, he took pleasure in handing his transfer papers to his commander, who was forced to sign them.[9]

Not all officers adhered to the War Department's warning against ethnic slurs. Morris Gutentag, a European immigrant who was a leather goods worker before the war, enlisted in the American Army to "fight and preserve the traditions of [his] adopted country." Private Gutentag served with the 308th Infantry Regiment, 77th Division. He recalled that there were many ethnic groups in his unit, and strong leadership was shown by reserve officers and noncommissioned officers—"everyone did his best." Gutentag recalled that his unit was drilled to a song with the phrase "The Jews and the wops and the dirty Irish cops."[10]

Common among the memoirs of these ethnic soldiers is pride in serving America. Gutentag praised his adopted country and concluded that foreign-born soldiers "realized that to 'go home' to the USA meant more to [them] as immigrants fighting for [their] adopted country."[11] J. Swietanka, director of the Czechoslovak National Council in Washington D.C., "translated and censored dozens of letters" written by Czech and Slovak soldiers for the Translation Section of the Army War College. He found that the soldiers "spoke highly of the treatment extended to [them], and manifested an eagerness to get at the Kaiser. Some of the letters made it evident that the writers were urged by a double motive, that of loyalty to his adopted country and full zeal for the liberation of his native country; but in most cases the tone of the letters was like that of the American soldier, anxious to do his full duty."[12]

Campanelli expressed his "love for America" but questioned what was gained by the war. DiFonzo enlisted even though he "didn't speak English well," because he was full of "pride in the U.S.A." and determined "to win [the] war." Van Iersel described his unit as a "close nit [sic]" group that helped one another and summed up his war experience this way: "I learned to get along and respect all people." An issue of the *Soldiers' Bulletin* that printed messages from Cardinal Gibbons; Maj. Gen. M. C. Gorgas, U.S. Army Surgeon General; and Samuel Gompers also included a statement from a Private Kaminski, 313th Machine Gun Battalion. Kaminski wrote: "I am proud of my uniform. This country gave me bread, and I am going to die for it with a smile, knowing that I have repaid the contracted debt for the Stars and Stripes, and at the same time helped Poland." Sgt. Albert Hocky, a Czech soldier at Camp Meade, expressed how anxious he was to go "over there" and considered it "a source of much pride to become a citizen." Hocky understood very little English when he was drafted, but he learned rapidly and was promoted to sergeant within sixteen days. Leon Rose, private first class, 106th Infantry, 27th Division, was a stock clerk in civilian life. Rose described himself as a "patriotic kid" and enlisted with a friend on a Jewish holiday. He was "happy to have served," and afterward became active in the American Legion and the Jewish War Veterans of the United States.[13]

New York's *Daily Slovak American* reprinted a letter from a son of Jewish immigrants in which the soldier reprimanded his parents for suggesting that he seek an early medical discharge from the army due to ear problems. The young man asked if his parents had forgotten why they came to the United States and reminded them of the tyranny, abuse, and intolerance found in Europe: "Jews especially, who have been in bondage or slaves in every country in the world except the United States, where they have been treated like white people ought to be among the first to offer their sons for service in the Army. . . . You ought to feel proud to have a son in the service of Uncle Sam and fighting for the ideals we are fighting for. . . . The Jews all over the world are doing their share now, with few exceptions, and I know you don't want any slacker in your family."[14]

While many German and Austrian soldiers joined the U.S. Army prior to the war, others were mistakenly drafted once the fighting began. The War Department asked all camp commanding generals to interview these soldiers to find out if they wanted to remain in service and to evaluate their loyalty. Pvt. Charles J. Gottwald of the 77th Division wrote an emotional letter (through military channels) to the adjutant general of the army. Gottwald, who took out his first papers in January, 1913, and took the oath of allegiance to the United States on September 14, 1917, wrote: "I made no reservations of any kind when I took this oath of allegiance; I stand willing in view of the fact that war is existing between Austria Hungary and United States, to take again the oath of allegiance to the United States; there is nothing in the country of my birth to cause me to have any hesitation in taking up arms against the government or the subject of that country. In view of the above facts, I pray that as soon as may be, I be granted by final papers establishing me as a citizen of the United States and I further pray that I be allowed to remain in the military service of the United States."[15]

Drafted primarily from New York City, the 77th Division reflected the multiethnic nature of the area, however, Jewish soldiers made up the largest group. The division was sometimes called the "Yaphank," named after the East Side of New York, and it was also referred to as the "Yiddish Division." The 77th included the famous 308th Battalion, which according to the Office of Jewish War Records, was "practically a Jewish battalion."[16] The 308th received national press when it became trapped in a hollow in the Argonne Forest, surrounded by the enemy. The battalion survived four days of heavy bombardment while cut off from their division. The *New York Globe* compared the bravery of these soldiers to that of those at the Alamo in 1836 and showed their surprise that former "tailors, factory workers, pushcart men, clerks . . . crowding the east side's streets would be capable of such a feat. . . . The Yiddishers fight like Wildcats? . . . But they did." The *Globe* congratulated the Russian Jews for ridding themselves of the tyranny and oppression of their native land and joining the American melting pot. Some 125 Jewish soldiers in the 77th Division received official citations for bravery. Among the list were a number of soldiers from the recent Jewish migration to the United States. Pvt. Abraham Krotoshinsky, formerly a barber in the Bronx, received the Distinguished Service Cross for extraordinary heroism in the Argonne Forest. Trapped by the enemy with the now famous "Lost Battalion," Krotoshinsky volunteered to run through the enemy lines to seek help for the troops. Runner after runner had been killed attempting to report the battalion's position before Krotoshinsky succeeded. Daniel Moskowitz of Company F, 108th Infantry (no rank listed), received the Distinguished Service Cross after he demonstrated exceptional bravery by rescuing wounded soldiers in an open field while under heavy machine-gun and artillery fire. Pvt. Isaac Stomersky of Company B, 106th Infantry, exhibited exceptional bravery when he volunteered as a runner during a barrage of heavy high explosives and gas shells. Stomersky managed to relay orders during the battle at considerable risk to his life. Sgt. Isie J. Herscovitz was cited for valor, and Sgt. Nizel Rafalsky received the Distinguished Service Cross. Joseph Bemowski, Silas Kantrowitz, Benjamin Shapiro, Isidore Studinski, all from the 104th Infantry, also received citations for bravery along with the rest of their regiment.[17]

With the Armistice in November, 1918, the War Department began a campaign for universal training of all young men in the United States. They also argued that the military could build from their World War I successes with ethnic groups by turning non-English-speaking immigrants into skilled soldiers. Postwar enlistment of immigrants into the United States Army continued since the Emergency Act, temporarily enacted to override the 1899 law excluding non-English-speaking persons (except Indians) from military service, was still in place. Congress began debating whether to repeal the act with the end of hostilities. In response, the War Department worked to educate the public to the benefits of a multiethnic army. With this in mind, they created a special group of immigrant soldiers trained at the Recruit Educational Center at Camp Upton, New York. This unit consisted of twenty-eight foreign-born soldiers from fourteen different nationalities who performed in major cities throughout the United States in an impressive "cadence system of close order drill." In demonstrations held twice a day at city parks and plazas in Providence, Boston, Buffalo, Cleveland, Detroit, Milwaukee, Cincinnati, Pittsburgh, Washington, Baltimore, Philadelphia, and Newark, the unit displayed "proficiency . . . worthy of veteran regulars and elicited hearty applause from the throngs who watched their snappy evolution."[18] In press releases, the War Department contended that in just a few months this group of "illiterates" became a positive force by learning English, military drill, and a vocational trade while serving their adopted country. Enlistment in the army also increased the likelihood of naturalization, since the soldiers could become citizens after only three years of service rather than five years of civilian residence. In only a few months, the army argued that they had taken a group of "classified illiterates" and turned them into productive future citizens. This, they maintained, was a "practical business proposition."

However, the continuance of a multiethnic army was not to be. Renewed anti-immigration hysteria fueled by postwar uncertainty and the turbulence of the 1920s Red Scare pushed Congress into enacting the 1924 National Origins Act. This law essentially closed the "Golden Doors" to future mass immigration. The military soon dropped its "Americans All" dream and supported the immigrant restriction movement.

Future conflicts would be fought with the sons, and now daughters, of the 23 million immigrants who came to the United States in the late nineteenth and early twentieth centuries. Today's military role call still reads like the First World War Victory Loan Drive poster: Du Bois, Smith, O'Brien, Cejka, Haucke, Pappandrikopolous, Andrassi, Villotto, Levy, Turovich, Kowalski, Chriczanevic, Knutson, Gonzales.[19] During World War I, a German officer noted with some complexity the ethnic diversity of the American Army: "Only a few of the troops are of pure American origin; the majority are of German, Dutch, and Italian parentage. But these semi-Americans . . . fully feel themselves to be true-born sons of their [adopted] country."[20] Despite the acute perception of this officer, he was wrong on one very important point. These men were not "semi-Americans," they were "Americans All!"

Notes

Abbreviations

AGO	Adjutant General's Office
CTCA	Commission on Training Camp Activities
HSP	Historical Society of Pennsylvania
MID	Military Intelligence Division
MID-WDGS	Records of the Military Intelligence Division of the War Department General Staff
NA	National Archives and Records Administration
RG	Record Group
U.S.A.M.H.I.	U.S. Army Military History Institute, Carlisle Barracks, Pennsylvania
WDGSS	Records of the War Department General and Special Staff
WDOR	War Department Organizational Records

Introduction

The document from which the epigraph is extracted is found in Serie 17N47, Archives de l'Armee de Terre, Chateau de Vinceness, Paris, Postal control, 28 Octobre 1917. Thanks to Jennifer Keene for sharing this quote with me. The French soldier goes on to mention: "This doesn't seem to bother them. But doesn't this appear to you like a bizarre mentality? As far as I'm concerned, I scarcely see myself fighting against my country, even if I had left it long ago. They don't seem to remember it. . . . Did I tell you the story of the soldier in my regiment disembarking in France who saw his brother, a boche prisoner, working in the port." Part of this manuscript appeared in Nancy Gentile Ford, "'Mindful of the Traditions of His Race': Dual Identity and Foreign-born Soldiers in the First World War American Army," *Journal of American Ethnic History* 16, no. 2 (winter, 1997): 35–57.

1. In all, the U.S. Selective Service registered 23,908,576 men. Every man considered physically and mentally fit and without a draft deferment was placed in the Class I "pool," from which the actual draftees were drawn. As of November 11, 1918, the total draftees in the American Army numbered 2,758,542 men. According to Selective Service reports, approximately 11 percent of the Class I registrants were noncitizens (aliens); naturalized citizens made up 6.67 percent of the remaining total. Therefore, 17.6 percent (11 percent aliens and 6.67 percent naturalized) of the 2,758,542 total draftees (487,434) were foreign born. (This does not include the thousands of immigrants who enlisted prior to the

draft.) *Second Report of the Provost Marshal General to the Secretary of War*, pp. 89–92, 163–401; *Final Report of the Provost Marshal General to the Secretary of War*, p. 14. These calculations match those made by Fred Davis Baldwin, who sampled approximately 100,000 white draftees and discovered that approximately 18 percent were foreign born. Fred Davis Baldwin, "The American Enlisted Man in World War I," p. 59. William Bruce White briefly examined immigrant soldiers in the First World War in his 1968 dissertation, but he did not have access to Military Intelligence Division records. He therefore concluded that since the army "contained large number of immigrants . . . during World War I and after, [the United States military] worked diligently for their Americanization." William Bruce White, "The Military and the Melting Pot: The American Army and Minority Groups, 1865–1924," pp. 5, 309–14.

2. For recent analyses of Progressivism, see Allen Dawley, *Struggle for Justice: Social Responsibility and the Liberal State*; Judith Ann Trolander, *Professionalism and Social Change: From Settlement House Movement to Neighborhood Centers 1886 to the Present*; Nell Irvin Painter, *Standing at Armageddon: The United States, 1877–1919*; and Michael B. Katz, *In the Shadow of the Poorhouse: A Social History of Welfare in America*. Older studies that offer solid interpretations of Progressivism include Roy Lubove, *The Professional Altruist: The Emergence of Social Work as a Career, 1880–1930*; Robert H. Wiebe, *The Search For Order, 1877–1920*; Allen F. Davis, *Spearheads for Reform: The Social Settlements and the Progressive Movement, 1890–1914*; Allen F. Davis, *American Heroine: The Life and Legend of Jane Addams*; Kenneth L. Kusmer, "The Functions of Organized Charity in the Progressive Era: Chicago as a Case Study," *The Journal of American History* 60, no. 3 (Dec., 1973); Paul Boyer, *Urban Masses and Moral Order in America, 1820–1920*.

3. Boyer, *Urban Masses*, p. 242. For details on women and social reform, see Nancy K. Bristow, *Making Men Moral: Social Engineering during the Great War*; Ruth Bordin, *Women and Temperance: The Quest For Power and Liberty, 1873–1900*; Ruth Rosen, *The Lost Sisterhood: Prostitution in America, 1900–1918*; Nancy Woloch, *Women and the American Experience*; Trolander, *Professionalism and Social Change*; and Kathryn Kish Sklar, "Hull House in the 1890s: A Community of Women Reformers," in *Women, Families, and Communities: Reading in American History*, ed. by Nancy A. Hewitt.

4. John Higham, *Send These to Me: Jews and Other Immigrants in Urban America*, p. 68; David Kennedy, *Over Here: The First World War and American Society*, p. 64.

5. Boyer, *Urban Masses*, pp. 236, 237–39; Jane Addams, *Twenty Years at Hull-House*, p. 169; Davis, *Spearheads for Reform*, pp. 46, 89; Addams, *Twenty Years*, pp. 46–50.

6. For discussions on scientific management and its relationship to Progressivism, see Weibe, *Search for Order*; and Samuel Haber, *Efficiency and Uplift: Scientific Management in the Progressive Era, 1890–1920*, pp. 75–98.

7. Peter Karsten, *The Military in America: From the Colonial Era to the Present*, p. 229; John M. Gates, "The Alleged Isolation of U.S. Army Officers in the Late 19th Century," *Parameters: Journal of the U.S. Army War College* 10 (Sept., 1980): 42. For an early study of the influence of Progressivism on the U.S. Army, see

Baldwin, "American Enlisted Man." For key debates over civil-military relationships, see Samuel P. Huntington, *The Soldier and the State: The Theory and Politics
of Civil-Military Relations;* Emory Upton, *The Military Policy of the United States;*
Morris Janowitz, *The Professional Soldiers: A Social and Political Portrait;* Allen
Guttmann, "Political Ideals and the Military Ethic," *The American Scholar* 3
(1965); Allen Guttmann, *The Conservation Tradition in America,* especially chap-
ter 4, "Conservatism and the Military Establishment"; Russell F. Weigley, ed.,
The American Military: Readings in the History of the Military in American Society
(Reading, Mass.: Addison-Wesley, 1969); Zeb B. Bradford Jr. and James R.
Murphy, "A New Look at the Military Profession," *Army* 19 (Feb., 1969); Jack C.
Lane, "The Military Profession's Search for Identity," *Marine Corps Gazette* 57
(June, 1973); and Russell F. Weigley, *History of the United States Army;* Russell F.
Weigley, "The Elihu Root Reforms and the Progressive Era," in *Command and
Commanders in Modern Warfare: Proceedings of the Second Military Symposium,
U.S. Air Force Academy,* ed. by William Geffen. Baldwin, Gates, Lane, and
Weigley also discuss military modernization and Progressivism.

8. Weigley, "Elihu Root Reforms," p. 12; Jack C. Lane, *Armed Progressive: General
Leonard,* pp. 107, 149, 155.

9. Elvid Hunt, *A Manual of Intensive Training,* pp. 7, 9, 39; William E. Dunn, *Scientific Management Applied to Instruction and Training in Field Artillery,* pp. 1–41.

10. David C. Shanks, *Management of the American Soldier* (distributed to morale
officers in Aug., 1918). See also memorandum concerning Maj. Gen. David C.
Shank's *The Management of the American Soldier,* Aug. 20, 1918, 80–78/2, MID-
WDGS RG 165, N.A.; Bruce W. Bidwell, *History of the Military Intelligence Divi-
sion, Department of the Army General Staff: 1775–1941,* p. 205; Edward L.
Munson, *The Management of Men: A Handbook on the Systematic Development of
Morale and Control of Human Behavior,* p. v. See also Munson's chapter "Morale
Methods and Scientific Management," p. 35.

11. Memorandum concerning Shank's *Management of the American Soldier,* 80–78/
1–3, MID-WDGS.

12. Frederick Palmer, *Newton D. Baker America at War;* Raymond B. Fosdick,
Chronicles of a Generation: An Autobiography; "The Commission on Training
Camp Activities," June, 1918, CTCA 33087, WDGSS RG 165, N.A., p. 1.

13. Bidwell, *Military Intelligence Division,* p. 205.

14. Ibid., pp. 124, 105, 185, 206; Charles D. Ameringer, *U.S. Foreign Intelligence: The
Secret Side of American History,* pp. 110–11; Lane, *Armed Progressive,* pp. 109–31,
205, 185.

15. Kennedy, *Over Here,* p. 67. See also Kennedy's chapter 1, "The War for the
American Mind"; and John Higham, *Strangers in the Land: Patterns of American
Nativism 1860–1925,* especially chaps. 8, "War and Evolution," and 9," Crusade
for Americanization."

16. Kathleen Neils Conzen, et al., "The Invention of Ethnicity: A Perspective from
the U.S.A.," *Journal of American Ethnic History* 12 (fall, 1992): 5; Victor R.
Greene, *American Immigrant Leaders, 1800–1910: Marginality and Identity,* pp. 3,
15, 45, 16. See also John Higham, ed., *Ethnic Leadership in America.*

17. John Bodnar, *Remaking America: Public Memory, Commemoration, and Patriotism in the Twentieth Century*, p. 16.

18. Robert Zecker, "The Activities of Czech and Slovak Immigrants during World War I," *Ethnic Forum* 15, nos. 1–2 (spring–fall, 1995): 36.

19. In past wars, the number of immigrant soldiers and their experience with the U.S. Army had been remarkably different. See chapter 3 for a more detailed treatment of this issue.

20. Bidwell, *Military Intelligence Division*, pp. 205, 185.

21. Jennifer Diane Keene, "Civilians in Uniform: Building an American Mass Army for the Great War," p. 161.

22. Copies of posters can be found in "Liberty Loans," Freeman Collection, HSP; C. A. Sienkiewica, "Fourth Liberty Loan, Foreign Language Division," Oct., 1917, Liberty Loan Collection, HSP; "Czech America Do Thy Duty: Let Shining Examples Demonstrate Loyalty to Our New Homeland and to President Woodrow Wilson," *Denni Hlasatel*, Apr. 7, 1917.

Chapter 1. "In the Family of One Nation"

1. "The War for the American Mind" was coined in Kennedy, *Over Here*, p. 45.

2. John Bodnar's work primarily deals with the post–World War I era, however, his theories help us reexamine the patriotic culture of the Great War. Bodnar, *Remaking America*, p. 16. Building on Bodner's study, Zecker connects public memory and the "language of Americanism" to the Czech and Slovak communities during the First World War. Zecker, "Czech and Slovak Immigrants," pp. 37, 35–54.

3. German American activities during World War I are covered in the following secondary sources: Clifton James Child, *The German-Americans in Politics, 1914–1917*; Carl Wittke, *German-Americans and the World War*; Frederick C. Luebke, *Bonds of Loyalty: German Americans and World War I; Deutsche-Amerikanischen National-Bundes*; and Sally M. Miller, *The Ethnic Press in the United States: A Historical Analysis and Handbook*, pp. 146–47.

4. *Deutsche-Amerikanischen National-Bundes*, pp. 3–5; Child, *German-Americans in Politics*, p. 4; Miller, *Ethnic Press*, pp. 146–47. According to Miller, subscriptions increased from an estimated 782,000 readers in 1914 to 950,000 in early 1917.

5. Miller, *Ethnic Press*, p. 146; Luebke, *Bonds of Loyalty*, pp. 162, 164; Child, *German-Americans in Politics*, p. 48; Edward Cuddy, "Irish-American Propaganda and American Neutrality," *Mid-America* 49 (1967): 261.

6. Miller, *Ethnic Press*, pp. 146–49.

7. Luebke, *Bonds of Loyalty*, pp. 166–67, 191; Wittke, *German-Americans and the World War*, p. 89; Miller, *Ethnic Press*, p. 147.

8. Child, *German-Americans in Politics*, p. 173.

9. *Liberty is Alive!!*, Balch Institute for Ethnic Studies, Philadelphia, pp. 15, 3, 11–14.

10. Miller, *Ethnic Press*, p. 149.

11. Kennedy, *Over Here*, p. 75; Luebke, *Bonds of Loyalty*, pp. 44–45; Miller, *Ethnic*

Press, pp. 148–49. See also U.S. Attorney and Marshals, "World War I Cases," World War I Manuscript Collection, National Archives and Records Administration Mid-Atlantic Branch, Philadelphia.

12. Thomas J. Rowland, "Irish-American Catholics and the Quest for Respectability in the Coming of the Great War, 1900–1917," *Journal of American Ethnic History* 15, no. 2 (winter, 1996); Thomas J. Rowland, "Strained Neutrality: Irish-American Catholics, Woodrow Wilson, and the *Lusitania*," *Eire-Ireland* 30, no. 4 (winter, 1996). By 1922 some 7 million Irish immigrants had come to America. Miller, *Ethnic Press*, p. 177.

13. Rowland, "Irish-American Catholics"; Rowland, "Strained Neutrality"; Miller, *Ethnic Press*, p. 177.

14. Cuddy, "Irish-American Propaganda," pp. 252–53, 231, 252–57, 275; Joseph P. O'Grady, ed., *The Immigrants Influence on Wilson's Peace Policies*, pp. 31, 4–5, 61.

15. Cuddy, "Irish-American Propaganda," pp. 256–57; Rowland, "Strained Neutrality," pp. 59–60.

16. Jeremiah A. O'Leary, *A Statement*, p. 1.

17. "Great Irish Meeting," *Irish Press*, Apr. 13, 1918, Irish Collection, Villanova University Library.

18. Rowland, "Irish-American Catholics," p. 9; Rowland, "Strained Neutrality," pp. 65–70, 21.

19. Kennedy, *Over Here*, pp. 82, 60–64.

20. Division of the Four-Minute Men, *The Meaning of America*, Bulletin 33, pp. 4, 15.

21. *American Loyalty by Citizens of German Descent*, pp. 2–3.

22. Ibid.

23. "Liberty Loans," Freeman Collection, HSP.

24. Zecker, "Czech and Slovak Immigrants," p. 36. While Zecker focuses on the agenda of Czech and Slovak immigrants, this same case certainly can be made for other ethnic groups.

25. "President Calls for July 4 Celebration," *New York Times*, May 24, 1918, p. 7; "Many Nations to Contribute to July 4 Celebration," *New York Herald*, June 29, 1918, World War History Newspaper Clippings Collection, vol. 344, U.S.A.M.H.I.

26. "In Congress, July 4, 1918," print #47/1, World War I Collection, the Balch Institute for Ethnic Studies, Philadelphia; "The Solemn Declaration of the Czechoslovak People to the Republic of the United States of American and its Great Present Woodrow Wilson," Immigration History Research Center, University of Minnesota, St. Paul; "American Indian to Lead All Races in Great Parade," *The Evening Telegram*, June 29, 1918, Newspaper Clippings Collection, vol. 344, U.S.A.M.H.I.

27. Photo from Rock Springs, Wyoming, "Slovene Organizations," Matt Leskovec Collection, Immigration History Research Center.

28. Bodnar, *Remaking America*, p. 83.

29. Robert Zecker used the phrase "language of Americanism" in "Czech and Slovak Immigrants," p. 39.

30. "To Tear 'Kaiser Page' from Schoolbooks," *Denni Hlasatel*, Apr. 23, 1917; "American-

ization of Immigrants," *Denni Hlasatel,* June 6, 1918; "Try to Keep the Light of Liberty in Full Blaze," *Denni Hlasatel,* Oct. 15, 1918; "A Star on the Service Flag," *Denni Hlasatel,* Oct. 11,1918; "From the Czech Campaign Office," *Denni Hlasatel,* Oct. 9, 1918; C. A. Sienkiewica, "Fourth Liberty Loan, Foreign Language Division," Oct., 1917, Freeman Collection, HSP.

31. Edvard Benes, *My War Memoirs,* pp. 98–101; Thomas Capek, *The Čechs in America,* pp. 265–78.

32. Capek, *Čechs in America,* pp. 265–78; Zecker, "Czech and Slovak Immigrants," pp. 37, 38–39; Capek, *Čechs in America,* pp. 267–74.

33. "Let's Do Our Duty!" *Denni Hlasatel,* Apr. 14, 1917.

34. Quoted in Zecker, "Czech and Slovak Immigrants," pp. 43, 37–43; Capek, *Čechs in America,* p. 268.

35. "Message to President Woodrow Wilson," *Denni Hlasatel,* Dec. 6, 1917.

36. Capek, *Čechs in America,* p. 268; "In the Sign of the War, Proclamation by the Ceske Narodni Sdruzeni," *Denni Hlasatel,* Apr. 8, 1917.

37. "To All American Czechs and Slovaks: To the Branches of the Bohemian National Alliance, Also to the Czech and the Slovak Sokols: Last Greetings," *Denni Hlasatel,* Apr., 1917; "We are Behind in Recruiting," *Denni Hlasatel,* Apr. 12, 1917; "Committee Reports on Enlistment," *Denni Hlasatel,* Apr. 11, 1917; "Recruiting in Progress," *Denni Hlasatel,* Apr. 13, 1917; "Greetings! Follow Our Examples!" *Denni Hlasatel,* Apr. 14, 1917; "Czech Americans Respond: Mass Meeting Identifies Itself with Hopes of Old Homeland," *Denni Hlasatel,* June, 1917; "Echo of Enthusiasm: Demonstration of Loyalty," *Denni Hlasatel,* Dec. 12, 1917; "To the Czech-Americans," *Denni Hlasatel,* Apr. 17, 1917.

38. "Editorial," *Denni Hlasatel,* May, 1917; "More about Patriotic Fervor," *Denni Hlasatel,* Apr. 28,1917; "Czech-American Soldiers: Czech Volunteers Enlist in Gratifying Numbers for Service in the U.S. Army," *Denni Hlasatel,* Apr. 22, 1918, "From Sokol Camp to Soldiers' Camp," *Denni Hlasatel,* Apr. 22, 1917. See also *Denni Hlasatel* from Apr. to June, 1917.

39. "Warriors for the Cause," *Denni Hlasatel,* Oct. 3, 1917; "A Powerful Demonstration, Parade and Meeting Attract Thousands," *Denni Hlasatel,* Dec. 3, 1917.

40. Despite the decision to exclude enemy aliens from the American draft, men who had been born in lands under the control of the Central Powers continued to be called up due to misunderstandings and mistakes. See chapter 2 for details.

41. Edvard Benes, *In His Own Words: Threescore Years of a Statesman, Builder, and Philosopher,* p. 6; Thomas Garrigue Masaryk, *The Making of a State: Memories and Observations, 1914–1918,* pp. 21–25; Brackett Lewis, *Eyewitness Story of the Occupation of Samara, Russia, by the Czechoslovak Legion in June, 1918,* pp. 5–7.

42. "Slavs Carried Away by Patriotic Spirit: Enormous Crowds Meet in Behalf of Creation of a Czechoslovak Army for France," *Denni Hlasatel,* Oct. 15, 1917.

43. Ibid.; "To Our Czechoslovak Volunteers," *Denni Hlasatel,* Feb. 5, 1918; "Our Soldiers to Be Readmitted in America," *Denni Hlasatel,* Mar. 6, 1918.

44. "Chicago Bids Farewell to Czechoslovak Volunteers," *Denni Hlasatel,* Nov. 5, 1917.

45. "Go to Fight with the Allies: Czechoslovaks, Austrian Subjects, Get Permission

to Depart," *New York Times,* Aug. 9, 1918; "On Their way to France," *New York Times,* Jan. 6, 1918.

46. Masaryk, *Making of a State,* p. 206.

47. "A Message from the Czechoslovak Army Conveyed by its Officers," *Denni Hlasatel,* June 22, 1918; "Go to Fight with Allies," *New York Times,* Aug. 8, 1918, p. 5.

48. "Message from the Czechoslovak Army."

49. "A Map of the Czechoslovak State," *Denni Hlasatel,* July 18, 1918; "Our Volunteers' Farewell," *Denni Hlasatel,* Aug. 14, 1918; "Visits Slovaks in Camp: Prof. Masaryk Tells His Followers of Hopes in Allied Cause," *New York Times,* Sept. 8, 1918, p. 12.

50. "Czech and Slovak Recruitment Postcards," folder 152/151–158, Political Activity during World War I, The Balch Institute for Ethnic Studies, Philadelphia; *Second Report of the Provost Marshal,* pp. 104–207; "The Czechoslovak Military Mission," *Denni Hlasatel,* July 11, 1918.

51. "To Czechoslovak Physicians and Nurses: Join the Czechoslovak Army in Siberia!" *Denni Hlasatel,* Sept. 17, 1918; "More Work: Concerning the Czechoslav Aid Committee," *Denni Hlasatel,* Aug. 18, 1918.

52. "Furlough for Czechoslovak Soldiers," *Denni Hlasatel,* Sept. 14, 1918; "From the Czech Campaign Office," *Denni Hlasatel,* Oct. 9, 1918.

53. Benes, *War Memoirs,* p. 101.

54. Joseph T. Hapak, "Recruiting a Polish Army in the United States, 1917–1919," pp. 1–6.

55. Joseph A. Borkowski, *City of Pittsburgh's Part in Formation of Polish Army—World War I, 1917–1920,* pp. 3–26. Also see Polish organizational activities in the Campbell Collection, HSP.

56. Borkowski, *City of Pittsburgh's Part,* pp. 3–26; Hapak, "Recruiting a Polish Army," pp. 25–28.

57. Hapak, "Recruiting a Polish Army," pp. 55, 195.

58. Hapak, "Recruiting a Polish Army," pp. 6, 14–16, 24–28, 195; Borkowski, *City of Pittsburgh's Part,* pp. 13–14.

59. Hapak, "Recruiting a Polish Army," pp. 54–61, 66–74.

60. From the "Official Bulletin of the Committee on Public Information," quoted in ibid., p. 96.

61. Hapak, "Recruiting a Polish Army," pp. 9, 116–18; Borkowski, *City of Pittsburgh's Part,* pp. 15–20.

62. Hapak, "Recruiting a Polish Army," pp. 195, 2–7, 195–201, 141–53.

63. "Jews to Aid Recruiting: But Patriotic League Will Not Form a Separate Regiment," *New York Times,* Apr. 6, 1917, p. 8; "The Jews in the World War: A Study in Jewish Patriotism and Heroism," Miscellaneous Papers and Pamphlets, 1938–1950, Jewish War Veterans Papers, U.S.A.M.H.I.; "Austrian Jews Would Aid: Rabbi Buchler to Enlist Them for the Army and Navy." *New York Times,* Apr. 7, 1917, p. 6.

64. "The Jew is No Slacker," *Sunday Jewish Courier,* June 9, 1918.

65. "The Word and the Deed," *Daily Jewish Courier,* May 30, 1918; "The Critical Hour," *Sunday Jewish Courier,* Oct. 13, 1918.

66. "$50,000 in Palestine Fund: Meeting of Jews Discusses Drive for $1,000,000 for Restoration," *New York Times*, Mar. 1, 1918.
67. Vladimir Jabotinsky, *The Story of the Jewish Legion*, pp. 29, 30. See also J. H. Patterson, *With the Judeans in the Palestine Campaign* (New York: Macmillan, 1932). Lieutenant Colonel Patterson served as the commander of the Jewish Legion of Palestine.
68. Jabotinsky, *Story of the Jewish Legion*, p. 83.
69. "Jews Eager to Enlist: Enthusiasm at Recruiting Offices in Jerusalem and Jaffa," *New York Times*, Aug. 17, 1918, p. 4; Roman Freulich, *Soldiers in Judea: Stories and Vignettes of the Jewish Legion*, pp. 25–26.
70. Freulich, *Soldiers in Judea*, p. 30.
71. "Flag for Jewish Unit: Presented to Recruits Who Will Go to Palestine," *New York Times*, Mar. 21, 1918, p. 7. See also Elias Gilner, *War and Hope: A History of the Jewish Legion*, p. 165. Gilner served with other American Jews in the legion. Later he became the head of the American Palestine Jewish Legion Organization, which published the 1945 translation of Jabotinsky's book, *The Story of the Jewish Legion*. Gilner's memoirs include information from two other remembrances written in Hebrew and some personal records of Jabotinsky.
72. "Court House Crater Easy for British Tank," *New York Times*, Mar. 1, 1918; Freulich, *Soldiers in Judea*, p. 11; William Braiterman, "Memories of the Palestine Jewish Legion of 1917," (n.p.: Jewish Historical Society of Maryland, 1967), American Jewish Historical Society Archives, Waltham, Mass., p. 4; "The Fire beneath the Melting Pot," *Daily Jewish Courier*, June 5, 1918; Dr. S. M. Melamed, "Help America to Victory! Help the Jewish People to Victory!" *Sunday Jewish Courier*, Oct. 13, 1918.
73. Gilner, *War and Hope*, p. 166; see especially chapter 15, "The Volunteers from America."
74. Ibid., pp. 31, 32.
75. "Jews Join British Army: 200 from Here Enlist in Force to Go to Jerusalem," *New York Times*, Feb. 26, 1918, p. 13; "Zionist Soldiers Dined: Battalion Going to fight in Palestine is Honored," *New York Times*, Feb. 28, 1918, p. 5; "Jews in Palestine Service: Squad of 350 Sworn in at British-Canadian Recruiting Office," *New York Times*, Mar. 20, 1918, p 14; "Jewish Soldiers Depart: Detachment of 200 Who Are to Serve in Palestine Leave New York," *New York Times*, Mar. 22, 1918, p. 24; "Jewish Legionnaires from Chicago Arrive in London," *Daily Jewish Courier*, June 27, 1918; Freulich, *Soldiers in Judea*, p. 31.
76. "Greets Jewish Recruits: Lord Reading Telegraphs Best Wishes to British Battalion," *New York Times*, Mar. 5, 1918, p. 11; "Sabath's Second Foreign-Soldiers Bill Passes in Senate," *Daily Jewish Courier*, June 20, 1918; "Boost Jewish Recruiting: British Mission and Heads of Zionist Organizations Join Forces," *New York Times*, Aug. 24, 1918, p. 14.
77. Braiterman, "Memories," p. 5; Address of Mr. M. Newman, chairman, Palestine Jewish Legion given at the Jewish War Veterans of the United States National Headquarters, Aug. 29, 1940, "Releases—National Affairs—Other Groups," 1940, Jewish War Veterans Papers, U.S.A.M.H.I.; Jabotinsky, *Story of the Jewish*

Legion, pp. 103–104, 164; "The Jews in the World War," Jewish War Veterans of the United States, Miscellaneous Papers and Pamphlets, 1938–1950, Jewish War Veterans Papers; Address of Mr. M. Newman.

78. Jabotinsky, *Story of the Jewish Legion*, pp. 121, 124, 164–65; Braiterman, "Memories," p. 6; Gilner, *War and Hope*, pp. 170, 174.

79. Jabotinsky, *Story of the Jewish Legion*, p. 182.

80. Office of the Chief of Staff, rpt. 13549, July 14, 1917, WDGSS RG 165, N.A.

81. Ibid., rpt. 14773, Jan. 4, 1918, WDGSS RG 165, N.A.

82. Office of the Chief of Staff, rpt. 14099, Oct. 16, 1917, WDGSS RG 165, N.A.

83. "War," Campbell Collection, HSP; *Philadelphia in the World War, 1914–1919*, pp. 16–45; Charles V. Vickrey, American Committee for Armenian and Syrian Relief, to Raymond C. Fosdick [hereafter Fosdick], CTCA 39804, WDGSS; Mrs. Mary Hatch Willard, chairman, America's Allies Co-operative Committed, to R. Mornhinveg, CTCA 42745, WDGSS.

84. "German Propaganda among Lithuanians," *Lietuva*, Sept. 17, 1918; Bodnar, *Remaking America*, p. 57.

85. Division of Four-Minute Men, *Meaning of America*, pp. 4, 15.

Chapter 2. Drafting Foreign-born Doughboys into the American Army

1. Weigley, *United States Army*, pp. 3–44.

2. John Whiteclay Chambers II, *To Raise an Army: The Draft Comes to Modern America*, pp. 21–22.

3. Charles Patrick Neimeyer, *America Goes to War: A Social History of the Continental Army*, pp. 160, 27–64. Martin quoted in Neimeyer, *America Goes to War*, pp. 197–98.

4. James B. Jacobs and Leslie Anne Hayes, "Aliens in the U.S. Armed Forces: A Historico-Legal Analysis," *Armed Forces and Society* 7 (winter, 1981): 188, 191.

5. Chambers, *To Raise an Army*, p. 34; Jacobs and Hayes, "Aliens in the U.S. Armed Forces," p. 190.

6. Chambers, *To Raise an Army*, pp. 35–38. Weigley, *United States Army*, p. 168.

7. Chambers, *To Raise an Army*, pp. 51, 59; Jacobs and Hayes, "Aliens in the U.S. Armed Forces," p. 192.

8. Jacobs and Hayes, "Aliens in the U.S. Armed Forces," p. 192; Weigley, *United States Army*, pp. 205, 208–10, 212. "Declarant alien" was the term used for any immigrant who had filed official papers proclaiming the intention to become a U.S. citizen after fulfilling the residency requirements. A "nondeclarant" was one who had not filed papers of citizenship intention.

9. Chambers, *To Raise an Army*, p. 41.

10. Jacobs and Hayes, "Aliens in the U.S. Armed Forces," pp. 188–89; Chambers, *To Raise an Army*, p. 51.

11. Chambers, *To Raise an Army*, pp. 49, 59; Jacobs and Hayes, "Aliens in the U.S Armed Forces," p. 190; William L. Burton, *Melting Pot Soldiers: The Union's Ethnic Regiments*, p. 51.

12. Chambers, *To Raise an Army*, p. 10; Jacobs and Hayes, "Aliens in the U.S. Armed

Forces," p. 188; Weigley, *United States Army*, pp. 296–97. National citizenship was defined under the 14th Amendment to the U.S. Constitution in 1868.

13. Chambers, *To Raise an Army*, p. 11; Weigley, *United States Army*, pp. 356–58.
14. Weigley, *United States Army*, p. 357.
15. *Second Report of the Provost Marshal*, p. 88. Officially, the term "alien" applied to "any person not a native-born or naturalized citizen of the United States; but did not include Indians of the United States not taxed or citizens of the islands under the jurisdiction of the United States." *United States Statutes at Large* 39 (1917): 874.
16. *Second Report of the Provost Marshal*, pp. 86–88; "Alien Citizenship and the Draft," *Infantry Journal* 15, no. 4 (Oct., 1918): 323.
17. Quoted in Chambers, *To Raise an Army*, p. 227.
18. Statements from major newspapers quoted in "To Draft Aliens," *The Literary Digest* 55 (Sept. 29, 1917): 14. Additional quotes can be found in "To Get the Alien Slacker," *The Literary Digest* 55 (Aug. 4, 1917): 22.
19. *Second Report of the Provost Marshal*, p. 94.
20. Ibid., pp. 93–94; Chambers, *To Raise an Army*, pp. 115, 129, 161, 208–209.
21. U.S. House Military Affairs Committee, *Drafting Aliens into Military Service, Hearings*, 65th Cong., 1st sess., Sept. 26, 1917, pp. 22, 1–43.
22. Ibid., pp. 6–8, 1–16.
23. Ibid., pp. 12, 1–16, 4–5, 1–16.
24. *Second Report of the Provost Marshal*, p. 93.
25. Ibid., pp. 96, 94–95.
26. Ibid., p. 81; "Amending Naturalization Laws," *Army and Navy Journal* (Apr. 20, 1918): 1274, *Second Report of the Provost Marshal*, pp. 96–97.
27. *Second Report of the Provost Marshal*, pp. 97–98; *Final Report of the Provost Marshal*, pp. 26–27, table 5.
28. *Second Report of the Provost Marshal*, pp. 97–98; *Final Report of the Provost Marshal*, pp. 26–27, table 5.
29. *General Orders and Bulletins*, General Order No. 91, Oct. 16, 1918 (Washington, D.C., 1919), pp. 1–3; *Second Report of the Provost Marshal*, pp. 98–99.
30. *Final Report of the Provost Marshal*, pp. 26–27, table 5; *Second Report of the Provost Marshal*, p. 99.
31. *Second Report of the Provost Marshal*, pp. 99–100; "Alien Citizenship and the Draft," p. 323; *Second Report of the Provost Marshal*, pp. 99–102.
32. *Second Report of the Provost Marshal*, p. 104; "Everyone Should Keep His Place," *Denni Hlasatel*, July 24, 1917.
33. *Second Report of the Provost Marshal*, p. 104; confidential memorandum from the Adjutant General, General Headquarters, American Expeditionary Forces, to Commanding General, 77th Division, July 17, 1918, 77th Division Records, WDOR RG 120, N.A.; the Adjutant General of the Army to the Commanding Generals of all departments, camps, and divisions in the United States, the Commanding Generals of the ports of embarkation, and the Commanding General, American Expeditionary Forces, July 15, 1918, Bulletin 284, 77th Division Records, WDOR.

34. E. H. Crowder, Adjutant General of the Army, to all department, division, and independent station commanders, Feb. 15, 1918, Dec. File 006.061.1 9, 29th Division Records, WDOR.

35. "Czech Soldiers, Editorial," *Denni Hlasatel*, Aug. 25, 1917. See also "Czech America Do Thy Duty!" *Denni Hlasatel*, Apr. 7, 1917; "Committee Reports on Enlistments," *Denni Hlasatel*, Apr. 11, 1917; "To All American Czechs and Slovaks!" *Denni Hlasatel*, Apr. 11, 1917; "Recruiting in Progress," *Denni Hlasatel*, Apr. 13, 1917; "Let's Do Our Duty!" *Denni Hlasatel*, Apr. 14, 1917; and "Czechs in the Army," *Denni Hlasatel*, Aug. 25, 1917.

36. *Second Report of the Provost Marshal*, pp. 104–105.

37. "'Foreign Legion Companies," *Infantry Journal* 15, no. 3 (Sept., 1918): 252–54.

38. "Aliens Who Seek Exemption from Military Service," *Denni Hlasatel*, Jan. 2, 1918.

39. *Second Report of the Provost Marshal*, pp. 104, 105; "Proclamation of Czechoslovak Independence by U.S. Government," *Denni Hlasatel*, Sept. 14, 1918; "Registration of Czechoslovaks," *Denni Hlasatel*, Sept. 17, 1918.

40. *Second Report of the Provost Marshal*, p. 105.

41. War Department memorandum to camp commanding officers, Mar. 4, 1918, 105654–26/1, MID-WDGS RG 165, N.A.; memo, Maj. Gen. William E. Bergin to President, Army Discharge Review Board, Oct. 16, 1953, Legislative and Policy Precedent Files, 1943–75, AGO Records RG 407, N.A.; item, Feb. 2, 1918, 10565–81/6, MID-WDGS; Office of the Chief of Staff, rpt. 14645, Jan. 2, 1918, WDGSS RG 165, N.A.

42. "Ethnic Bulletin: Austrian-born Solders Serving in the U.S. Army," undated (filed on Apr. 15, 1919), 10565–110/28, MID-WDGS. Internal evidence clearly indicates that the bulletin was distributed prior to the end of the war, since a number of references are made to "the war in progress."

43. Brig. Gen. Marlborough Churchill [hereafter Churchill], chief, Military Intelligence Branch, to Adjutant General of the Army, June 20, 1918, 10438–24/1, MID-WDGS; Mitchell Yockelson, "The Ghosts of Ft. Oglethorpe," *North Georgia Journal* 14, no. 2 (summer, 1997): 57, 54–58.

44. The Jugoslav National Council to the Secretary of War, Aug. 31, 1918, 10565–487a, MID-WDGS; memorandum on the Slavic Legion, Sept. 24, 1918, 10565–500/5, MID-WDGS; Hapak, "Recruiting a Polish Army," p. 51.

45. War Department, General Order No. 91 (Washington, D.C.: Oct. 5, 1918), pp. 1–4; memorandum, Churchill to the Adjutant General, Nov. 13, 1918, 10565–501/8, MID-WDGS; "To All American Czechs and Slovaks!" *Denni Hlasatel*, Apr. 11, 1917; "Committee Reports on Enlistment," *Denni Hlasatel*, Apr. 11, 1917; "Recruiting in Progress," *Denni Hlasatel*, Apr. 13, 1917; to C.O. 1st Prov. Co., Slavic Legion, "Roster of Officers and Enlisted Men, assigned and attached to 1st Prov. Company, Slavic Legion," Sept. 25, 1918, 1st Provisional Company, Slavic Legion Organizational File, 27th Division Records, WDOR. The number of men and officers changed over time, and some records indicate 113 men and eighteen officers.

46. *Second Report of the Provost Marshal*, p. 101.

47. Office of the Chief of Staff, memorandum no. 79, May 21, 1918, 77th Division Records, WDOR.

48. War Department, Bulletin 28 (Washington, D.C.: May 18, 1918), pp. 1–8; War Department, General Order No. 151 (Washington, D.C.: Sept. 9, 1918), p. 1; *Second Report of the Provost Marshal*, p. 101.

49. War Department, General Order No. 151, pp. 1–2; War Department, General Order No. 74 (Washington, D.C.: Aug. 14, 1918), p. 1; War Department, Bulletin 68 (Washington, D.C.: Sept. 9, 1918), pp. 1–5; War Department, Bulletin 28, pp. 1–8; *Second Report of the Provost Marshal*, pp. 101–104.

50. Roger Baldwin to Embassy of the Netherlands, Nov. 16, 1917, Conscientious Objectors file, American Civil Liberties Cases, 1917–18, Seeley G. Mudd Manuscript Library, Princeton University, vol. 15, roll 2 (microfilm); Netherlands Minister to Roger Baldwin, Nov. 19, 1917, Conscientious Objectors file, American Civil Liberties Cases, vol. 15, roll 2 (microfilm).

51. Morris Tasken, 154 Depot Brigade, Camp Meade, to the National Civil Liberties Bureau, Jan. 7, 1918, Conscientious Objectors file, American Civil Liberties Cases, vol. 10, roll 2 (microfilm); William M. Kantor, 154 Depot Brigade, Camp Meade to Mr. [Roger] Baldwin, Feb. 7, 1918, Conscientious Objectors file, American Civil Liberties Cases, vol. 10, roll 2 (microfilm); Roger Baldwin to Frederick P. Keppel, Feb. 12, 1918, Conscientious Objectors file, American Civil Liberties Cases, vol. 10, roll 2 (microfilm).

52. Roger Baldwin to Honorable Joseph P. Tumulty, Oct. 11, 1917, Conscientious Objectors file, American Civil Liberties Cases, vol. 19, roll 3 (microfilm); Joseph P. Tumulty to Roger Baldwin, Oct. 13, 1917, Conscientious Objectors file, American Civil Liberties Cases, vol. 19, roll 3 (microfilm).

Chapter 3. The Camp Gordon Plan

1. "Eradicating Illiteracy in the Army," *Infantry Journal* 17, no. 4 (Oct., 1920): 353; Willis Fletcher Johnson, "Students at Camp Upton," *North American Review* 211 (Jan., 1920): 47; Frederick Harris, *Service with Fighting Men: An Account of the Work of the American Young Men's Christian Association in the World War*, vol. 1, p. 344.

2. Padgett, "Camp Gordon Plan," p. 334; "Making Americans of Alien Soldiers: By Method Known as Camp Gordon Plan," *Trench and Camp*, Camp Devens, no. 16 (Sept. 25, 1918); Johnson, "Students at Camp Upton," p. 47. The number of immigrants in the military after the first draft (76,545) comes from Bidwell, *Military Intelligence Division*, p. 185.

3. "'Foreign Legion' Companies," *Infantry Journal* 15, no. 3 (Sept., 1918): 252; Extract from M.I.3 Bulletin 17, "'Foreign Legion' Companies," July 15, 1918, 10565–414, MID-WDGS RG 165, N.A.; James J. Cooke, *The All-Americans at War: The 82nd Division in the Great War, 1917–1918*, pp. viii, 17.

4. "Making Americans of Alien Soldiers," *Trench and Camp*, Camp Devens, no. 16 Sept. 25, 1918); "'Foreign Legion' Companies," pp. 252–54; "Camp Gordon Plan," pp. 334–40; "Foreign-Speaking Officers," *Infantry Journal* 15, no. 5 (Nov.,

1918): 436; "The Camp Gordon Plan," p. 437; William Howard Taft, *Service with Fighting Men: An Account of the Work of the American Young Men's Christian Association in the World War*, vol. 1, p. 344.

5. Brig. Gen. Marlborough Churchill [hereafter Churchill], director, Military Intelligence Division, to Intelligence Officer, Camp Beauregard, Louisiana, Nov. 6, 1918, 10565–562, MID-WDGS; Churchill, memorandum for the Chief of Staff, "Extract from Confidential Bulletin No. 17," July 17, 1918, 10565–414/1, MID-WDGS. The military used the term "races" when referring to the various ethnic and racial groups.

6. G. J. A. O'Toole, *The Encyclopedia of American Intelligence and Espionage: From the Revolutionary War to the Present*, pp. 461–63.

7. Col. R. H. Van Deman [hereafter Van Deman.], chief, Military Intelligence Branch, to Mr. John J. Coss, State War and Navy Building, Mar. 6, 1918, 10565–111/4, MID-WDGS; Higham, *Strangers in the Land*, pp. 236, 237–39; NACL quoted in John F. McClymer, *War and Welfare: Social Engineering in America, 1890–1925*, p. 110.

8. Discussed later in extract from M.I. 3 Bulletin 17, "'Foreign Legion' Companies," July 15, 1918; Foreign-speaking Soldier Subsection, "Camp Gordon Plan," Sept. 7, 1918, CTCA 40824, WDGSS RG 165, N.A.

9. Lt. Stanislaw A. Gutowski [hereafter Gutowski], "Report on the Observations in Camp Devens, Massachusetts," Dec. 28, 1917, CTCA 15667, WDGSS, p. 1.

10. Ibid.

11. "Officers from Various Camps to Meade to Observe and Assist with Development Battalions," Sept. 6, 1918. 10565–525/6, MID-WDGS.

12. Ibid.

13. Gutowski to D. Chauncy Brewer [hereafter Brewer], Feb. 1, 1918, 10564–17/4, MID-WDGS; Lt. F. Swietlik, assistant acting division intelligence officer, to Chief, Military Intelligence Section, Mar. 4, 1918, 10564–26/1, MID-WDGS.

14. Gutowski to Brewer, Feb. 1, 1918; Major Crawford, acting intelligence officer, to Van Deman, Jan. 24, 1918, 10565–85, MID-WDGS.

15. Charles C. T. Lull, Headquarters 86th Division, to Van Deman, G.S.C., War College Division, Feb. 26, 1918, 10565–110/2, MID-WDGS. For a description of camps see World War I Training Camp Index, N.A.

16. Brewer to Henry S. Drinker, principal, Lehigh University, Feb. 7, 1918, and Feb. 11, 1918, 10565–112, MID-WDGS; Capt. Eugene C. Bryan, intelligence officer, Camp Gordon, Georgia, to Chief, Military Intelligence Branch, 10565–110/12, MID-WDGS.

17. Gutowski, "Report on the Observations in Camp Devens."

18. Raymond C. Fosdick [hereafter Fosdick], memorandum for Dr. Keppel, Apr. 5, 1918, and Keppel to Fosdick, Apr. 8, 1918, CTCA 36779, WDGSS; Brewer to Fosdick, May 7, 1918, CTCA 27894, WDGSS.

19. Capt. George B. Perkins [hereafter Perkins] and Lt. Herbert A. Horgan [hereafter Horgan] to Camp Commanders, Aug. 9, 1918, 80–55/1, MID-WDGS; Bidwell, *Military Intelligence Division*, p. 185; Churchill to Camp Commanders, Oct. 22, 1918, 10564–587/4, MID-WDGS.

20. O'Toole, *Encyclopedia,* p. 114; *The United States in the First World War,* (New York: Garland Publishing, 1995), p. 148.

21. "Perkins, Grafton Brookhouse," and "Horgan, Herbert A.," Commission Records, National Army, First World War Commission Records, N.A.

22. War Department, General Order 45, May, 1918, CTCA, WDGSS RG 165, N.A. Correspondence discussing plans for the development battalions include: Brig. Gen. Henry Jervey, acting assistant chief of staff, memorandums for the Adjutant General, Apr. 17, 1918, CTCA, WDGSS; Jervey, memorandum for the Executive Assistant to the Chief of Staff, May 17, 1918, CTCA, WDGSS; Col. Lutz Wahl, chair, Operations Branch, memorandum for the Chief of Staff, Apr., 6, 1918, CTCA, WDGSS.

23. Churchill, memorandum for the Chief of Staff: "Extract from Confidential Bulletin No. 17," July 17, 1918, 10565–414/1, MID-WDGS; "'Foreign Legion' Companies," pp. 252–54; "Camp Gordon Plan," pp. 334–40; "Foreign-Speaking Officers," p. 436; "Camp Gordon Plan," p. 437; General Order No. 45, May 9, 1918; Perkins and Horgan to Col. Harry Cutler, Jewish Welfare Board, Aug. 5, 1918, 10565–533, MID-WDGS, N.A.

24. Padgett, "Camp Gordon Plan," p. 336.

25. Extract from M.I. 3 Bulletin 17, "'Foreign Legion' Companies," July 15, 1918; "Foreign-Speaking Officers," p. 436; Padgett, "Camp Gordon Plan," p. 334.

26. Gutowski to Perkins, Aug. 17, 1918, 10565–559/7, MID-WDGS; extract from M.I. 3 Bulletin 17, "'Foreign Legion' Companies," July 15, 1918; Churchill to Chief of Staff, Camp Meade, Maryland, Aug. 14, 1918, 10565–495/7, MID-WDGS; "Foreign-Speaking Officers," p. 436.

27. E. G. Moyer, intelligence officer, Camp Gordon, Georgia, to Acting Director, Military Intelligence Division, "Report on Past Activities," Jan. 23, 1919, 10565–515/21, MID-WDGS; extract from M.I. 3 Bulletin 17, "'Foreign Legion' Companies," July 15, 1918; Churchill, "Extract from Confidential Bulletin No. 17," July 17, 1918; "Foreign-Speaking Officers," p. 436.

28. Capt. Eugene C. Bryan, intelligence officer, Camp Gordon, Georgia, to Perkins, MID memorandum 10930–22/1, July 22, 1918, MID-WDGS; Perkins to Capt. Ernest J. Hall, intelligence officer, Camp Devens, Massachusetts, Aug. 6, 1918, 10565–512/3, MID-WDGS; Churchill, memorandum for the Chief of Staff, Aug. 6, 1918, 10565–515, MID-WDGS.

29. FSS memorandum, July 22, 1918, 10930–22/1, MID-WDGS.

30. Capt. E. R. Padgett, to Perkins, Sept. 6, 1918, 10565–581, MID-WDGS.

31. FSS memorandum, Aug. 30, 1918, 10565–506/8, MID-WDGS; "Foreign-Speaking Officers," p. 436; Churchill, "Extract from Confidential Bulletin No. 17," July 17, 1918; Office, Chief of Staff, Executive Division, memorandum for Captain Hale, Aug. 14, 1918, 10565–559/11, MID-WDGS.

32. Perkins and Horgan to Miss Edith Terry Bremer, Sept. 9, 1918, 10565–532, MID-WDGS; Perkins to Fosdick, Sept. 9, 1918, 10565–501G/29, MID-WDGS; Gutowski to Perkins, Aug. 17, 1918, 10565–559, MID-WDGS; Horgan to Gutowski, Nov. 1, 1918, 10565–110/21, MID-WDGS.

33. Perkins to Fosdick, Sept. 9, 1918; Gutowski to Perkins, Aug. 17, 1918; Horgan to

Gutowski, Nov. 1, 1918; Churchill, memorandum for the Chief of Staff, Aug. 24, 1918, 10565–517/16, MID-WDGS; Churchill to Maj. A. J. Deering, Oct. 28, 1918, 10565–525/7, MID-WDGS; Horgan, memorandum for Captain Hale, Aug. 27, 1918, 10565–559/12, MID-WDGS; Churchill to Chief of Staff, Camp Meade, Maryland, Aug. 14, 1918, 10565–495/7, MID-WDGS.

34. Louis Zara to Churchill, "Personal Report and Statement of Preferences for Reserve Officers," Nov. 1, 1918, 10565–512/23, MID-WDGS; Churchill to Commanding General, Camp Dix, New Jersey, Nov. 8, 1918, 10565–525/29, MID-WDGS; Col. John M. Dunn, acting director of military intelligence, to Commanding General, Camp Devens, Massachusetts, Nov. 6, 1918, 10565–472, MID-WDGS.

35. Churchill, memorandum for the Adjutant General of the Army from the War Department, Aug. 31, 1918, 10565–465, MID-WDGS.

36. Ibid.

37. Horgan, memorandum for Captain Hale, Aug. 27, 1918, 10565–559/12, MID-WDGS; Perkins and Horgan to intelligence officer, Camp MacArthur, Texas, Sept. 4, 1918, 10565–520/1, MID-WDGS.

38. Ibid.

39. Perkins to Chief of Staff, Camp Meade, Maryland, Aug. 14, 1918, 10565–495/7, MID-WDGS; Brig. Gen. Henry Jervey, assistant chief of staff, memorandum for the Chief, Military Intelligence Branch, Aug. 26, 1918, 10565–414/37, MID-WDGS; Perkins and Horgan to John Kliniewski, Sept. 4, 1918, 10–565–4927, MID-WDGS; Churchill to Major Dearing, Camp Meade, Maryland, Sept. 10, 1918, 10435–77, MID-WDGS; memorandum, Oct. 17, 1918, 10565–446, MID-WDGS; War Department, Special Order No. 225 [enclosure], Sept. 25, 1918, 10565–472, MID-WDGS.

40. Horgan, memorandum for Captain Hale, Aug. 27, 1918, 10565–559/12, MID-WDGS; Intelligence Officer, auxiliary units, Camp Devens, Massachusetts, to Chief, Military Intelligence Branch, July 22, 1918, 10565–414/9, MID-WDGS; Perkins to Intelligence Officer, Camp Devens, Massachusetts, Aug. 20, 1918, 10565–512/12, MID-WDGS; Churchill to Chief of Staff, Camp Devens, Massachusetts, (telegram) Aug. 23, 1918, Aug. 23, 1918, 10565–512/8, MID-WDGS; Intelligence Officer, auxiliary units, Camp Devens, Massachusetts, to Chief, Military Intelligence Branch, July 22, 1918, 10565–414/9, MID-WDGS.

41. Horgan, memorandum for Captain Hale, Aug. 27, 1918, 10565–559/12, MID-WDGS; Perkins to Intelligence Officer, Camp Upton, New York, Aug. 8, 1918, 10565–523/3, MID-WDGS.

42. Churchill to Lieutenant O'Connell, morale officer, Camp Dix, New Jersey, Oct. 28, 1918, 10565–514/25, MID-WDGS; Capt. J. Joseph Lilly, camp intelligence officer, Camp Dix, New Jersey, to Director of Military Intelligence, Nov. 9, 1918, 10565–111, MID-WDGS; Brig. Gen. E. L. Munson, General Staff, to Intelligence Officer, Camp Lee, Virginia, Oct. 16, 1918, 10565–517, MID-WDGS; Churchill to Commanding Generals, Camp Custer, Michigan; Camp Grant, Illinois; and Camp Dodge, Iowa, Oct. 30, 1918, 10565–468/1, MID-WDGS; Horgan to Gutowski, Nov. 12, 1918, 10565–110/25, MID-WDGS; Churchill to Lt. Felix

Mateia, Camp Gordon, Georgia, Nov. 11, 1918, 10565–601/1, MID-WDGS; Horgan to Gutowski, Sept. 7, 1918, 10565–110/27, MID-WDGS.

43. Perkins to Intelligence Officer, Camp Lee, Virginia, Oct. 3,1918, 10565–517/218, MID-WDGS; Warren Vanozne, secretary, Democratic State Committee, Pennsylvania, to Mr. T. A. Huntley, Oct. 3, 1918, 10565–517; Horgan, memorandum for Colonel Masteller, Nov., 1918, 10565–517/26, MID-WDGS; Horgan to Lt. E. C. Weiscz, Oct. 16, 1918, 10565–528, MID-WDGS.

44. Churchill to Intelligence Officer, Camp Sherman, Ohio, Nov. 8, 1918, 10565–582, MID-WDGS; Churchill to Intelligence Officer, Camp Taylor, Kentucky, Nov. 8, 1918, 10565–583/4, MID-WDGS.

45. Churchill, memorandum for the Chief of Staff, Nov. 11, 1918, 10565–524/9, MID-WDGS; Churchill to Capt. J. Mott Dahlgren, Camp Travis, Texas, Nov. 11, 1918, 10565–575/18, MID-WDGS; Churchill to Commanding Officer, Camp Wadsworth, South Carolina, Nov. 11,1918, 10565–524/8, MID-WDGS; Churchill to Commanding Officer, Camp Jackson, South Carolina, Nov. 12, 1918, 10565–573, MID-WDGS; Churchill to Commanding Officer, Camp Sevier, South Carolina, Nov. 12, 1918, 10565–580, MID-WDGS; Churchill to Commanding Officer, Camp Taylor, Kentucky, Nov. 1, 1918, 10565–525/18; Horgan to Gutowski, Nov. 1, 1918, 10565–110/21, MID-WDGS; Horgan to Gutowski, Nov. 12, 1918, 10565–110/25, MID-WDGS.

46. "Report of Aliens at Camp Gordon, Georgia," Oct. 15, 1918, 10565–515/11, MID-WDGS; Churchill to Intelligence Officer, Camp Gordon, Georgia, Nov. 1, 1918, 10565–515/18, MID-WDGS.

47. Correspondence regarding Kracha, Nov. 8, 1918, Jan. 20. 1919, Jan. 7, 1919, Jan. 13, 1919, and Mar. 14, 1919, 10565–471, MID-WDGS; and Oct. 28, 1918, Nov. 5, 1918, Nov. 16, 1918, and Jan. 13, 1919, 10565–466, MID-WDGS; Horgan to Gutowski, Nov. 12, 1918, 10565–110/25, MID-WDGS; Churchill to Lt. C. Walczynski, Nov. 13, 1918, 10565–470/5 MID-WDGS; Churchill, memorandum for the Director of Operations, Nov. 15, 1918, 10565–470/8, MID-WDGS.

48. Words by Billy Frisch and Archie Fletcher, music by Alex Mar, "When Tony Goes Over the Top," 1918.

49. Padgett, "Camp Gordon Plan," p. 335; "Making Americans of Alien Soldiers," *Trench and Camp*, Camp Devens, Sept. 25, 1918; "Foreign-Born Soldiers are Taught Language," *Trench and Camp*, Camp Kearny, July 24, 1918.

50. Horgan, memorandum for Captain Hale, Aug. 27, 1918, 10565–559/12, MID-WDGS; Perkins and Horgan to Intelligence Officer, Camp MacArthur, Texas, Sept. 4, 1918, 10565–520/1, MID-WDGS.

51. Padgett, "Camp Gordon Plan," p. 335.

52. "Camp Gordon Plan," Foreign-Speaking Soldier Sub-section, Sept. 7, 1918, CTCA 40824, WDGSS RG 165, N.A.

53. "'Foreign Legion'" Companies," p. 253; extract from M.I. 3 Bulletin 17, "'Foreign Legion' Companies," July 15, 1918; Perkins and Horgan to Col. Harry Cutler, Jewish Welfare Board, Sept. 9, 1918, 10565–533, MID-WDGS; memorandum, Nov. 7, 1918, 10565–584/4, MID-WDGS; memorandum, Nov. 12, 1918,

10565–577, MID-WDGS; 10565–414/1, Churchill, "Extract from Confidential Bulletin No. 17," July 17, 1918; memorandum, July 31, 1918, 10565–515, MID-WDGS.

54. Churchill, "Extract from Confidential Bulletin No. 17," July 17, 1918; memorandum, July 31, 1918, 10565–515, MID-WDGS.

55. Moyer to Acting Director, Military Intelligence Division, "Report on Past Activities," Jan. 23, 1919.

56. Weibe, *Search for Order,* p. viii; Churchill, "Extract from Confidential Bulletin No. 17," July 17, 1918; Padgett, "Camp Gordon Plan" p. 335; "The Camp Gordon Plan," p. 437; "'Foreign Legion' Companies," pp. 252–53.

Chapter 4. Military Moral Uplifting

1. "The Committee on Training Camp Activities Report," June, 1918, CTCA 33087, WDGSS RG 165, N.A., p. 1; Fosdick, *Chronicle of a Generation,* p. 143.

2. Fosdick, *Chronicle of a Generation,* p. 143.

3. Boyer, *Urban Masses,* p. 221.

4. *Weekly Training Program for U.S. Army Units,* pp. 1–10; *Handbook and Instructions to Enlisted Men; Infantry Drill Regulations* (New York: Army and Navy Journal, 1911).

5. "Commission on Training Camp Activities Report," June, 1918.

6. Donald Smythe, "Venereal Disease: The AEF's Experience," *Prologue* 9, no. 2 (summer, 1977): 66. This article provides an excellent account of the American fight against venereal disease in the American Expeditionary Forces.

7. "Commission on Training Camp Activities Report," June, 1918; Wood quoted in Smythe, "Venereal Disease," p. 66.

8. Palmer, *Newton D. Baker,* vol. 1, pp. 298, 297.

9. Raymond Fosdick [hereafter Fosdick], CTCA, to Brig. Gen. Edward L. Munson [hereafter Munson], Morale Section, undated, CTCA 44184, WDGSS, pp. 1–6.

10. Quoted in Boyer, *Urban Masses,* pp. 222, 194, 212, 220, 222; War and Navy Departments, *Commissions on Training Camp Activities* (Washington, DC: Government Printing Office, 1917), pp. 25–26.

11. *Commissions on Training Camp Activities,* pp. 18–24; "Memorandum Outlining the Various Activities," CTCA 44140, WDGSS; Fosdick, *Chronicle of a Generation,* pp. 145–46.

12. *Commissions on Training Camp Activities,* p. 20, RG 165, WDGSS, N.A.; Fosdick, *Chronicle of a Generation,* p. 147; Palmer, *Newton D. Baker,* p. 310.

13. "Report from Raymond B. Fosdick to Frederick P. Keppel," Feb. 7, 1919, CTCA, WDGSS, p. 22; "Memorandum Outline the Various Activities," CTCA 33140, WDGSS, p. 24.

14. Palmer, *Newton D. Baker,* 310; Fosdick, *Chronicle of a Generation,* p. 144; "Memorandum Outlining the Various Activities," CTCA 44140, WDGSS, p. 23.

15. *History of the Seventy-Seventh Division,* p. 14; CTCA, "Report from Raymond B. Fosdick to Frederick P. Keppel," Feb. 7, 1919, p. 5.

16. *Commissions on Training Camp Activities,* pp. 1–31; Raymond R. Fosdick testimony in U.S. House Committee on Military Affairs, *Hearings before the Committee on*

Military Affairs, Camp Activities (Washington, D.C.: Government Printing Office, Mar. 14, 1918), pp. 1–21; Boyer, *Urban Masses*, p. 242.

17. YMCA, "Report from the War Camp Community Service," CTCA, WDGSS; *Commissions on Training Camp Activities*, 31; "Commission on Training Camp Activities," p. 31; YMCA, "Report from the War Camp Community Service," pp. 3–6.

18. YMCA, "Report from the War Camp Community Service," pp. 3–6, 31.

19. Ibid., pp. 6–8; "Report from Playground and Recreation Association of America," Dec., 1917, CTCA 27333, WDGSS; "Memorandum Outlining the Various Activities," CTCA 44140, WDGSS.

20. Quoted in Boyer, *Urban Masses*, p. 110.

21. Harris, *Service with Fighting Men*, pp. 94, 103.

22. *Commissions on Training Camp Activities*, pp. 25–26; "Fosdick Testimony," *Hearings before the Committee on Military Affairs*, pp. 1–21.

23. *Commissions on Training Camp Activities*, pp. 25–26.

24. Anna V. Rice, *A History of the World's Young Women's Christian Association*, pp. 36–49. "Report from Katharine Scott, National War Work Council, YWCA, to Major Jason S. Joy," CTCA, WDGSS, p. 29.

25. "Report from Katharine Scott," pp. 3, 44.

26. Ibid., pp. 1–4, 19, 29, 32, 29–30.

27. Ibid., p. 17; Dr. Katharine B. David, "How Women Can Cooperate with the Government in Carrying out its Educational Program For Combating Vice and Disease" [speech], CTCA 41533, WDGSS, pp. 1–2.

28. David, "How Women Can Cooperate," pp. 1–2; "Report from Katharine Scott," pp. 17–18, 37–40; Taft, *Service with Fighting Men*, vol. 1, p. 94.

29. Taft, *Service with Fighting Men*, vol. 1, p. 29.

30. "Books not Desirable for Camp Libraries" [undated attachment to a memorandum dated Aug. 13, 1918], 10175–582/14, MID-WDGS RG 165, N.A; Capt. G. B. Perkins [hereafter Perkins], chief, Military Morale Section, to Library War Service, Sept. 6, 1918, 10175–582/24, MID-WDGS; *Commission on Training Camp Activities*, pp. 7–9, 25–26; "Memorandum Outlining the Various Activities," CTCA 44140, WDGSS, p. 21; "The War Department Goes to Work," *The War Cry*, May 5, 1917, p. 9; "Salvation Army Officer Holds Meeting in Front Line Trenches," *The War Cry*, p. 4.

31. *Commissions on Training Camp Activities*, p. 6; "Fosdick Testimony," *Hearings before the Committee on Military Affairs*, pp. 1–21, 13; "Memorandum on Present Situation of the Commission on Training Camp Activities," CTCA 44124, WDGSS, p. 2.

32. Capt. Eugene C. Bryan, Camp Gordon, to Perkins and Lt. Herbert A. Horgan [hereafter Horgan], July 22, 1918, 10930–22/1, MID-WDGS; Capt. Frank Glick, athletic aide to commanding general, to Robert Edgren, *New York Evening World*, Mar. 21, 1918, 77th Division Records, WDOR RG 120, N.A.

33. CTCA, *Camp Music Division of the War Department*, (Washington D.C.: Government Printing Office, 1919), pp. 9–10, 43. See also Raymond Fosdick Papers, Seeley G. Mudd Manuscripts Library, Princeton University.

34. "Memorandum Outlining the Various Activities," CTCA 44140, WDGSS, pp. 9–10.
35. Greene, *American Immigrant Leaders*, p. 13. See also Higham, *Ethnic Leadership.*
36. *Keeping Fit to Fight* (New York: The War Department, Commission on Training Camp Activities, Prepared by the American Social Hygiene Association, undated), CTCA 26204, WDGSS, pp. 3, 4.
37. *Keeping Fit to Fight*, pp. 5–6; American Association of Foreign Language Newspapers to War Department Committee on Training Camp Activities, May 3, 1918, CTCA 33061, WDGSS; American Association of Foreign Language Newspapers to War Department Commission on Training Camp Activities, June 22, 1918, CTCA 27385, WDGSS; Perkins and Horgan to Commission on Training Camp Activities, May 22, 1918, CTCA 30038, WDGSS; Perkins and Horgan to Lt. Walter Clarke [hereafter Clarke], director, Social Hygiene Section, July 17, 1918, 10565–501G/42, MID-WDGS.
38. Perkins and Horgan to Clarke, Social Hygiene Division, July 30, 1918, CTCA 36669, WDGSS; Perkins and Horgan to Clarke, July 30, 1918, CTCA 36669B, WDGSS; Perkins and Horgan to Clarke, Aug. 9, 13, 29, Sept. 6, 1918, CTCA 36820, WDGSS; correspondence with the American Association of Foreign Language Newspapers, Aug. 21, 1918, 10565–533/1, MID-WDGS; correspondence with the American Association of Foreign Language Newspapers, Aug. 24, 1918, 10565–495A/13, MID-WDGS.
39. Perkins and Horgan to Intelligence Officer, Camp Meade, Aug. 12, 1918, 10565–495A, MID-WDGS; Perkins to Clarke, July 30, 1918, 10565–501/8, MID-WDGS; memorandum, Aug. 20, 1918, 10565–501/12, MID-WDGS; memorandum, Aug. 24, 1918, 10565–495/13, WDGSS.
40. Perkins and Horgan to Clarke, Mar. 8, 1918, CTCA 26147, WDGSS; Perkins and Horgan to Clarke, July 30, 1918, CTCA 36669B, WDGSS; Clarke to Lieutenant Long, Aug. 13, 1918, CTCA 36819, WDGSS.
41. Perkins and Horgan to Clarke, July 30, 1918, CTCA 36669B, WDGSS; Perkins and Horgan to Clarke, Aug. 9, 13, 29, Sept. 6, 1918, CTCA 36820, WDGSS; Perkins and Horgan to Jewish Welfare Board, Aug. 21, 1918, 10565–533/1, MID-WDGS; Perkins to Intelligence Officers, Camp Meade, Aug. 24, 1918, 10565–495A/13, MID-WDGS; undated memorandums, 10565–455 to 460, MID-WDGS; memorandum, Jan. 26, 1918, 10565–81/2, MID-WDGS; Perkins to Camp Intelligence Officer, Camp Meade, Aug. 24, 1918, 10565–495/12, MID-WDGS; "Social Hygiene Lectures in Foreign-languages," Sept. 4, 1918, CTCA 38349, WDGSS; Royce R. Long, assistant director, Army Section, Social Hygiene Division, to Capt. J. E. Preucel, Coastal Defenses, and Capt. William Summerall, base hospital, Camp Wheeler, Georgia, Sept. 11, 1918, CTCA 38343, WDGSS; Capt. Frank J. Maha, Camp Greenleaf, Georgia, to Army Section, Social Hygiene Division, Sept. 8, 1918, CTCA 39234, WDGSS.
42. *The Girl You Leave behind You*, CTCA 35095, WDGSS; Perkins and Horgan to Joseph Spano, Oct. 5, 1918, 10565–91/49, MID-WDGS; Perkins to Erich Bernhard, Oct. 5, 1918, 10565–121/41, MID-WDGS.
43. Correspondence between the Illinois Vigilance Association and Clarke, Feb. 28, and Mar. 18, 1918, CTCA 26203 and CTCA 18190, WDGSS; Perkins and Horgan

to Eric Bernhard, Sept. 28, 1918, 10565–121/40, MID-WDGS; Perkins and Horgan to Clarke, Sept. 17, 1918, 10565–501/23, MID-WDGS.

44. Perkins and Horgan to Clarke, Sept. 17, 1918, 10565–501/23, MID-WDGS, pp. 33, 8, 18.

45. YMCA, "Report from the War Camp Community Service," p. 34.

46. Perkins to YWCA [attn: Miss Justine Klotz], New York, July 30, 1918, 10565–532/1, MID-WDGS, pp. 34, 44; Dr. Justine Klotz, Special Worker, Division on Work for Foreign-Born Women, to Perkins, Aug. 12, 1918, 10565–532/2, MID-WDGS.

47. Perkins to Mrs. H. W. Bremer, Division on Work for Foreign-Born Women, YWCA, New York, Aug. 22, 1918, 10565–532, MID-WDGS; Brig. Gen. M. Churchill [hereafter Churchill], director of military intelligence, to Mr. Vincent G. Parisi, Headquarters, Prov. Depot, Camp Wadsworth, South Carolina, Oct. 31, 1918, 10565–218, MID-WDGS; D. Chauncy Brewer [hereafter Brewer], in charge of the Foreign-speaking Soldier Subsection, to Acting Division Intelligence Officer, 76th Division, Camp Devens, Massachusetts, May 15, 1918, 10565–239/2, MID-WDGS; Mrs. M. Abby Staunton Shafroth, Camp and Community Service, Division on Work for Foreign-born Women, to Horgan, Sept. 11, 1918, 10565–532, MID-WDGS.

48. YMCA, "Report from the War Camp Community Service," p. 34.

49. Perkins to Fosdick, July 16, 1918, CTCA 37905, WDGSS, p. 3.

50. Ameen Rihani to Horgan, Aug. 30, 1918, 10565–500B, MID-WDGS; Perkins and Horgan to John R. Mott, War Work Council, Sept. 5, 1918, 10565–531, MID-WDGS; Perkins and Horgan to John R. Mott, Aug. 30, 1918, 10565–531/15, MID-WDGS; Horgan, liaison memorandum, YMCA, July 31, 1918, 10565–531, MID-WDGS; Brig. Gen. E. L. Munson, chief, Morale Branch, to Prof. Ernest H. Wilkins, director, Bureau of Education, YMCA, Oct. 16, 1918, 10565–539, MID-WDGS; Churchill, to Mr. C. A. Vyshla, Oct. 24, 1918, 10565–461, MID-WDGS.

51. Quoted in Christopher J. Kauffman, *Faith and Fraternalism: The History of the Knights of Columbus,* p. 214.

52. Kauffman, *Faith and Fraternalism,* p. 213; Michael Williams, *American Catholics in the War: National Catholic War Council, 1917–1921,* p. 395; Kauffman, *Faith and Fraternalism,* pp. 217, 230; "Memorandum Outlining the Various Activities," CTCA 44140, pp. 9–10, 26–27.

53. Memorandum regarding foreign-speaking soldiers, YMCA, and K of C Hut, July 16, 1918, 10565–501G, MID-WDGS; The National Catholic War Council to Fosdick, Oct. 12, 1918, CTCA 42734, WDGSS.

54. Charles E. Shulman, "Rabbis in Uniform," *Congress Bi-Weekly,* Apr. 2, 1962, Informal Committee on Commemoration of the Centennial of the Jewish Military Chaplaincy Records, 1961–63, American Jewish Historical Society Archives; *Commissions on Training Camp Activities Report,* p. 27.

55. Mr. Frank L. Tolman, camp librarian at Camp Upton, New York, to Perkins and Horgan, Aug. 12, 1918, 10565–531/12, MID-WDGS.

56. Perkins to John W. Jenusaitis, July 11, 1918, 10564–10/14, MID-WDGS; Perkins

to George A. Spannon, July 11, 1918, 10564–52/6, MID-WDGS; Perkins and Horgan to Mr. V. G. Parisi, intelligence officer, Camp Wadsworth, South Carolina, July 11, 1918, 10564–50/19, MID-WDGS; Perkins to Vincent Schultze, July 11, 1918, 10564–45/33, MID-WDGS; Perkins to Arthur Jacoby, July 11, 1918, 10564–51/5, MID-WDGS.

57. "Making Americans of Alien Soldiers," *Trench and Camp* no. 16, Sept. 25, 1918, reprinted in *The Boston Daily Globe*; Prof. Ernest H. Wilkins, director of education, YMCA, to Perkins and Horgan, Sept. 16 and 19, 1918, 10565–531, MID-WDGS; Perkins and Horgan to Mr. A. Bruce Bielaksi, chief, Bureau of Investigation, Department of Justice, Aug. 9, 1918, 10565–507/1, MID-WDGS; Churchill to Joseph Spolansky, Russian Bureau, Nov. 14, 1918, 10565–510, MID-WDGS; Perkins and Horgan to Prof. Ernest H. Wilkins, Aug. 14, 1918, 10565–531, MID-WDGS.

58. "Report from Playground and Recreation Association of America," Dec. 1917, CTCA 27333, WDGSS, pp. 5, 9, 11.

59. Brewer to Mrs. Florence M. Beacon, June 12, 1918, 10565–346/1, MID-WDGS; E. G. Moyer, intelligence officer, Camp Gordon, Georgia, to Acting Director, Military Intelligence Division, "Report on Past Activities," Jan. 23, 1919, 10565–515/21, MID-WDGS; YMCA, *Manual of Young Men's Christian Association Educational Work*, 3rd ed. (New York: The Educational Bureau of the National War Work Council of Young Men's Christian Associations of the United States, 1918), p. 7.

60. Board of Instruction, Office of the Provost Marshall General, "Teaching English to Non-English Speaking Selective," Bulletin 6 (Washington, D.C.: War Department, n.d.), p. 1; A. W. Castti, assistant superintendent, Board of Education, Cleveland, to Brewer, Aug. 13, 1918, 10565–530/2, MID-WDGS; Churchill to Mr. M. J. Downey, director of evening schools, Boston, Nov. 5, 1918, 10565–530, MID-WDGS; Taft, *Service with Fighting Men*, vol. 2, p. 249.

61. Harris, *Service with Fighting Men*, pp. 349, 349–51; Walter A. Davis, *Spelling Book for Soldiers* (San Antonio, Tex.: National War Work Council of the Young Men's Christian Association of the United States Southern Department, 1919); memorandum, July 17, 1918, 10565–414/1, MID-WDGS; YMCA, *Manual*, p. 1; Perkins to Bureau of Education, Department of Interior, Sept. 19, 1918, 10565–546/4, MID-WDGS; Horgan to Mr. Michael J. Downey, director of evening schools, Boston, Oct. 25, 1918, 10565–500B/32, MID-WDGS; Churchill to Dr. Charles William Dahney, president, University of Cincinnati, July 23, 1918, 10565–439/1, MID-WDGS; "Teaching English to Non-English Speaking Selective," pp. 5–29.

62. Harris, *Service with Fighting Men*, p. 350.

63. Christina Krysto, "Bringing the World to our Foreign-language Solders: How a Military Training Camp is Solving a Seemingly Insurmountable Problems by Using the Geographic," *National Geographic Magazine* 34, no 2 (Aug., 1918): 82, 81–90, 83, 89–90.

64. YMCA, *Manual*, pp. 1–5; "Report from Katharine Scott," p. 8; YMCA, *Manual*, p. 7.

65. CTCA, *Report from the Camp Music Division of the War Department* (Washington D.C.: GPO, 1919), pp. 10, 22–25. Gen. Lytle Brown, Adjutant General of the Army, memorandum, "Instruction of Non-English Speaking Men and Native-

born Illiterates," June, 27 1918; Col. D. W. Ketcham, acting director, War Plans
Division, "Memorandum," Apr. 29, 1918; and Gen. Peyton C. March, chief of
staff, "Instruction in English of Soldiers who have not Sufficient Knowledge of
that Language," July, 1918, CTCA 44183, WDGSS; *Jewish Welfare Board, Purpose
Scope and Achievements* (New York: Jewish Welfare Board National Headquarters, n.d.), pp. 1–7; Perkins and Horgan to Bureau of Education, 19 Sept. 1918,
10565–546/4, MID-WDGS; Col. John M. Dunn, to Intelligence Officer, Camp
Devens, Massachusetts, Dec. 1918, 10565–512/39, MID-WDGS; Munson to Intelligence Officer, Camp Dix, New Jersey, Oct. 15, 1918, 10565k-514/20, MID-
WDGS.
66. Fosdick, *Chronicle of a Generation*, p. 144.

Chapter 5. "Mindful of the Traditions of His Race"

1. Padgett, "Camp Gordon Plan," p. 437; "'Foreign Legion' Companies," pp. 252–53.
2. "Treatment of New Men," *Infantry Journal* 15, no. 4 (Oct., 1918): 341–42; Brig.
Gen. Marlborough Churchill [hereafter Churchill] to Lt. M. A. Viracola, Nov.
18, 1918, 10565–473, MID-WDGS RG 165, N.A.
3. For an example of correspondence with an "inside camp" agent, see D. Chauncy
Brewer [hereafter Brewer] to Erich Bernhard, May 10, 1918, 10565–121/4; Erich
Bernhard to Capt. George A. Perkins [hereafter Perkins], June 29, 1918, 10565–
121/9; and Bernhard to Perkins, June 29, 1918, 10565–40/72, MID-WDGS.
4. Perkins to Maj. Nicholas Biddle, intelligence officer, Eastern Department, Aug.
13, 1918, 10565–552/1, MID-WDGS; Lt. Herbert A. Horgan [hereafter Horgan]
and Perkins, to Baker D. Bairam, Sept. 16, 1918, 105650–407, MID-WDGS;
Horgan and Perkins to Baker D. Bairam Aug. 28, 1918, 10565–407/8, MID-
WDGS; Perkins and Horgan to Mr. Gaspare M. Cusumano, Aug. 15, 1918,
10565–458/3, MID-WDGS; Perkins and Horgan, to Mr. John A. Stalinski, July
19, 1918, 10564–46/22, MID-WDGS.
5. War Department investigation of Frank Kerzie, agent reports and correspondence between Kerzie and MID, Apr. 1–Sept. 16, 1918, 10565–170/4, MID-
WDGS; War Department investigation of Joseph Spano, agent reports and correspondence between Spano and MID, July 19–Nov. 1, 1918, 10565–91/21,
MID-WDGS; War Department investigation of Erich Bernhard, agent reports
and correspondence between Bernard and MID, Jan.–Nov., 1918, 10565–121,
MID-WDGS; War Department investigation of Baker D. Bairam, agent reports
and correspondence between Bairam and MID, Sept.–Nov., 1918, 10565–49,
MID-WDGS.
6. War Department investigation of Vincent Schultz, agent reports and correspondence between Schultz and MID, July–Oct., 1918, 10565–253, MID-WDGS;
War Department investigation of Sarkis Albarian, agent reports and correspondence between Albarian and MID, July–Aug., 1918, 10565–303, MID-WDGS;
War Department investigation of Prof. H. A. Miller, agent reports and correspondence between Miller and MID, [dates unknown] 10565–120, MID-WDGS;
War Department investigation of John A. Stalinski, agent reports and corre-

spondence between Stalinski and MID, May 3–Oct. 17, 1918, 10565–303, MID-WDGS; Rev. S. M. Albarian, Pastor, Armenian Presbyterian Church, to Lieutenant Colonel Campbell, Bureau of Military Intelligence, Apr. 28, 1918, 10565–286, MID-WDGS. An examination of the letters given to immigrant agents with their paychecks indicates that the FSS employed a total of forty-seven intelligence agents. Memorandum regarding paychecks, Jan.–Nov., 1918, 10636–40, MID-WDGS.

7. Reports from volunteer "cooperating doctors" can be found throughout the "FSS Bulletin" (composite of agent's reports). For examples, see "F.S.S. Bulletin, Outside Camp News," May 23, 1918, 10564–43/34, MID-WDGS; and "F.S.S. Bulletin," June 5, 1918, 10564–43/40, MID-WDGS. For examples of MID's requests to physicians, see Brewer to President, American Medical Association, Chicago, Illinois, Apr. 18, 1918, 10565–228/1, MID-WDGS; and Brewer to Dr. William G. Wulfahrt, June 12, 1918, 10565–228/47, MID-WDGS.

8. Greene, *American Immigrant Leaders*, p. 142; Horgan, memorandum regarding Foreign-Speaking Soldiers, YMCA, and K of C Hut, July 16, 1918, 10565–501G, MID-WDGS.

9. Brewer to Pvt. Elie Calentane, Camp Devens, Massachusetts, June 7, 1918, 10565–348/1, MID-WDGS; Brewer to Pvt. Saul Kaufman, Camp Upton, May 22, 1918, 10565–315/2, MID-WDGS; FSS memorandum, June 6, 1918, 10565–361/1, MID-WDGS; Brewer, to Pvt. A. Barnett, Camp Grant, Illinois, June 22, 1918, 10565–/1, MID-WDGS; Brewer to Lt. Ben Venuto Borella, Camp Wadsworth, South Carolina, June 22, 1918, 10565–395, MID-WDGS; Perkins to Cpl. Joseph Novick, Camp MacArthur, Texas, Aug. 6, 1918, 10565–458/11, MID-WDGS.

10. Fosdick, *Chronicle of a Generation*, p. 184; Perkins to Col. Harry Cutler, Jewish Welfare Board, Aug. 20, 1918, 80–81, MID-WDGS.

11. The Union of Orthodox Rabbis of the United States and Canada, the Association of Orthodox Rabbis of New York, and the Rabbinical College of America (through the Commanding General of Camp Upton) to The Honorable Secretary of War, Sept. 6, 1918, Dec. 004.3–012.2, 77th Division Records, WDOR RG 120, N.A; and H. G. Learnard, Adjutant General, to Commanding General, 77th Division, Sept. 8, 1917, Dec. 004.3–012.2, 77th Division Records, WDOR.

12. Lt. Col. E. E. Booth, General Staff, to General Manager, Long Island R.R. Sept. 17, 1917, Dec. 004.3–012.2, 77th Division Records, WDOR; Dr. G. Bacarat, the Mayor's Committee on National Defense, to Maj. C. Garlinton, Camp Upton, New York, Sept. 14, 1917, Dec. 004.3–012.2, 77th Division Records, WDOR; Rabbi Nathan Blechman, "Services for Jewish New Year Holy Days," Sept., 1917, Jewish Welfare Board, American Jewish Historical Society Archives.

13. Bulletin No. 7, Sept. 14, 1917, 27th Division Records, WDOR; Bulletin 79, Dec. 6, 1917, 27th Division Records, WDOR.

14. Pastor of the Hellenic Orthodox Church of New York to Headquarters, 77th Division, Camp Upton, New York, Dec. 28, 1917, Dec. File 004.3–012.2, 77th Division Records, WDOR; Nicholas Lazaris, Greek Orthodox Community "Evangelismos," to Commanding Officer, Camp Upton, New York, Jan. 3, 1918, Dec. File 004.3–012.2, 77th Division Records, WDOR; Maj. John Richardson,

assistant to chief of staff, to Reverend Lazaris, Jan. 6, 1918, Dec. File 004.3–012.2, 77th Division Records, WDOR.

15. Henry G. Sharpe, quartermaster general, to Rabbi M. Zaimon, July 31, 1917, Dec. File 004.3–012.2, 77th Division Records, WDOR; Cooke, *All-Americans at War*, p. 15.

16. John H. Gregory, adjutant general of the army, to Commanding General, Camp Gordon, Jan. 9, 1918, Dec. File 000–014.31, 82nd Division Records, WDOR; "Religious Statistics, 82nd Division, Camp Gordon," Jan. 15, 1918, Dec. Files 000.2 through 000.5, 82nd Division Records, WDOR; Commanding General Bell to Camp Chaplain, Nov. 26, 1917, 82nd Division Records, WDOR; Mr. J. F. Muller to Raymond B. Fosdick [hereafter Fosdick], Nov. 7, 1917, CTCA 13877, WDGSS RG 165, N.A.; Fosdick to J. F. Muller, Dec. 19, 1917, CTCA 13877, WDGSS.

17. *Commissions on Training Camp Activities*, Raymond B. Fosdick, *Report to the Secretary of War on the Activities of Welfare Organizations serving with the A.E.F.* (Washington, D.C.: War Department, undated); Perkins to Reverend O'Hearn, Aug. 7, 1918, 10565–500D/2, MID-WDGS.

18. Perkins to O'Hearn, Aug. 7, 1918.

19. Quoted in Kauffman, *Faith and Fraternalism*, p. 213.

20. Perkins and Horgan to Rev. Louis Ahern, Aug. 20, 1918, 10565–500D/5, MID-WDGS; Brewer to *New York Greek National Herald*, Apr. 2, 1918, 10565–185/1, MID-WDGS; Cooke, *All-Americans at War*, p. 68.

21. Major General Burnham, Headquarters, 82nd Division, Confidential Memorandum 121, Aug. 26, 1918, Dec. File 000–014.31, 82nd Division Records, WDOR; Jewish Welfare Board, "Final Report of War Emergency Activities," New York, 1920, American Jewish Historical Society Archives, Waltham, Massachusetts; War Department Correspondence, Mar., July 10, and Dec. 31, 1918, Isaac Siegel Papers, 1897–1944, American Jewish Historical Society Archives; The War and Navy Departments, *Commissions on Training Camp Activities*, pp. 26–27; Fosdick, *Report to Secretary of War*, pp. 6–7, 9–10, 26–27; War Department, General Order No. 46, May 9, 1918, (Washington, D.C.: GPO, 1919), p. 1; and War Department, Bulletin 25, May 3, 1918, (Washington, D.C.: GPO, 1919), pp. 1–2.

22. Jewish Welfare Board, "Final Report of War Emergency Activities."

23. Jewish Welfare Board, *Abridged Prayer Book for Jews in the Army and Navy of the United States*, American Jewish Historical Society Archives; The Jewish Welfare Board, *United States Army and Navy: Purpose, Scope, Achievement*; Jewish Welfare Board, Army-Navy Division, 1919–1939, "Graves," World War I Collection, American Jewish Historical Society Archives; *The War Record of American Jews*, pp. 10, 14–15; *Prayer Book for Jews in the Army and Navy of the United States* (Philadelphia, Issued for the Jewish Welfare Board), pp. v–vi; Jewish Welfare Board, "Manual for Speakers in the United War Work Campaign," American Jewish Historical Society Archives; Perkins to Col. Harry Cutler, Jewish Welfare Board, Aug. 20, 1918, 80–81, MID-WDGS.

24. Commanding General Bell, Camp Upton, to The Reverend Edmund Banks Smith, Nov. 26, 1917, Dec. File 000.2 to 000.5, 77th Division Records, WDOR.; Perkins to Cutler, Aug. 20, 1918; Major General Bell, to Mr. Ralph A. Hayes,

    private secretary to the secretary of war, Dec. File 000.2 to 000.5, 77th Division Records, WDOR; Fosdick, memorandum for Secretary Keppel, Sept. 13, 1918, CTCA 38630, WDGSS.

25. Memorandum no. 121, HDQRS, Aug. 26, 1918, 82nd Division Records, WDOR.

26. Dr. Antonio Grasso to Horgan, Aug. 17, 1918, 80–92, MID-WDGS; Perkins to Intelligence Officer, Camp Meade, Maryland, Aug. 23, 1918, 80–92/2, MID-WDGS; Perkins and Horgan to Intelligence Officer, Camp Sheridan, Alabama, Aug. 2, 1918, 10565–522/1, MID-WDGS.

27. Churchill to Intelligence Officer, Camp Lee, Virginia, June 8, 1916, 10564–3/83, MID-WDGS; Horgan, memorandum for Perkins, July 11, 1918, 80–18/1, MID-WDGS; Churchill, memorandum for the Chief of Staff, "Extract from Confidential Bulletin No. 17," July 17, 1918, 10565–414/1, MID-WDGS; Perkins and Horgan to Intelligence Officer, Camp Sheridan, Alabama, Aug. 2, 1918, 10565–522/1, MID-WDGS.

28. Perkins to Mr. W. P. Sangers, Commission on Training Camp Activities, July 18, 1918, CTCA 35294, WDGSS; Arbib Costa, associate director, Italian Bureau of Information, to Capt. Joseph J. Marino, Hoboken, New Jersey [forwarded to MID], July 18, 1918, 10565–243, MID-WDGS; Perkins to Mr. Denis McCarthy, Knights of Columbus, July 10, 1918, 10565–535, MID-WDGS; Perkins to Prof. E. H. Wilkins, War Work Council, YMCA, July 30, 1918, 100565–531/4 MID-WDGS; Director, Military Intelligence Division, to Mr. Edgar Sisson, Committee on Public Information, Sept., 28 1918, 10565–243, MID-WDGS.

29. FSS memorandum, July 30, 1918, 10565–535/2, MID-WDGS; Perkins to Chairman, July 4th Celebration Committee, Kansas City, Missouri, July 20, 1918, 10565–485A/2, MID-WDGS; Costa to Marino, July 18, 1918.

30. Perkins and Horgan to Fosdick, Aug. 24, 1918, CTCA 37645, WDGSS; Perkins to Life Publishing Company, Aug. 6, 1918, 80–18/1, MID-WDGS; Life Publishing Company to Perkins, Aug. 9, 1918, 80–18–5, MID-WDGS; Perkins to Life Publishing Company, Aug. 12, 1918, 80–18/6, MID-WDGS; Perkins and Horgan to Fosdick, Aug. 24, 1918, 10565–501/17, MID-WDGS.

31. Perkins and Horgan to John Kliniewski, Sept. 4, 1918, 10565–492B/3, MID-WDGS.

32. FSS memorandum, Oct. 8, 1918, 10565–523/11, MID-WDGS.

33. Perkins to Intelligence Officer, Camp Meade, Maryland, Aug. 6, 1918, 10565–495A/4, MID-WDGS.

34. Major Bonsel to Col. R. H. Van Deman [hereafter Van Deman], Jan. 29, 1918, 10565–86/1, MID-WDGS; Van Deman, memorandum for the Chief of War College Division, Feb. 1, 1918, 10565–86/2, MID-WDGS; Van Deman to Chief, War College Division, Feb., 1918, 10565–86/2, MID-WDGS.

35. Col. John M. Dunn, acting director, Military Intelligence, to Maj. H. L. Barnes, intelligence officer, Fort Sam Houston, Texas, Dec. 2, 1918, 10565–598/3, MID-WDGS; Perkins to Chaplain S. C. Black (telegram), Sept. 20, 1918, 10565–515/8, MID-WDGS; FSS memorandum, Jan. 31, 1919, 10565–520, MID-WDGS.

36. Churchill to Intelligence Officer, Camp Meade, Maryland, Oct. 22, 1918, 10565–587/4, MID-WDGS.

37. Agent Alfonso Lambiase to Perkins, Aug. 26, 1918, 10564–55, MID-WDGS; Perkins to Mr. Denis McCarthy, Knights of Columbus, Sept. 5, 1918, 10565–535, MID-WDGS. A number of these ethnic patriotic and entertainment events took place under Brewer's leadership. See various documents in MID-WDGS RG 165, N.A.

38. Perkins to Provost Marshal General, Oct. 9, 1918, 10565–501/15, MID-WDGS; Brig. Gen. E. L. Munson [hereafter Munson], General Staff, "Memorandum for Personnel Branch Operator, Division, General Staff," Oct. 15, 1918, 10565–500A, MID-WDGS; Churchill to Mr. Vincent G. Parisi, Headquarters, Prov. Depot, Camp Wadsworth, South Carolina, Oct. 31, 1918, 10565–218, MID-WDGS; Churchill to Mr. Ludwyk Kradyna, Oct. 31, 1918, 10565–195/19, MID-WDGS.

39. Churchill to Ludwyk Kradyna, Oct. 31, 1918, 10565–195/19, MID-WDGS; Perkins to Personnel Branch, Operations Division, General Staff, 18 Oct. 1918, 10565–500A, MID-WDGS; Churchill to Ludwyk Kradyna, Oct. 31, 1918, 10565–195/19, MID-WDGS.

40. Churchill to Parisi, Oct. 31, 1918; M. Lincoln Schuster to Perkins, Aug. 23, 1918, 10565–545/3, MID-WDGS; Director, Military Intelligence Division, to Maj. H. G. Adams, Bureau of War Risk Insurance, Oct. 31, 1918, 10565–543, MID-WDGS.

41. War Department, General Order No. 33, Apr. 6, 1918; Lambiase to Perkins, Aug. 26, 1918.

42. Munson to Intelligence Officer, Camp Merritt, New Jersey, Oct. 15, 1918, 10565–578, MID-WDGS; Dr. Justine Klotz, Special Workers, Division on Work for Foreign-Born Women, to Perkins, Oct. 31, 1918, 10565–532/2, MID-WDGS.

43. Perkins, memorandum for the Adjutant General, Aug. 6, 1918, 10565–501/1, MID-WDGS; Churchill, memorandum for the Chief of Staff, "Naturalization—Foreign-speaking Soldiers," Sept. 18, 1918, 10565–506/7, MID-WDGS; Perkins and Horgan to Pvt. Chiueri Baccash, Camp Upton, New York, Aug. 28, 1918, 10565–500B/3, MID-WDGS.

44. Major Bonsal, S.O.R.C., to Major Masteller, General Staff, Jan. 29, 1918, 10565–84/1, MID-WDGS; Brig. Gen. Lytle Brown, memorandum for the Chief of Staff, Sept. 4, 1918, 10565–492A/2, MID-WDGS; Benedict Crowell, acting secretary of war, to Col. James Martin, French Military Mission, Sept. 5, 1918, 10565–492A/4, MID-WDGS.

45. "Beware of Foreign Agitators!" *Denni Hlasatel*, Feb. 15, 1917; "German Propaganda among Lithuanians," *Lietuva*, Sept. 17, 1918; "F.S.S Bulletin, July 8, 1918, 10564–43/135, MID-WDGS, p. 3; "F.S.S Bulletin," July 3, July 8, 1918, 1056–45/135, MID-WDGS; "F.S.S. Bulletin," May 11, 1918, 10564–43/29, MID-WDGS.

46. "F.S.S Bulletin," Apr. 20, 1918, 10564–43, MID-WDGS, p. 1; "F.S.S Bulletin" July 3, 1918, pp. 4, 3; "F.S.S. Bulletin," June 5, 1918, 10564–43/47, MID-WDGS, p. 1.

47. Dr. Buna Seymour to Brewer, June 1, 1918, 10565–255/14, MID-WDGS; Drs. F. D. & A. H. LaRochelle to War Department, June 22, 1918, 10565–255/89, MID-WDGS; Dr. Bernard Klein, to Brewer, June 20, 1919, 10565–255/75, MID-WDGS; Dr. F. J. Lepak to Brewer, June 19, 1918, 10565–255/74, MID-WDGS.

48. Brewer to Eugene Braslansky, Russian-American Bureau, June 7, 1918, 10565–355, MID-WDGS; Perkins and Horgan to M. Kaupas, Lithuanian National Council, Aug. 14, 1918, 10565–538/2, MID-WDGS; Brewer to Mr. J. B. Kaupas, July 2, 1918, 10565–412/1, MID-WDGS.

49. Lt. Stanislaw Gutowski, Headquarters, 85th Division, Intelligence Section, Camp Custer, Michigan, to Brewer, Feb. 1, 1918, 10564–17/4, MID-WDGS; Perkins and Horgan to Dr. John Mott, Aug. 8, 1918, 10565–531/7, MID-WDGS.

50. Institute for Public Service, *Ten Reasons Why We Are at War,* War Camp Leaflet No. 1 (undated), CTCA 36669, WDGSS; William H. Allen, director, Institute for Public Service, to Asst. Secretary of War Frederick P. Keppel, Sept. 4, 1918, CTCA 36669C, WDGSS.

51. Van Deman to Rev. Alex. Syaki, editor, *Polish Daily News,* Jan. 12, 1918, 10565–57/1, MID-WDGS; Perkins to Intelligence Officer, Camp Dix, New Jersey, 10565–514/2, Aug. 2, 1918, MID-WDGS; Perkins to Intelligence Officer, Camp Upton, New York, Aug. 3, 1918, 10565–523/2, MID-WDGS; Perkins to Intelligence Officer, Camp Humphrey, Virginia, July 24, 1918, 10565–516, MID-WDGS; A. V. Pipe, Committee on Classification of Personnel in the Army, to Perkins, Aug. 7, 1918, 80–58/2, MID-WDGS.

52. Perkins to Rev. William Rosenau, Aug. 9, 1918, 80–55, MID-WDGS; Perkins to Ameen Rihani, Sept. 18, 1918, 10565–534, MID-WDGS.

53. Perkins to *Baltimore Sun,* July 22, 1918, 80–68, MID-WDGS; "Extract from *Boston Globe,* 'Absorbing Alien Rookies,'" Aug. 3, 1918, 10565–535/6, MID-WDGS; FSS memorandum, undated, 10565–455/460, MID-WDGS; Horgan to Mr. Joseph Mayper, commissioner of education, War Work Extension, Aug. 14, 1918, 10565–546/2, MID-WDGS; Lt. H. O'Reardon, intelligence officer, Camp Merritt, New Jersey, to Perkins, Sept. 6, 1918, 10565–578, MID-WDGS.

54. Horgan to R. J. Foster, Speakers' Bureau, U.S. Treasury, Jan. 9, 1918, 10565–602/6, MID-WDGS.

55. Ernest J. Hall, Camp Devens, Massachusetts, to Perkins, July 15, 1918, 80–70, MID-WDGS; Horgan to Miss Mabel B. Ury, executive clerk, Conference on Publicity Methods, Oct. 15, 1918, 10565–590/6, MID-WDGS; Brewer to Royal Italian Embassy, Washington, D.C., 10565–261/2, May 13, 1918, MID-WDGS; Perkins and Horgan to Lt. Bruno Rosselli, July 16, 1918, 19565–261/4, MID-WDGS; Perkins to Capt. E. J. Hall, July 18, 1918, 80–70/2, MID-WDGS.

56. Perkins and Horgan to Pvt. Chiueri Baccash, Camp Upton, New York, Aug. 28, 1918, 10565–500B/3, MID-WDGS; Perkins to Intelligence Officer, Camp Upton, Aug. 29, 1918, 10565–523/6, MID-WDGS; Pvt. Shurcri Baccash to Camp Intelligence Officer, Camp Upton, Oct. 19, 1918, 10565–523/13, MID-WDGS; Horgan to Pvt. Shurcri Baccash, Camp Upton, Oct. 19, 1918, 10565\500B/28, MID-WDGS; FSS memorandum, Jan. 3, 1919, 10565–522/22, MID-WDGS.

57. "Extract from *Boston Globe,* 'Absorbing Alien Rookies,'" Aug. 3, 1918, 10565–535/6, WDGS.

58. FSS memorandum, May 9, 1918, 10565–236/1, MID-WDGS; Division Intelligence Office, Camp Devens, Massachusetts, to Van Deman, 10565–239/1, May 9, 1918, MID-WDGS; Intelligence Officer, Fort McPherson, Georgia, to Commanding Officer, Fort McPherson, Georgia, Apr. 16, 1918, 10565–201/1, MID-WDGS; Perkins to Rev. Fan S. Noli, Sept. 17, 1918, 10565–534, MID-WDGS; Perkins and Horgan to Intelligence Officer, Camp Upton, New York, Sept. 5, 1918, 10565–523/7, MID-WDGS.

59. Perkins to Intelligence Officer, Camp Dix, New Jersey, Aug. 24, 1918, 10565–

514/8, MID-WDGS. For examples of speaker recruitment, see Brewer to President, University of Georgia, Apr. 26, 1918, 105655–201/5, MID-WDGS; and Brewer to Lt. Col. Charles G. Lawrence, Fort McPherson, Georgia, Apr. 26, 1918, 10565–301/2, MID-WDGS; FSS memorandum, Sept. 17, 1918, 10565–535, MID-WDGS.

60. Perkins to Intelligence Officers, Camps Lee, Dix, Meade, Lewis, Gordon, Grant, Sherman, Wadsworth, McArthur, Upton, Sheridan, Pike, and Devens, Sept. 12, 1918, 10565–458, MID-WDGS; Perkins to Intelligence Officer, Camp Lee, Virginia (telegram), Sept. 17, 1918, 10565–517, MID-WDGS; J. Krausnick, Camp Intelligence Section, Camp Grant, Illinois, to Director of Military Intelligence, Sept. 18, 1918, 10565–541/7, MID-WDGS.

61. FSS memorandum, Aug. 17, 1918, 10565–559/12, MID-WDGS; Intelligence Officers, Foreign Legion, to Commanding Officer, Military Morale Section, Oct. 10, 1918, 10565–525/17, MID-WDGS; Capt. E. R. Padgett, memorandum for Perkins, "Report of One-Day Trip to Camp Meade," Sept. 7, 1918, 10901–22, MID-WDGS.

62. Cooke, *All-Americans at War*, p. 124; "Leave Train For Italy: Memorandum Re: Italian Leave Train," memorandum no. 54, Mar. 19, Mar. 21,1919, 82nd Division Records, WDOR.

Conclusion

1. Baker, *America at War*; "From the Beseda Fresl," *Denni Hlasatel*, July 29, 1917.
2. Greene, *American Immigrant Leaders*, p. 10.
3. Ibid.
4. "Louis Van Iersel, 93, Immigrant Hero of WWI," *Los Angeles Times*, June 16, 1987; Sgt. Louis Van Iersel, Company M, 9th Infantry, 2nd Division, Army Service Experiences Questionnaires, U.S.A.H.M.I. The "Army Service Experiences" questionnaires were sent out by the U.S. Army Military History Institute, Carlisle Barracks, Pennsylvania, in the 1970s. It should be noted that by then over five decades had passed since the end of the First World War, and time may gave distorted the memories of the soldiers filling out the forms.
5. "Louis Van Iersel, 93, Immigrant Hero of WWI," *Los Angeles Times*, June 16, 1987; Sgt. Louis Van Iersel, Company M, 9th Infantry, 2nd Division, Army Questionnaires.
6. "An Old New Jersey Soldier to get World War I Medal at Last," *The Philadelphia Bulletin*, Aug. 22, 1980.
7. Pvt. Salvatore Campanelli, Headquarters Company, 306th Infantry, 77th Division, Army Questionnaires.
8. Pvt. John L. DiFonzo, Company C, 9th Infantry Regiment, 2nd Division, Army Questionnaires.
9. Pvt. George Dongarra, Company B, 2nd Ammunition Train, 2nd Division, Army Questionnaires.
10. Pvt. Morris Gutentag, Company C, 308th Infantry Regiment, 77th Division, Army Questionnaires.
11. Ibid.

12. J. Swietanka, director, Czechoslovak National Council, Washington Office, to Lt. Col. Graham D. Fitch, chief, Translation Section, Army War College, Aug. 16, 1918, 10565–537/1, MID-WDGS RG 165, N.A.

13. Swietanka to Fitch, 10565–537/1, MID-WDGS; *Soldiers Bulletin* 1, 10565–455 to 460, MID-WDGS; Intelligence Officer, Camp Meade, Maryland, to Perkins, Aug. 6, 1918, 10565–495A/4, MID-WDGS; Pvt. Leon Rose, Company M, 106th Infantry, 27th Division. Army Questionnaires.

14. FSS bulletin, July 6, 1918, 10565–447/1, MID-WDGS.

15. Pvt. Charles J. Gottwald, Headquarters Troop, 77th Division, to the Adjutant General of the Army, Dec. 19, 1917, Dec. File 014.32, 77th Division Records, WDOR RG 120, N.A.

16. *The War Record of American Jews*, pp. 39, 15.

17. "Fruit of the Melting Pot," *New York Globe*, Oct. 11, 1918, quoted in *War Record of American Jews*, pp. 39, 21, 14–29. Rank and unit are not listed for all soldiers. In some cases the birthplace of the soldier was not listed. Most of the names indicate that the men or their families originated in southern or eastern Europe, but it is not clear whether the soldiers were first- or second-generation Americans.

18. "Aliens of Army Melting Pot Win Applause in Exhibition Drills," *New York Herald*, Sept. 16, 1919; Brig. Gen. W. J. Nicholson, U.S. Army commanding, memorandum to Commanding General of Camp Upton, New York (report "Our Army as an Americanization Agency" enclosed), undated, 52296, WDGSS RG 165, N.A.

19. Copies of posters can be found in "Liberty Loans," Freeman Collection, HSP; C. A. Sienkiewica, "Fourth Liberty Loan, Foreign Language Division," Oct., 1917, Campbell Collection, HSP.

20. Quoted from Von Berg, lieutenant and intelligence officer, "Extracts from a German Document Recently Captured" [enclosure to an untitled document], June 17, 1918, 80–71, MID-WDGS. The German officer noted with some exaggeration, but with general accuracy, the number of first- and second-generation immigrants found in the American Army.

Selected Bibliography

Archives and Collections

Abridged Prayer Book for Jews in the Army and Navy of the United States. American Jewish Historical Society Archives, Waltham, Massachusetts.

Army and Navy Journal. U.S. Army Military History Institute, Carlisle Barracks, Carlisle, Pennsylvania.

Army Service Experiences Questionnaires. U.S. Army Military History Institute, Carlisle Barracks, Carlisle, Pennsylvania.

Calmenson, Jesse B. Papers (1902–1952), Palestine & Israel. American Jewish Historical Society Archives, Waltham, Massachusetts.

Camp Activities: Hearing before the Committee on Military Affairs. Washington, D.C.: Government Printing Office, 1918. Raymond Fosdick Collection. Seeley G. Mudd Manuscript Library, Princeton University Archives, Princeton, New Jersey.

Commission on Training Camp Activities. The War Department. Washington, D.C.: Government Printing Office, 1917. Raymond Fosdick Collection. Seeley G. Mudd Manuscript Library, Princeton University Archives, Princeton, New Jersey.

Committee on Training Camp Activities. Records of the War Department. General and Special Staff, War College and War Plans Division, Subordinate Offices Education and Recreation Branch. Record Group 165. National Archives, Washington, D.C.

Daily Jewish Courier. Immigration History Research Center, University of Minnesota, St. Paul.

Denni Hlasatel. Immigration History Research Center, University of Minnesota, St. Paul.

Department of the Army. *General Orders and Bulletins.* Washington, D.C., GPO, 1919. U.S. Army Military History Institute, Carlisle Barracks, Carlisle, Pennsylvania.

Evening Telegram. World War History Newspaper Collection. U.S. Army Military History Institute, Carlisle Barracks, Carlisle, Pennsylvania.

Final Report of the Provost Marshal General to the Secretary of War. Washington, D.C.: Government Printing Office, 1920. Government Records Department, The Free Library of Philadelphia, Pennsylvania.

Fosdick, Raymond. Collection. Seeley G. Mudd Manuscript Library, Princeton University Archives, Princeton, New Jersey.

Freeman Collection. Historical Society of Pennsylvania, Philadelphia.

Infantry Journal. U.S. Army Military History Institute, Carlisle Barracks, Carlisle, Pennsylvania.

Informal Committee on Commemoration of the Centennial of the Jewish Military Chaplaincy Records. American Jewish Historical Society Archives, Waltham, Massachusetts.

Irish Collection. Villanova University Library, Philadelphia, Pennsylvania.

Irish Press. Villanova University Library, Philadelphia, Pennsylvania.

Jewish War Veterans Papers, 1938–1950. U.S. Army Military History Institute, Carlisle Barracks, Carlisle, Pennsylvania.

Jewish Welfare Board. "Final Report of War Emergency Activities." American Jewish Historical Society Archives, Waltham, Massachusetts.

———. "Manual for Speakers in the United War Work Campaign." American Jewish Historical Society Archives, Waltham, Massachusetts.

Leskovec, Matt. Collection. Slovene Organizations. Immigration History Research Center, University of Minnesota, St. Paul.

Liberty Loan Collection. Information on Philadelphia's Participation in the First World War. Historical Society of Pennsylvania, Philadelphia.

Lietuva. Immigration History Research Center, University of Minnesota, St. Paul.

Office of the War Records of the American Jewish Committee Collection. American Jewish Historical Society Archives, Waltham, Massachusetts.

Philadelphia Bulletin. Urban Archives, Temple University, Philadelphia, Pennsylvania.

Philadelphia Gazette Democrat. Balch Institute for Ethnic Studies, Philadelphia, Pennsylvania.

Political Activity during World War I. Czech and Slovak Recruiting Posters. Balch Institute for Ethnic Studies, Philadelphia, Pennsylvania.

Prayer Book for Jews in the Army and Navy of the United States. American Jewish Historical Society Archives, Waltham, Massachusetts.

Records of the Military Intelligence Division of the War Department General Staff, 1917–1941, General Correspondence. Record Group 165. National Archives, Washington, D.C.

Records of the War Department General and Special Staff, War College and War Plans Division, Subordinate Officers' Education and Recreation Branch. Record Group 165. National Archives, Washington, D.C.

Second Report of the Provost Marshal General to the Secretary of War. Washington, D.C.: Government Printing Office, 1918. Government Records Department, The Free Library of Philadelphia, Pennsylvania.

Serie 17N47. Archives de l'Armee de Terre, Chateau de Vinceness, Paris.

Siegel, Isaac. Papers, 1897–1944. War Department Correspondence. American Jewish Historical Society Archives, Waltham, Massachusetts.

Sunday Jewish Courier. Immigration History Research Center, University of Minnesota, St. Paul.

Trench and Camp. U.S. Army Military History Institute, Carlisle Barracks, Carlisle, Pennsylvania.

U.S. House Military Affairs Committee. "Drafting Aliens into Military Service." Hearings, 65th Cong., 1st sess., September 26, 1917. Government Records Department, The Free Library of Philadelphia, Pennsylvania.

United States Statutes at Large 39 (1917): 874. Government Records Department, The Free Library of Philadelphia, Pennsylvania.

War and Navy Departments. *Commissions on Training Camp Activities.* Washington, D.C.: Government Printing Office, n.d. Raymond Fosdick Collection. Seeley G.

Mudd Manuscript Library, Princeton University Archives, Princeton, New Jersey.
War Department Organizational Records. 27th Division Records, Headquarters, Miscellaneous Orders, Memos, and Bulletins. Record Group 120. National Archives, Washington, D.C.
———. 29th Division Records, Headquarters, Miscellaneous Orders, Memos, and Bulletins. Record Group 120. National Archives, Washington, D.C.
———. 77th Division Records, Headquarters, Miscellaneous Orders, Memos, and Bulletins. Record Group 120. National Archives, Washington, D.C.
———. 82nd Division Records, Headquarters, Miscellaneous Orders, Memos, and Bulletins. Record Group 120. National Archives, Washington, D.C.
World War History Newspaper Clippings Collection. U.S. Army Military History Institute, Carlisle Barracks, Carlisle, Pennsylvania.
Young Men's Christian Association Report to the Commission on Training Camp Activities. World War I Collection. Young Men's Christian Association Archives, University of Minnesota, St. Paul.
Young Women's Christian Association Report to the Commission on Training Camp Activities. World War I Collection. Young Women's Christian Association Archives, New York City.

Books, Articles, and Other Publications

Addams, Jane. *Twenty Years at Hull-House.* New York: New American Library, 1910.
American Loyalty by Citizens of German Descent. War Information Series No. 6. Washington, D.C.: Committee on Public Information, 1917.
Ameringer, Charles D. *U.S. Foreign Intelligence: The Secret Side of American History.* Lexington, Mass.: Lexington Books, 1990.
Baker, Newton. *America at War.* New York: Dodd, Mead, 1931.
Baldwin, Fred Davis. "The American Enlisted Man in World War I." Ph.D. diss., Princeton University, 1965.
Benes, Edvard. *My War Memoirs.* 1920. Reprint, New York: Arno Press, 1971.
———. *In His Own Words: Threescore Years of a Statesman, Builder, and Philosopher.* New York: Czech-American National Alliance, 1944.
Bidwell, Bruce W. *History of the Military Intelligence Division, Department of the Army General Staff: 1775–1941.* Frederick, Md.: University Publications of America, 1986.
Bodnar, John. *Remaking America: Public Memory, Commemoration, and Patriotism in the Twentieth Century.* Princeton, N.J.: Princeton University Press, 1992.
Bordin, Ruth. *Women and Temperance: The Quest For Power and Liberty, 1873–1900.* Philadelphia: Temple University Press, 1981.
Borkowski, Joseph A. *City of Pittsburgh's Part in Formation of the Polish Army—World War I, 1917–1920.* Pittsburgh: Central Council of Polish Organizations, 1956.
Boyer, Paul. *Urban Masses and Moral Order in America, 1820–1920.* Cambridge, Mass.: Harvard University Press, 1978.
Bradford, Zeb B., Jr., and James R. Murphy. "A New Look at the Military Profession." *Army* 19 (February, 1969).
Bristow, Nancy K. *Making Men Moral: Social Engineering during the Great War.* New

York: New York University Press, 1996.

Burton, William L. *Melting Pot Soldiers: The Union's Ethnic Regiments.* Ames: Iowa State University Press, 1988.

Capek, Thomas. *The Čechs in America.* Boston: Houghton Mifflin, 1920.

Chambers, John Whiteclay, II. *To Raise an Army: The Draft Comes to Modern America.* New York: Free Press, 1987.

Child, Clifton James. *The German-Americans in Politics, 1914–1917.* Madison: University of Wisconsin Press, 1939.

Coffman, Edward M. *The War to End All Wars: The American Military Experience in World War I.* Madison: University of Wisconsin Press, 1986.

Conzen, Kathleen Neils, et al. "The Invention of Ethnicity: A Perspective from the U.S.A." *Journal of American Ethnic History* 12 (fall, 1992).

Cooke, James J. *The All-Americans at War: The 82nd Division in the Great War, 1917–1918.* Westport, Conn.: Praeger, 1999.

Cuddy, Edward. "Irish-American Propaganda and American Neutrality, 1914–1917." *Mid-America* 49 (1967).

Davis, Allen F. *Spearheads for Reform: The Social Settlements and the Progressive Movement, 1890–1914.* New York: Oxford University Press, 1967.

———. *American Heroine: The Life and Legend of Jane Addams.* New York: Oxford University Press, 1973.

Dawley, Alan. *Struggle for Justice: Social Responsibility and the Liberal State.* Cambridge, Mass.: Harvard University Press, 1991.

Deutsche-Amerikanischen National-Bundes. Philadelphia, 1905.

Division of the Four-Minute Men. *The Meaning of America.* Bulletin 33. Washington, D.C.: Committee on Public Information, 1918.

Dunn, William E. *Scientific Management Applied to Instruction and Training in Field Artillery.* Philadelphia: J. B. Lippicott, 1916.

Ford, Nancy Gentile. "War and Ethnicity: Foreign-born Soldiers and United States Military Policy during World War I." Ph.D. diss., Temple University, 1994.

Fosdick, Raymond B. *Chronicle of a Generation: An Autobiography.* New York: Harper and Brother, 1958.

Freulich, Roman. *Soldiers in Judea: Stories and Vignettes of the Jewish Legion.* New York: Herzel Press, 1964.

Frisch, Billy, and Archie Fletcher (words); Alex Mar (music). "When Tony Goes Over the Top." New York: Joe Morris Music, 1918.

Gates, John M. "The Alleged Isolation of U.S. Army Officers in the Late 19th Century." *Parameters: Journal of the U.S. Army War College* 10 (September, 1980).

Gilner, Elias. *War and Hope: A History of the Jewish Legion.* New York: Herzel Press, 1969.

Greene, Victor R. *American Immigrant Leaders, 1800–1910: Marginality and Identity.* Baltimore, Md.: Johns Hopkins University Press, 1987.

Guttmann, Allen. "Political Ideals and the Military Ethnic." *The American Scholar* 3 (1965).

———. *The Conservation Tradition in America.* New York: Oxford University Press, 1967.

Haber, Samuel. *Efficiency and Uplift: Scientific Management in the Progressive Era, 1890–*

1920. Chicago: University Chicago Press, 1964.

Hapak, Joseph T. "Recruiting a Polish Army in the United States, 1917–1919." Ph.D. diss., University of Kansas, 1985.

Harris, Frederick. *Service with Fighting Men: An Account of the Work of the American Young Men's Christian Association in World War I.* New York: Associated Press, 1922.

Higham, John. *Send These to Me: Jews and Other Immigrants in Urban America.* New York: Athenaeum, 1975.

―――. *Strangers in the Land: Patterns of American Nativism 1860–1925.* New York: Athenaeum, 1969.

―――, ed. *Ethnic Leadership in America.* Baltimore, Md.: Johns Hopkins University Press, 1978.

History of the Seventy-Seventh Division. New York: Hynkoop, Hallenbeck, and Crawford, 1919.

Hunt, Elvid. *A Manual of Intensive Training.* Honolulu, 1916.

Huntington, Samuel P. *The Soldier and the State: The Theory and Politics of Civil-Military Relations.* Cambridge, Mass.: Harvard University Press, Belknap Press, 1957.

Jabotinsky, Vladimir. *The Jewish Legion and the Palestine Questions.* New York: New Zionists Organization of America, 1945.

―――. *The Story of the Jewish Legion.* New York: Bernard Ackerman, 1945.

Jacobs, James B., and Leslie Anne Hayes. "Aliens in the U.S. Armed Forces: A Historico-Legal Analysis." *Armed Forces and Society* 7 (winter, 1981).

Janowitz, Morris. *The Professional Soldiers: A Social and Political Portrait.* New York: Free Press, 1960.

The Jewish Welfare Board, United States Army and Navy: Purpose, Scope, Achievements. New York: Jewish Welfare Board, n.d.

Karsten, Peter. *The Military in America: From the Colonial Era to the Present.* New York: Free Press, 1980.

Katz, Michael B. *In the Shadow of the Poorhouse: A Social History of Welfare in America.* New York: Basic Books, 1986.

Kauffman, Christopher J. *Faith and Fraternalism: The History of the Knights of Columbus.* New York: Simon and Schuster, 1992.

Keene, Jennifer Diane. "Civilians in Uniform: Building an American Mass Army for the Great War." Ph.D. diss., Carnegie-Mellon University, 1991.

Kennedy, David. *Over Here: The First World War and American Society.* New York: Oxford University Press, 1989.

Kohn, Richard H., ed. *The United States Military under the Constitution of the United States, 1789–1989.* New York: New York University Press, 1991.

Kusmer, Kenneth L. "The Functions of Organized Charity in the Progressive Era: Chicago as a Case Study." *The Journal of American History* 60, no. 3 (December, 1973).

Lane, Jack C. "The Military Profession's Search for Identity." *Marine Corps Gazette* 57 (June, 1973).

―――. *Armed Progressive: General Leonard Wood.* London: Presidio Press, 1978.

Lewis, Brackett. *Eyewitness Story of the Occupation of Samara, Russia, by the Czechoslovak Legion in June, 1918.* Washington, D.C.: Czechoslovak Society of Arts and

Sciences in America, 1977.

Lubove, Roy. *The Professional Altruist: The Emergence of Social Work as a Career, 1880–1930.* Cambridge, Mass.: Harvard University Press, 1965.

Luebke, Frederick C. *Bonds of Loyalty: German Americans and Work War I.* DeKalb: Northern Illinois University Press, 1974.

Masaryk, Thomas Garrigue. *The Making of a State: Memories and Observations, 1914–1918.* New York: Howard Fertig, 1969.

McClymer, John F. *War and Welfare: Social Engineering in America, 1890–1925.* Westport, Conn.: Greenwood Press, 1980.

McCollun, Lee Charles. *History and Rhymes of the Lost Battalion.* Chicago: Foley, 1919.

Miller, Sally M. *The Ethnic Press in the United States: A Historical Analysis and Handbook.* New York: Greenwood Press, 1987.

Munson, Edward L. *The Management of Men: A Handbook on the Systematic Development of Morale and Control of Human Behavior.* New York: Henry Holt, 1921.

Neimeyer, Charles Patrick. *America Goes to War: A Social History of the Continental Army.* New York: New York University Press, 1996.

O'Grady, Joseph P., ed. *The Immigrants Influence on Wilson's Peace Policies.* Lexington: University of Kentucky Press, 1967.

O'Leary, Jeremiah A. *A Statement.* New York: American Truth Society, n.d.

O'Toole, G. J. A. *The Encyclopedia of American Intelligence and Espionage: From the Revolutionary War to the Present.* New York: Facts on File, 1988.

Painter, Nell Irvin. *Standing at Armageddon: The United States, 1877–1919.* New York: W. W. Norton, 1987.

Palmer, Frederick. *Newton D. Baker: America at War.* New York: Dodd, Mead, 1931.

Philadelphia in the World War, 1914–1919. New York: Wynkoop, Hallenbeck, Crawford in association with the Philadelphia War History Committee, 1922.

Plan and Scope of the American Truth Society. New York: American Truth Society, n.d.

Rice, Anna V. *A History of the World's Young Women's Christian Association.* New York: Woman's Press, 1947.

Rosen, Ruth. *The Lost Sisterhood: Prostitution in America, 1900–1918.* Baltimore, Md.: Johns Hopkins University Press, 1982.

Rowland, Thomas J. "Irish-American Catholics and the Quest for Respectability in the Coming of the Great War, 1900–1917." *Journal of American Ethnic History* 15, no. 2 (winter, 1996).

———. "Strained Neutrality: Irish-American Catholics, Woodrow Wilson, and the *Lusitania*," *Eire-Ireland* 30, no. 4 (winter, 1996).

Shanks, David C. *Management of the American Soldiers.* N.p., n.d.

Sklar, Kathryn Kish. "Hull House in the 1890s: A Community of Women Reformers." In *Women, Families, and Communities,* edited by Nancy A. Hewitt. Glenview, Ill.: Scott, Foresman, 1990.

Smythe, Donald. "Venereal Disease: The AEF's Experience." *Prologue* 9 (summer, 1977).

Taft, William Howard. *Service with Fighting Men: An Account of the Work of the American Young Men's Christian Association in the World War.* New York: Associated

Press, 1922.

Trolander, Judith. *Professionalism and Social Change: From Settlement House Movement to Neighborhood Centers, 1886 to the Present.* New York: Columbia University Press, 1987.

U.S. House. *Extended Further Time for Naturalization to Alien Veterans of the World War,* H.R. 1625 and H.R. 4291. 75th Cong., 1st sess., 1918. H. Rept. 487, part 2.

U.S. House Select Committee on Expenditures in the War Department. *War Expenditures: Hearings before Subcommittee (Foreign Expenditures) of the Select Committee on Expenditures in the War Department.* 1919. Vol. 227, pt. 1.

Upton, Emory. *The Military Policy of the United States.* 1904. Reprint, New York: Greenwood Press Publishers, 1968.

The War Record of American Jews. New York: American Jewish Committee, 1919.

Weigley, Russell F. *History of the Unites States Army.* Bloomington: Indiana University Press, 1967.

———. "The Elihu Root Reforms and the Progressive Era." In *Command and Commanders in Modern Warfare: Proceedings of the Second Military Symposium, U.S. Air Force Academy,* edited by William Geffen. Washington, D.C.: United States Air Forces, 1969.

———. *The American Way of War: A History of United States Military Strategy and Policy.* Bloomington: Indiana University Press, 1973.

White, William Bruce. "The Military and the Melting Pot: The American Army and Minority Groups, 1865–1924." Ph.D. diss., University of Wisconsin, 1968.

Wiebe, Robert H. *The Search for Order, 1877–1920.* New York: Hill and Wang, 1967.

Williams, Michael. *American Catholics in the War: National Catholic War Council, 1917–1921.* New York: Macmillan, 1921.

Wittke, Carl. *German-Americans and the World War.* Columbus: Ohio State Archaeological and Historical Society, 1936.

Woloch, Nancy. *Women and the American Experience.* New York: McGraw-Hill, 1984.

Yockelson, Mitchell. "The Ghosts of St. Oglethorpe." *North Georgia Journal* 14 (summer, 1997).

Zecker, Robert. "The Activities of Czech and Slovak Immigrants during World War I." *Ethnic Forum* 15, nos. 1–2 (spring–fall, 1995).

Index